P9-DFL-072

Our Towns

Remembering Community in Indiana

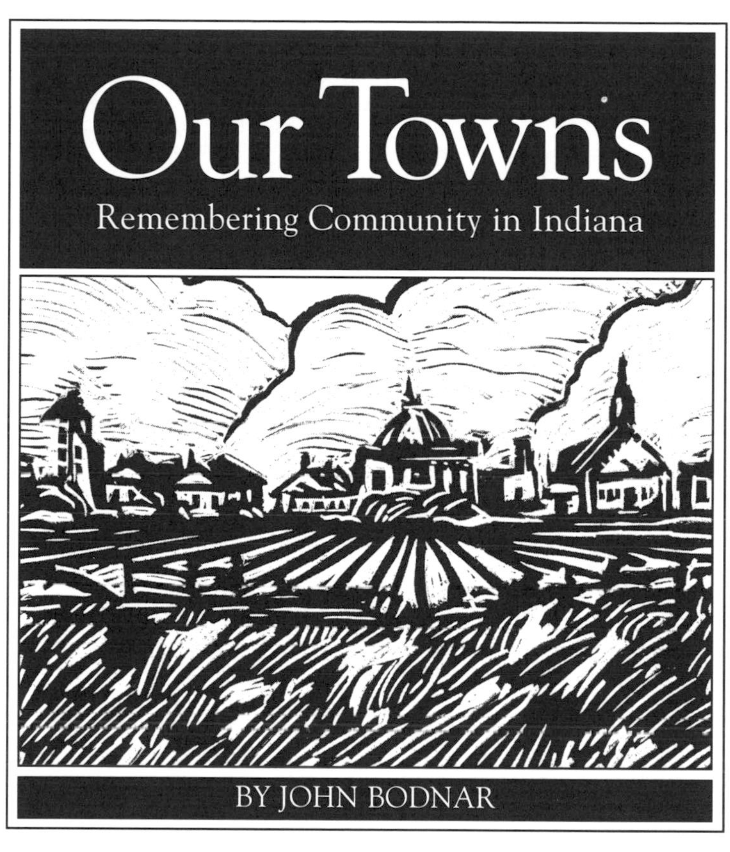

INDIANA HISTORICAL SOCIETY
INDIANAPOLIS 2001

Printed in the United States of America

The paper in this publication meets the minimum requirements of American National Standard for Information Sciences—Permanence of Paper for Printed Library Materials, ANSI Z39.48–1984. ∞

Library of Congress Cataloging-in-Publication Data

Bodnar, John E., 1944-
Our towns: remembering community in Indiana / John Bodnar.
p. cm.
Includes bibliographical references and index.
ISBN 0-87195-149-5 (alk. paper)
1. Indiana—Biography. 2. Indiana—Social life and customs—20th century. I. Title.

CT233 .B63 2001 00-063377
977.2'043'0922—dc21

Contents

Preface

This book is based upon oral history interviews with people who lived in Indiana towns throughout most of the twentieth century. These recollections of individual lives come not from any single research project but were collected over a period of twenty years from 1976 to 1996 by scholars at the Indiana University Oral History Center who pursued a number of topics relating to social and economic life in the state. This effort resulted in hundreds of recordings from rural townships, industrial cities, urban neighborhoods, and small towns. From these recordings at the center, thirty-one were selected from six different communities for presentation in this volume. The life histories here remember both the past of individuals and the collective experience of communities in Anderson, Evansville, Indianapolis, Paoli, South Bend, and Whiting.

A number of scholars participated in these oral history projects, and a list of the role each one played in the interview process is to be found in the appendix to this book. Catherine Jones and Maria Green, individuals trained in anthropology and folklore, conducted the interviews used here from Paoli. Barbara Truesdell and Samuel White, a folklorist and a labor historian, contributed the stories from Evansville. Greg Stone and Richard Pierce, both graduate students in history at the time of their respective work, did the interviews with the African-American community in Indianapolis. The tales of life and work in Anderson were collected by Greer Warren, a folklorist, and historians Karen Gatz and R. T. King. Folklore and history also contributed to the interviewing process in South Bend where conversations were carried on over a period of five years by Robin Lee Zeff, John Wolford, John Bodnar, and R. T. King. Bodnar also taped conversations with current and former residents of Whiting. The entire effort also benefited greatly from the administrative talents of Jeanne Harrah and Barbara Truesdell, who coordinated grant and contract activity at the Oral History Center over these many years. Graduate students such as Chad Berry and Patrick Ettinger also contributed many additional interviews from some of these communities. Timothy Borden did expert work in making editorial revisions and finding just the right photographs to accompany the text.

Support for all of this work came from many sources. Indiana University and various deans responsible for research centers, such as Mort Lowengrub and George Walker, provided a firm foundation for our endeavors. At various times crucial grants were awarded from the National Endowment for the Humanities and the Spencer Foundation. Robert M. Taylor, Jr., and the Indiana Historical Society were among the chief sponsors of much of this work, and they were indispensable in sustaining our attempts at oral history on numerous occasions. We could not have completed all that went into this book without them.

Introduction

In 1940 Americans could view the movie version of Thorton Wilder's play *Our Town* and reflect upon the capacity of ordinary people to create virtuous lives by accepting traditional models of marriage, family, religion, and American nationalism. Framing the idea of a nation through the lens of a mythical small community, a common practice in American film in the 1930s and 1940s, this story created a portrait of citizens in Grover's Corners, New Hampshire, who revered their nation's history, valued social cohesion over divisiveness, exhibited a deep level of religious faith, and were staunchly democratic. Without a doubt the context of this story was the deteriorating international situation in the late 1930s when Wilder wrote his play. Totalitarian regimes were rising in power in Europe, and many in the world feared the possibility of a war. In Wilder's story there was seriousness of purpose about representing America and Americans as good and decent people in both the past and the present in comparison to the practices of ruthless, godless, and antidemocratic dictators. Wilder's narrative idealized communal life and the nation. In his imagination citizens held no doubts about the value of the dominant ideas that patterned their lives: patriotism, religion, and community. The linkages between people in this locale and between local thought and national institutions were firm and unbroken. This was exactly the type of cultural solidarity that America would need as it stood ready to act in concert to fight Japan and Germany in World War II.

Initial reactions to Wilder's story were often critical. Some felt it offered an overly tragic view of Americans because it concentrated so heavily on the repetitive nature of everyday life: birth, marriage, and death. Critics felt such a narrative failed to capture adequately the creative capacity that people had to improve both their own lives and the life of their nation.

But Wilder was not interested in endorsing visions of progress and dreams of self-improvement as much as he was in exploring how common people in a democracy possessed the freedom to give meaning to their daily existence. For Wilder progress was best measured not by technological change, success, or abundance but by the preservation of an ideal of free choice that allowed people—even in small towns—to choose the ways they would live their lives. If that independence led them to reaffirm conventions and resist innovations, so be it. The point was that in democracies people could at least make choices about what they believed and who they wanted to be. In autocratic regimes such decisions were imposed.[1]

In *Our Town* institutional loyalty, patriotism, mutualism, and self-sacrifice were presented as natural qualities of Americans. These attributes were embedded in the relationships of everyday life: marital, communal, and religious. Unlike people living in totalitarian regimes, American men and women felt they were part of a caring community where ties between the sexes, between the classes, and between the dead and the living were vital and unbroken. Not surprisingly, relationships in Grover's Corners were marked by high degrees of equality, unity, and love. There were mild deviations from these norms: some people drank too much, and ethnic minorities like the Poles and the French Canadians lived apart from the rest of the town, "beyond the railroad tracks." But audiences learned that the town was essentially cohesive. Old-line residents, generally Protestant and Republican in this section of America, had accepted the immigrants, and the local newspaper editor claimed that there was hardly any variety at all in the local culture, except "Robinson Crusoe and *The Bible*."

While this narrative of America had democratic intentions in 1940, we should remember that it was ultimately mythical because it drained away almost all evidence of local conflict, politics, and tension and made consensus appear inevitable. *Our Town* was a story that rendered citizens, town, and nation exemplary. It did not invoke memories of traumatic events or speak about ways in which the community or the nation may have inflicted suffering in the past. Although it served very well as a basis to defend America against external enemies in the 1940s, its reaffirmation of everything traditional did not offer any formula for how America might solve domestic problems if they were acknowledged sometime in the future.[2]

Town citizens also clearly embraced their place within a highly structured and traditional narrative of American history. Reasserting the power of national culture to shape local thought, Wilder's story took pains to show how tombstones at the local cemetery were dated from the beginnings of American life in the seventeenth century, and a section of the burial ground was given over to Civil War veterans who "had a notion that the union had to be kept together. . . . And they went and died about it." People knew the exact location where William Jennings Bryan once delivered an oration in the town, and a young girl in the story is depicted as busily working on a speech about the Monroe Doctrine and the Louisiana Purchase. In this place the local and national versions of cultural memory are in agreement; harmony reigns between the past and the present and between the national and the local.

Much of the early part of the story centers on relations between a young man and woman, George Gibbs and Emily Webb. George dreams about going away to college, while Emily appears to enjoy studying American history and making speeches. She sees her future as a wife and a mother and even warns Gibbs that if he goes away to school he might entirely forget about his hometown and about her. She also tells him that she is looking for a man with "character," a trait that is exemplified in the story by men who work at creating caring relationships with women in marriage. Emily's father, the town editor, ultimately reaffirms this goal for adult men by telling George that his father once advised him to start a union with his spouse by "showing her who's boss." But the editor claimed that he realized such an attempt to exercise dominion over a partner was foolish and asserted that his own happy marriage

[1] Thorton Wilder, *American Characteristics and Other Essays* (New York: Harper and Row, 1979), 73; Donald Haberman, *Our Town: An American Play* (Boston: Twayne Publishers, 1989), 2–7, 69.

[2] On the definition of mythical see Roland Barthes, *Mythologies* (New York: Hill and Wang, 1994), 143. Barthes understands the political to encompass the whole of human relations including tensions over social structure and power. For him myth is "depoliticized speech." On the idea of communal memory and "dangerous memory" preventing future change and alterations, see Robert N. Bellah et al., *Habits of the Heart: Individualism and Commitment in American Life* (Berkeley: University of California Press, 1985), 152–53.

was based more upon a sense of equality. In Grover's Corners, as in the 1946 mythical town of Bedford Falls depicted in the film *It's a Wonderful Life*, selflessness won out over individual ambition.

George learns this lesson well. He tells Emily that establishing a relationship with someone "you are very fond of" is just as important as going to college. In this simple decision to pursue a loving relationship within his community rather than a career through college, the tale manages to head off any potential conflict between communal and national harmony and individual ambition, a resolution that would obviously serve the effort to mobilize the country during the war. On the eve of the wedding Emily and George reveal that both had contemplated lives without marriage but ultimately elected to join together rather than stand alone; this is their contribution to the preservation of local and national society.

At the end of *Our Town* Emily, now living in a "happy home" on a farm with George, has a dream sequence. In a stark scene on a hilltop where townsfolk have gathered to commemorate her death, she imagines she can see beloved ancestors who have passed away. She tells her deceased mother-in-law that she and George have managed to make their marriage and farm work. And she is able to observe her own parents when she was a child and the scenes of other contented households where married adults remained committed to one another. Such images were designed not only to foster attachments to forefathers and foremothers but to all Americans who came before them. We can love our town and our nation and defend it in the war to come because these are places where people we cared about lived and defended themselves. *Our Town* is a narrative that aspires to make the individual, the community, and the nation one and argues that the best of all possible futures will depend more on mutualism than individualism and more on continuity than change.

Stories told in this book, however, by residents of towns in Indiana, offer a more critical view of American life. They retain some of the mythical qualities of Wilder's vision and recall the existence of a caring community, but they also contain "dangerous memories" or remembrances of economic and communal degeneration. They contest, in other words, positive and sentimental views of the society and the nation in which these citizens lived. And they find fault with many of the changes that have marked American life since World War II. They even indicate that individuals resented some of the personal sacrifices they were forced to make for others. Taken together, the ordinary people of Evansville, Paoli, Indianapolis, Anderson, South Bend, and Whiting do, indeed, reveal attachments to the idea of America and to its history, but ultimately in the last decades of the twentieth century they remember lives with narratives that are less cohesive than Wilder's and disrupted by significant amounts of regret. Many of these stories mourn what has been lost more than they exalt what has been gained. Ultimately these tales from the heartland reject any effort to view the past in terms of nostalgia or celebration. Rather, after the traumatic years of depression and war, they tend to come to terms with life in America by discussing something of the cost of progress and change.

Personal accounts of remembering, like other expressions of local history, can be seen as forms of resistance to ways of knowing the world that are constructed by powerful institutions like political parties, religious bodies, and corporations. Scholars often use the term metanarratives or grand narratives to refer to comprehensive stories that attempt to organize the way we understand the past, the present, and the future. Such stories usually endorse powerful ideals like nationalism, Christianity, free-market capitalism, or individualism and can render personal outlooks as secondary. When a scholar like John Fiske, for instance, argued that "popular knowledges are localizing ones," he meant that individuals are always forced to make sense of the vastness of their "social experience" from a subordinate point of view. Thus, schoolteachers who lived through most of this century in Paoli, Indiana, for instance, must attempt to understand their experiences by reconciling in the best way they can the life they have actually lived with grand narratives of what has transpired over time, such as the interpretation that the American economy has made things better for us all. They must connect all they know with knowledge derived from their family's past, nation's history, work, and religion, from their television watching, and from what they have seen in consumer advertising in order to shape some sort of story that makes sense to them. No small feat. But the task is made easier because their stories are inevitably highly selective and subjective. Personal and local narratives of remembering are never designed to account for all that has happened; they do not aspire to be comprehensive or accurate in the way a history textbook or a political or religious doctrine might. Rather, they reshape grand narratives, select from them what appears useful, and condense the full sweep of history into tales and anecdotes that constitute a point of view.

Oral histories are one way to examine how individuals manage to connect personal and local experience with larger historical ideas and events. Thus, the fictitious schoolteachers from Paoli might tell how they desired to serve their students and at the same time felt the need to support their nation in World War II. One could feel local and national attachments at the same time. Alessandro Portelli calls such histories a "composite genre" that reveal the correlation between biography and history. As such they allow us to see how people felt they were tied to others in the community and their nation. These stories offer us clues of how local people situate themselves in the sweep of change over time and become active agents in the process of creating meaning or producing a cultural story. They reaffirm the point made by James Wertsch that the human mind is constantly mediating between individual and social levels of experience. For Fiske and others this means that individuals must resist to some extent some of the powerful ideologies that pervade their lives like nationalism or even Christianity for that matter, even as they accept some of what they teach. They must do this he feels in order to "extricate" from those ideas something that will prove to be compatible with what they have learned from the actual lives they have lived. For individual memories and life stories to embrace uncritically powerful ideological statements—such as the American economy will bring material advancement for all or that individual happiness can best be realized through the fulfillment of personal goals—would mean that people would have to screen out counter experiences in which they suffered economic reversals or experienced happiness by serving others. Complete harmony would have to exist between powerful collective myths and the intricate nature of daily life. This would be difficult; it would mean that life in these Indiana towns was as harmonious and mythical as Wilder's representation of town and nation had been.[3]

In stories from Indiana towns offered here, we can see human minds striking some middle ground between Fiske's idea of resistance and Wilder's dream of acceptance. These recollections defy myths that say Americans have enjoyed only material progress over most of this century but reveal an acceptance of the ideal that personal happiness should be attainable in America. The point of view from these towns is ultimately ironic for it says that American communal life in this century was marked by both moral and communal decline, on the one hand, and progress and improvement on the other. The political and economic institutions of the American nation certainly rewarded its citizens with a better life, as these voices tell it. But this progress was attained at the expense of attachments to communal and national institutions that these citizens of Indiana felt deeply. That is why they talk so much about betrayal, decline, and disunity in a society that ultimately defeated totalitarianism and gave them abundance. These recollections of anonymous people from Paoli, Evansville, Indianapolis, Anderson, South Bend, and Whiting tell us that at the end of the twentieth century the quest for a harmonious and caring society—something Wilder and millions of other Americans wanted in this century—was only partially realized. Invariably these narrators recalled families that cooperated to survive hard times and confront life's problems. Much of their version of the past tells of individuals who felt they counted only because they were part of a larger, collective identity such as a family or a labor union and not because they were a successful person. And, yet, the people speaking here did not deny that material changes in their lives constituted a distinct improvement and that they held some resentment toward limits placed on desires they once had. In a way we can argue that their personal testimony, with its deep sense of uncertainty, very much resisted any effort to create a history of the twentieth century in terms that

[3] John Fiske, *Power Plays, Power Works* (London: Verso, 1993), 206. For a treatment of local memories and knowledge as tools of resistance to the "imperial designs" of more powerful political forces, see Joanne Rappaport, *The Politics of Memory: Native Historical Interpretation in the Colombian Andes* (Durham and London: Duke University Press, 1998). Also see Alessandro Portelli, *The Battle of Valle Giulia: Oral History and the Art of Dialogue* (Madison: University of Wisconsin Press, 1997), 3–6, and James Wertsch, *Mind as Action* (New York: Oxford University Press, 1998), 4, 13–14.

would simply venerate the good qualities of life in either Indiana or America.[4]

The image of a moral community in the past—infused with caring families, corporations, and citizens—that slowly withered away is the most powerful component of cultural memory these people articulate. They clearly felt part of a collective entity, but they argue that such a unity no longer exists. This is the most dominant way that these people defined what they thought the community of the past was and tell us of what they might hope it can be again. Their stories confirm the point made by Thomas Bender in his study of the idea of community in America. Bender argued, correctly I believe, that a community is not simply a place in which a group lives, but it is a subjective feeling or an emotional attachment that carries a sense of mutual obligations and common understandings. And we can extend this point to suggest that it resides, therefore, primarily in the mind and in the memories and stories people tell. Admittedly, the intervening hand of the historian pulls these local stories and fragments of remembering together from the thousands of hours of taped recordings collected from these towns. Wertsch might argue that the historian brings these personal tales to a level of "full narrativity." Nevertheless, the collective power of their myth of mutualism commands our attention because it is so fully developed as a story and so pervasive in the hundreds of life stories collected for this project.[5]

It is not possible to determine from these stories all of the possible explanations for the power of this collective myth. But we can certainly see traces of some of the sources of this point of view in these recollections. All but two of the narrators in this book were born before 1930, and most were born between 1900 and 1920. The identity and memory of these individuals were imprinted heavily by ideals and events that took place during the half century after World War I. In their life stories, collected from 1976 to 1996, they compare those formative years with recent times and offer us an overall perspective on the twentieth century. They lived during a period when wild swings in economic and political life pushed people off farms and into factories and forced citizens to fear for both their economic and political survival in sustained episodes of depression and war. In this era powerful ideologies and political mobilizations impacted upon the lives and locales described here. Family solidarity was encouraged to meet the realities of economic scarcity; political mobilizations called upon thousands of Hoosiers to join unions or parties that endorsed the idea that the government and authorities needed to assist them; large companies like Studebaker and General Motors offered workers paternalistic promises of steady work and benefits; and the United States government articulated emotional calls to serve and sacrifice during the greatest war of the twentieth century. In short, these people were exposed to constant reminders in their lives of the ideal of mutualism or reciprocal obligations. They were told that they had a debt to other citizens and to their nation and were led to believe that their employers, communities, and nation owed them something in return. Clearly, however, they saw significant reversals in all of these patterns, a point they made forcefully in their stories. The outlook of their generation was fashioned from the interplay of ideological expression and personal experience and not from any single event like the Great Depression, but it was also rooted in the comparison they were able to make between the age of mutualism they recall and the one that they feel has replaced it.

Consider some of the discrete aspects of this collective story and central characters who were invoked to exemplify this ideal of mutualism. Alice Hottenstein, born in 1918, recalled that her father was "a warm and caring person." She emphasized that he had little wealth, "but did many nice things for people" during the 1930s. In Paoli, Owen Stout, born in a log cabin in 1903, told of his father taking care of his parents in their old age. "There were no such things as nursing homes; that was unknown in those days. There was no welfare. There was no help of any kind except the neighbors. And the neighbors then were very cooperative and very helpful." Stout is a good example of how memories were retrieved as ways of interpreting what individuals were encountering in the present. He even described cooperative ventures among neighbors to cut timber and clear land for farming. Elizabeth

[4] Luisa Passerini, "Mythbiography in Oral History," in Raphael Samuel and Paul Thompson, *The Myths We Live By* (London: Routledge, 1990), 49–69. This volume offers excellent evidence of how the past is used as a benchmark to mark both progress and decline.

[5] Thomas Bender, *Community and Social Change in America* (New Brunswick, N.J.: Rutgers University Press, 1978), 6–8. Wertsch, *Mind as Action*, 78–80.

Cornwell, who taught school in the same town, characterized her neighborhood as "close-knit." She recalled that people would help each other out and visit almost every night even if they were not related. Anne Malott, in describing patterns of life in the Stringtown section of Indianapolis in the 1950s, claimed that "Stringtowners were like a large family." In Anderson, Naomi Wilson explained how she and her oldest brother worked to support her younger siblings after their father had died. On the assembly line of an Anderson auto plant she recalled women celebrating each other's birthday and offering kindness when someone had an operation or a car accident. The family metaphor was frequently used to describe relations between workers and management at the Studebaker Company in South Bend. In Whiting, Sophie Gresko told a story of how her aunt's tavern served as a supportive enterprise for newly arrived immigrants who were looking for kin or for jobs in a new country. And Leo Kus carefully explained how men of modest means in northwest Indiana helped each other by offering their skills cooperatively to build family homes.

Invariably, in the minds of these citizens of Indiana, the imagined community of cohesion and helpfulness did not last. A decline in communal attachments and sense of obligations to help others inevitably took place in their collective version of cultural memory. One woman lamented the deterioration of downtown Evansville in her lifetime. "There's nobody downtown. . . . You go downtown and there will be a few people sitting watching a water fountain while they eat their sandwich but that isn't what a town should be." Louanne Rutherford noted that Paoli is not what it used to be. She explained:

> For one thing the kids aren't as well behaved as they used to be. . . . We have a lot more people from the city. Names that we don't recognize. That's something else. When you were a kid in Paoli everybody knew everybody else.

Several residents indicated the demise of civic and social activities over time on the Paoli town square. Joe Wilson thought that feelings of solidarity among workers in the Anderson auto plants dwindled over time. He felt that as some workers acquired more seniority they did not care about more recent arrivals who lost their jobs. "These people are not grouped together like we was [*sic*] when we formed this union," Wilson lamented. In South Bend evidence of a deteriorating communal life was massive during the course of their lives. The closing of the Studebaker plant, the loss of pension benefits, and erosion of self-respect among town workers were all duly noted. A former resident of Whiting, Bill Curosh, claimed that in the present "everybody wants their own way now, and I don't think people [in the 1990s] respect the law like we used to."

We should not be surprised that the memory narratives of ordinary Americans who lived through most of the twentieth century were created from an uneasy mixture of ideas of progress and decline and reflect a strong element of regret. Cultural memory, that level of memory defined by Marita Sturken as one fashioned on a cultural field between the idiosyncratic rememberings of individuals and the formal constructions of institutions, has been highly debated in our times. Thus, when the Smithsonian Institution wanted to blend an account of America's dropping of the atomic bomb and the ending of World War II with a depiction of the devastation the bomb brought to the Japanese, a fierce political battle broke out. Individual veterans who fought the war shared a memory of their actions that would not tolerate a sympathetic attitude toward the Japanese that they perceived in the Smithsonian plans. Such contests over meaning did not exist in the mythical world of *Our Town*, but they occur frequently in the post-Vietnam nation where sentimental ideas of America as a good society and Americans as good people—something that would have been readily accepted in the 1940s—find strong opposition from those who feel America has been unfair to them and to others in the world. The point can be made easily by thinking for a minute about the symbols expressed by the Iwo Jima Memorial and the Vietnam Veterans Memorial in Washington, D.C. The World War II monument stands as a sign that Americans pulled together and were united in their effort to win the war that Wilder wanted them to win. At the Vietnam memorial ideals of a united nation and victory are disputed by names of those who died and the acts of public sorrow and regret that have been expressed over the war at the site. Sturken sees public forms of remembering "entangled" in our age. That is to say that extensive intermingling of personal and official and positive and negative versions of the past have taken place. All Americans do not see the nation or its history in the same way as they did in Grover's Corners. Some see only noble patriots and a venerable nation as did the veterans who criticized the Smithsonian's initial plans to exhibit the *Enola Gay*. Others see the American past as one that was marked by unfairness and the creation of victims as do some of the veterans of the Vietnam War or marchers for civil rights.[6]

Despite the strong affirmation of the ideal of a cooperative society, entanglement definitely characterizes these stories from Indiana. They demonstrated one significant difference from Sturken's account of modern American cultural memory, however. Sturken feels that ambivalent and contested views of what this nation and its history have meant are products of a more contentious era after the traumatic events like Vietnam and the AIDS epidemic that forced citizens to confront the existence of pain and suffering within their own communities and within their nation. But stories from Indiana towns reveal that the production of a conflicted cultural memory—one with critical and positive dimensions—was well under way before these events and was driven by the traumas of corporate plant shutdowns, technological change, human migrations, and racism in places such as Indiana.

Thus, at the end of the twentieth century no one narrative appears to determine American history or its political culture. Wilder's dream of consensus, shared by many Americans of all backgrounds over time, is now not so readily accepted. The attempt to create consensual narratives of cultural memory that incorporate and subdue the vagaries of personal experience and desires seems to be unattainable. Human minds continue to mediate various layers of reality as they have always done. Certainly if one walks about the Washington Mall today, as central a site to our national collective memory as there is, the sense of ambiguity and uncertainty is evident. Alongside the monuments to the famous men who founded our nation, saved it, and made it more democratic are images of victims: the dead from Vietnam, the unemployed from the Great Depression, and soldiers with uncertain looks on their faces proceeding cautiously through a battlefield in Korea. Images of Holocaust victims from the 1940s have now penetrated this sacred space as well. In an age when films, television, textbooks, and memorials cannot agree on one view of America and its past, we should not be surprised to find misgivings in personal stories from the nation's heartland.[7]

But the lack of narrative coherence in these stories should not obscure the effort and the thought that has gone into them over a long period of time. Oral histories are able to uncover some of the process of creating cultural memories that took place over time in these towns and suggest that these ordinary people considered the issues they raised extensively and offered a variety of explanations for why things evolved in the way that they did. Communal decline, for instance, was attributed to a number of factors. A woman in Evansville blamed the demise of the city's downtown on federal urban renewal programs that tore down too many buildings. Sometimes critical references would be made to the expansion of federal welfare programs that were often seen as promoting moral decline by fostering laziness. But a more common explanation for the deterioration of the moral and communal fiber of these towns was grounded in the introduction of new technologies. Paul Waynick felt that people were less likely to gather in churches and schools in Paoli than they used to because they were now attracted to a variety of new forms of entertainment. "The people watch television, they have more entertainment, and they don't work as hard," he reasoned. Another woman felt that civic activities on the Paoli square had degenerated in part due to the advent of television and the widespread use of automobiles that allowed citizens to leave the community for more activities. Others associated automobiles with moral decline; younger people were chastised for having too many cars and too much sex. In fact, the widespread criticism of the social impact of television and automobiles demonstrated how these local stories could, indeed, resist powerful interpretations in their culture—mostly from advertisers—that had claimed such inventions were simply keys to greater personal happiness. At times these devices were certainly seen as evidence of material abundance, but they were also interpreted with considerable skepticism.

Finally, in towns like Anderson and South Bend,

[6] Marita Sturken, *Tangled Memories: The Vietnam War, the AIDS Epidemic, and the Politics of Remembering* (Berkeley: University of California Press, 1997), 3–5, 13–15.

[7] On the ability of powerful narratives to subdue the force and unpredictability of personal forms of memory, see Michael S. Roth, *The Ironist Cage: Memory, Trauma, and the Construction of History* (New York: Columbia University Press, 1995), 209.

corporate practices and decisions were also held responsible for the deterioration of moral and communal life. Capitalism was not put up for review in *Our Town*, but it was evaluated in the cultural memory of thousands of Americans who lived through most of this century. They revealed that they had placed faith in the promise of this economic system to deliver security and prosperity and had often felt betrayed when it did not. People who lived through the prosperity and the decline of the Studebaker plant in South Bend or the Standard Oil Refinery in Whiting knew very well that investors and company officials often made decisions that were detrimental not only to their own welfare but also to the welfare of their towns. Their collective memories tell us that corporate capitalism was seen as a mixed blessing: able to deliver a better life and economic security on the one hand and capable of destroying the moral basis of community life on the other.

Stories of communal decay, however, were entangled with tales of personal anguish over the need to serve others. Despite the veneration of the ideal of a cooperative community, they revealed that their lives and their towns were sites of personal and social turmoil as well. Individuals expected to serve the needs of families and communities under conditions of economic scarcity but often expressed regret over the costs of such obligations to their own sense of personal desire. Alice Hottenstein wanted to be a nurse as a young woman but was forced to enter an Evansville factory. Ralph Dorris gave up his idea to become an electrical engineer when his father was injured and he had to go to work. When a man in Paoli expressed a desire to go to law school, his father told him that he simply did not have the money to help him. One woman in Paoli recalled that her father would not speak to her mother for a long period of time because she had registered to vote. That same woman expressed frustration that she did not get the opportunities to enter professions as women do today. In this case the present was better than the past. Naomi Wilson wanted to become a nurse during the Great Depression but was forced to do housework and take care of children in order to earn money.

Bitterness over personal sacrifices was reinforced by memories of class and economic conflict. In Paoli there were signs of a social divide in the local schools between people who lived in town and those, deemed inferior, who came from the surrounding countryside. Men on the General Motors assembly lines in Anderson complained about the arbitrary manner in which managers fired workers and the difficult conditions under which they toiled. Women at Studebaker expressed dissatisfaction when they were told they would have to relinquish their jobs to returning veterans after World War II. And residents of Whiting were critical of company decisions to lay off employees after the great fire at the local refinery in 1955.

Memories of racial exclusion were additional deterrents to any attempt to recall town life as simply cohesive and harmonious. In towns like Indianapolis, where there was a fairly substantial population of African Americans, it was impossible to dismiss the fault line of race. African Americans remember all kinds of barriers to social integration. Listen to W. B. Ransom, a black lawyer in the city, explain the matter of equal access to housing.

> There was a long fight here on housing discrimination. We were fighting all the time. Blacks were fighting to get housing accommodations and there was a good deal of residential segregation.

Ransom added that he could recall how "jubilant" blacks were when they were able to buy property north of Thirty-eighth Street in the city. And he detailed how this split in the town's residential patterns was enforced by the prejudicial lending practices of institutions that favored whites over blacks. For Alberta Murphy, a black migrant from Tennessee to Indianapolis, it would have been difficult to create a story in which the past was better than the present because she had suffered so much as a young person. In her lifetime she explained how she experienced change from being treated as a second-class citizen to a person who could expect some acceptance in the world in which she lived. Although, even in stories of African Americans that are dominated by accounts of unfairness, there are hints of nostalgia for the segregated community, as when Indianapolis blacks expressed pride in their academic achievement at an all-black high school.

The "dangerous" past was also marked by memories of deprivation and stories of improvement. Most of the people who lived through the depression and the postwar era were struck by the obvious advancements in material and economic life. They frequently noted the expanded use of cars and television sets in their daily lives. Owen Stout measured material progress over time by recalling the fact that he was born in a log cabin in 1903 near Paoli. His fellow townsman, Benjamin Minton, created a portrait that could have been applied to hundreds of people interviewed in these oral history projects:

> I grew up during the depression, and it took no money to keep a family going. . . . [My parents] did have a little money in the bank when the depression started, but when the bank closed, why they lost all that money. There was no money anywhere.

When he thought about his life in Kentucky before moving to Anderson, Joe Wilson admitted that "there wasn't no work down there and . . . you'd starve to death on a farm." Life in Anderson was not much better in the 1930s. Wilson recalled living in a house where the walls were so thin that a person "about froze to death." Sometimes deprivation was judged to be a life without Social Security or reliable retirement programs. It was the expectation of security raised by government and corporate welfare practices that made the loss of jobs and pensions such a traumatic experience for many. Some of these people actually moved from deprivation to economic security and back to deprivation in one lifetime. At some level they reveal that they felt victimized by American life itself.

But the ironic nature of remembering community here—both the lament over its demise and the critique of its power—should not obscure the fact that these local histories still manage to convey a sense that their narrators felt themselves part of a larger, imagined community or nation. To some extent Wilder's dream did live in Indiana. People like Alice Hottenstein offered histories of the settlement of their ancestors in the Evansville area and also volunteered their time to perform work for a local chapter of the Daughters of the American Revolution, which had decided to commemorate those from Vanderburgh County who had died in the war that created the American nation. She also revealed how clearly she recalled a moment of national tragedy—the assassination of President John F. Kennedy. She recalled crying because "he was around my age," an indication that shared feelings could transcend geographical boundaries. And she felt the killing suggested that America would have to alter some of its violent ways. Ralph Dorris, who lived in the same town, said that he measured progress in his life by the achievements of Franklin D. Roosevelt's New Deal and federal programs for Social Security and the support of labor unions. Owen Stout blended images of his personal history and national history when he told a story of how his grandfather served in the Civil War and then deserted his military unit to be with his wife when she delivered a baby. Stout's own effort at historic preservation included keeping part of the log cabin in which he was born and the honorable discharge papers of his grandfather. A woman in Stout's hometown of Paoli marked the moment of her birth as "three weeks before the Armistice was signed" to end World War I. "My daddy had been wounded actually about a month before I was born," she related. This woman also kept a bust of John Kennedy and a print of Dwight Eisenhower in her home. Lotus Dickey told interviewers about his grandfather's trek from Ohio to Indiana by covered wagon and in the same story emphasized his great-grandfather's participation in the American Revolution.

Sometimes the presentation of patriotic identities and the attachment to the idea of an American nation took the form not of ancestor reverence but actual participation in crusades to affirm one's rights. This was a version of American identity not really possible in Wilder's story because the overwhelming goodness of the society and people he mythologized inferred that there was no basis for militant political action at home. But in stories about the Anderson sit-down strike we hear of citizen strikers riding in automobile caravans and waving American flags. Studebaker workers revealed the pride they took in helping to build bombers during World War II—an indication that personal stories did not always resist the dominant narratives of American nationalism. Otto Klausmeyer thought that the mutualism he remembered from Studebaker was very much an American trait. He noted a strong "father-son heritage" in the corporation; sons followed their fathers into the plant. "I think that's part of America . . . this kind of relationship," he observed, "and I think the proprietors of the business really had a fatherly feeling of responsibility for the employees." In a sense, Klausmeyer's view of the nation and the paternalistic corporation was grounded in the idea of a moral community in which family members, employers, and workers took an interest in each other's welfare. Some workers in South Bend recalled that the plant actually closed only a month after the assassination of John Kennedy and noted that they had hoped that both the president and the corporation would work to bring economic stability to their lives.

It is no wonder that people who saw their lives, communities, and nation tied together in this way were devastated by the reality of corporate shutdowns and economic decline. In Whiting, Joe Sotak observed that layoffs of loyal workers in the 1950s and the hiring of younger workers less committed to their employers in the 1960s would harm the American nation itself. "This country will go to hell. I really think so," he asserted, "[the younger generation] are living for today and the hell with tomorrow. I would think that if we were in a real big war . . . we would have more people running across the border being chicken." Sotak feared for the future of his country if the ideal of mutual obligation were abandoned.

These people, who lived through much of the twentieth century in Indiana communities, further revealed their lasting feelings of attachment to family, town, and nation by presenting themselves as individuals who were highly moral. That is to say that they described themselves essentially as people who were more concerned about the welfare of others than of themselves. They refused to accept completely modern ideas—widely distributed through our culture today in advertising, film, and television—that celebrated personal satisfaction as the highest goal of one's life. In this regard they used their cultural memory and local history to resist powerful ideologies of individualism and consumer capitalism that marked the nation at the end of the twentieth century. They thought they were more principled and righteous than the generations of Americans born after them. They tell us over and over that they took up family obligations over personal ambition, hard work over laziness, friendliness over hatred, and duty over rebelliousness. They certainly disclosed that life could be difficult under such circumstances by lamenting at times the sacrificing of personal ambitions. And they tell of problems of alcoholism and racism in their towns. But generally the contradictions in their stories are resolved by the affirmation that mutualism should stand above individualism. That is why they present themselves as people who supported the major institutions that patterned their lives: church, family, corporation, and nation. In the words of Paul John Eakin, their self-portrayals involved "culturally sanctioned models of identity."[8] But these were models rooted in a particular age; they are much less sanctioned today. The moral conservatism they exhibited through their tales of selflessness, mutualism, and patriotism was countered somewhat by hints that they were politically liberal. That is to say they did not tend to defend individualist behavior in the marketplace and repeatedly had positive things to say about New Deal programs, corporate welfare plans, and unions. Moral conservatives and political liberals also distinguished most of them from the generation of both conservatives and liberals that followed. The former would not tend to sanction their desire for intervention into market forces, and the latter would not share their limited sense of personal fulfillment. The community they reconstructed worked for them precisely because people and institutions cared for each other; consequently, they are alarmed by the thought of a society and a nation driven by unconnected individuals pursuing wealth and personal dreams and by corporations and government disavowing the needs of employees and citizens. They offer us a version of community that saw person, town, and nation fully integrated. Not only do they regret that those bonds appear to be weakened, but they also do not think a world without their values and memories will work. And that is why they remembered their towns in ways that they did. They feel more connected to us than we do to them and feel obliged to caution us about what they think we are doing with the towns and the nation they left us. Their cultural memory is constructed not only to affirm their collective identity but also to join debates now taking place concerning the moral and economic direction of the American nation.[9]

[8] Paul John Eakin, *Touching the World: Reference in Autobiographies* (Princeton, N.J.: Princeton University Press, 1992), 72.

[9] John Bodnar, "Generational Memory in an American Town," *Journal of Interdisciplinary History* 26 (spring 1996): 619–37.

Paoli

is a small town in the central portion of southern Indiana. In this chapter seven residents reconstruct patterns of daily life and social change in the community and in the surrounding rural region throughout most of the twentieth century. They offer vivid glimpses of family life and relate how the courthouse square was seen as an important center of civic activity. They tell us what it was like to attend school in this area before World War II and how some people saw the need to make "moonshine whiskey." Excellent descriptions of how people made a living are also provided. Owen Stout conveys some of the rigors of sustaining a farm, and others describe toil in a local basket factory. Overall, these individuals assert their view that the communal ties they felt in the Paoli of their youth have dissipated and that the town no longer appears to be as isolated and cohesive as it once was.

***Born in 1917, Paul Waynick grew up on a farm in Greenfield Township. He later owned an insurance agency in Paoli.*[1]**

Waynick: My paternal great-grandfather, Joshua Waynick, came to Orange County in 1847 with two first cousins, George and Solomon Waynick. They settled in a little village of Valeene.

And my maternal great-grandfather came ahead and settled in Greenfield Township. He homesteaded land there in 1854. I still have ownership of that forty acres. His daughter wound up with it and then I got it through her.

They were just looking for better land. Just everybody was on the move. They came by the Cumberland Gap, with horses. They came here, and he first homesteaded land. Land was getting scarce, I suppose, in North Carolina. And my maternal grandparents, of course, were Jordan and Minnie Seybold. And his great-grandfather was Thomas R. Seybold, who founded and bought land at Helix, the community of Helix, which is no longer in existence.

Well, then, he had a son, Robert, that homesteaded land in what is now known as Greenbrier. You'll find it on the road map here. It had a post office here named Greenbrier. When Joshua came here, he worked for Robert Seybold. And he eventually married his daughter. And they, of course, built a log cabin first and they pulled it down, moved it, and made a barn out of it. That barn was sold in, let's see, in 1981—I think it was. And it's now a log house on the west edge of Paoli.

And then, of course, he had one son, my grandfather, Daniel Waynick. And their house still stands. Many parts of it is log, but it's still standing.

When I got out of common school, in the eighth grade, I wanted to go forward in education. Well, that year they got a school bus to haul you into Paoli. And I hadn't been to town except for two or three times. Scared me to death.

Now what year was this?

It was in 1931. We went to town maybe once a month to buy groceries. I hadn't been here hardly any time. It was a large bus. As a matter of fact, at that time there was nothing against allowing other people to ride it. We had more riders than we did students most times.

Paul Waynick
Waynick family

I really enjoyed my four years of schooling. I'd taken bookkeeping and started out with a farm course and saw I didn't like that. And then I wanted to go to law school. And my dad said, "We haven't got the money. You don't need to go to law school." So I didn't. But I've always been sorry that I didn't go ahead and carry on. But I didn't.

And, of course, I married at the age of twenty-four. Had bought my own farm then and tried to farm for a few years. I became disenchanted with it, didn't make any money, and didn't enjoy it.

So Ralph Fleming owned a Fleming Insurance Agency. My wife and I talked about it. I came up and talked to Ralph in 1957. Well, he'd had an operation. He had cancer in one leg, melanoma. And so they'd taken his leg off up to his hip. Well, he was very glad to hire me as solicitor.

So I went selling life insurance, hospital insurance, automobile insurance, everything there was to go. I was

[1] Interviewed by Catherine A. Jones, 8 and 15 July 1988, Paoli.

Revival meeting, early twentieth century
Orange County Historical Society

out working every day and every day, and every day. Well, in February in 1958, Ralph called me in and said, "I want you to take care of the office for a few days. I've got an appointment for a checkup."

I came in one morning two or three days afterward, came in the office, opened up. He was already there. He said, "Well, I want to sell you my interest." Said, "I've only got a short time to live." Said he had an inoperable tumor behind his lungs.

I said, "You know, Ralph, I don't have any money."

He said, "You don't need any money." He said, "I'll settle for $100 a month with no interest." Which is a pretty good deal for me.

I said, "I want to talk with my wife. And I want to talk with my dad."

My dad said, "Well, you better not do that, you'll go broke."

What did people do for entertainment in Paoli?

They used to hold religious debates. This was about 1911 to 1913, in that territory somewhere. And the first one was at the old Hickory Ridge School, which was in Greenfield Township. My father would take a horse and buggy to these debates.

People became very exited about [religion]. [One Reverend] said, "Now, if you could ever find just *one* item in that Bible that wasn't the way you thought it was, what would you do?"

Fellow said, "If they'd ever find one thing in there that was wrong, I'd still believe it."

That shows the depth of the feeling in this situation.

And they did become very loud. Walt Stout, who lived about a half a mile down the creek from the school where they debated down in Greenville, said he could hear them nights just roaring, just debating. So, I'm sure it was a very exciting time. It was great entertainment.

Yes. I really get that impression.

You see, it had originally been the Christian church, and then some of them broke off. And that's when they formed the Church of Christ—which is still in existence today, in Paoli and different places. And that church is still in Unionville, believe it or not.

Where Youngs Creek is now. And the old church is still there. And there used to be a church on the hill. It was a Baptist church. It's now torn down.

My family was always Methodist. My mother and father belonged to Moores Ridge Methodist Church.

It's a very, very old church. As a matter of fact, I wrote a brief history of it—last year or the year before. I dug up quite a bit of research. It started down off of State Route 145. And then it burned or something.

I can remember it very well. It had two front doors and the men sat on one side of the church and the women sat on the other side of the church. Yes, I was just a very small child. They built the new church in 1924, I believe.

How many acres did your father have?

He had eighty acres. Well, it would be subsistence today. He generally had a team of horses and he'd put out a little corn—tried to raise enough corn to feed his horses. And he had two or three cows. And had about 100 or 150 hens, laying hens. And then, of course, he yarded logs. He'd take his team and pull logs into piles for trucks to haul. He'd take his team, work hard. Made quite a bit of money yarding logs. He liked to do that. He'd yard logs for sawmills.

He was not at all like his father. He was like his mother—his mother was very practical. Very hard worker. He never read. He didn't care about reading.

My grandfather—maternal grandfather—was a character. His name was Jordan. They called him Jorde. He was a heavyset, heavy, big man. Big arms, big hands.

He liked to drink. They said of him, tie one hand behind him and get him half drunk—replace three good men [laughs]. He liked to fight, and he liked to drink. He tried—after his wife died in 1924—he tried to move in with our folks. But my dad didn't believe in drinking, and they just didn't get along, period.

Did you have brothers and sisters?

I had two sisters. They both died in infancy. I have one brother, seven years younger than I am.

Now, my younger brother is very practical. He works the farm. He's like my dad. He farms—that's all he wants to do and that's all he's ever been interested in. Of course, he's retired now, but that's all he always wanted to do. And he was doing pretty well at farming.

Oh, he had milk cows and had a dairy barn, raised a lot of crops too. He bought the Joshua Waynick farm, and then he bought some other acreage, and then he rented a good bottom farm. So, he'd done pretty well in life farming. He really did.

But I wasn't cut out to be a farmer. And I think I could have been successful much younger if I'd have started . . .

But I'd done so much work on so many of the families, and got so many stories. That's rather interesting. And I've got fifteen scrapbooks, big scrapbooks, full of material. When they were building Tucker Lake, I was down there. They tore the old house down, and I accidentally found a big old chest. I thought it was something that, just chuck-jammed full of papers. So I brought it home with me; it was full of letters, advertising, deeds, et cetera, with just a few watermarks on them. But they hadn't really [been] damaged. And out of that I got seventy-odd letters dating back to 1871 that was written in ink. They were in a good state of preservation. A couple of old almanacs, 1890s. I've got advertisements for all kinds of old farm implements. I've got ledgers. I've got about six or eight ledgers dating back into [the] 1850s. Ledgers of the sawmill, the distillery.

The area that you lived in, did you have neighbors close by?

Charlie McBride, he been married five times. His fourth marriage ended in divorce, his first ended in divorce, and two had died. And to get everybody, he'd been married five times. And then he and his fourth wife was divorced, so he would come out about every night and entertain us with stories. He was a great storyteller. He was a wonderful mimic. He could mock other people—talk in their voice.

Women, men—and I wish that I could have had a tape recorder back in those days. I could have given a hundred dollars to heard him talk about the old-timers. He would come on every night with his trusty lantern. Used to see us just practically every night of the week. He'd be out there because he was a single man and I guess he was lonesome.

Well, he'd tell wonderful stories. Indian stories, lost gold mines, lost silver mines, lost lead mines, everything imaginable he would tell about.

Do people still tell stories the same way, do you think?

I don't believe that such a hurried world and so much going on, I don't believe they tell them *exactly* like they did then. There's not the visiting that there was in those days and ages.

People don't stop by and visit and tell tales like they did in those days. It's just a different world. A different society.

And I know, he told stories of caves. One of the caves is on my farm. Well, I rented it before I ever bought it. I bought it from an old lady by the name of Celia Parks. Well, there was a better man rented it and plowed their rows up and down the hill and the land eroded. When it ran up to a cave, the dirt ran over and filled it up. And I started to excavate it a few years ago, and it cost too much money. And since it's such an awful job, I let it go.

But anyway, he told stories about what was in that cave. Supposed to have been some lost gold stored in the cave, one thing and another. And I doubt if he'd have found anything, but I was just going to excavate it to see what I might find. But there was so much trouble, going to take so awful long, I let it drop.

I've probably told you the story about old man Hopper. I don't know whether it's in the Orange County history—about him—or not. But anyhow, he would carry a needle and thread and different items throughout the country selling. He was a pack-peddler. And he lived in this cave and so became known folkwise as Hopper's Cave.

And Celia Parks lived adjoining us on the east side. Well, her husband had died—I think maybe the flu or something—around 1917 or '18. Well, their house had burned and then she lived in a little two-room house. Well, I'd walk through the fields over to the road to get the *Indiana Farmers' Guide*—which incidentally I have two volumes bound, *Indiana Farmers' Guide*, 1928 and 1929 and 1930.

Well then, the farm on the southwest corner, Tom Allen lived. He raised a family of about seven or eight children and lived right on the corner of our farm. Well, the way they had to get out was they had an old dirt road that went out to the main road. Or most of the time, they walked up through our farm to get to go up to what they called Queen City or Greenbrier—where the store was: where Bert Weeks had a country store.

Well then, when I was eight years old, my dad bought this farm off his brother-in-law, and we moved over there. It was like heaven to me. I really enjoyed it. It had a big spring. We had to carry our water from a little spring. The water was warm always. Almost got dry in the summertime.

I carried the water in the dry weather. It wasn't that we didn't have enough rain to catch enough water in the tub for the wash, but I'd go to the spring to carry the water for the washwomen. Oh, about a thousand feet, I think. [Up a] steep hill. You had to go down and, of course, it was a big spring: plenty of water.

In the depression you were about thirteen or fourteen, fifteen years old? What do you remember of that time?

What I can remember is very, very difficult. But I think we carried it better than a lot of people. We had our own food and our own clothes. My dad trapped and they were generous in logs being done, so we done reasonably well. My dad bought a 1923 Chevrolet and then he bought a 1928—and was able to pay for them. He was never in debt, you know. He wasn't rich, I don't mean that. But he was able to subsist, to make a living. He was strict and a good manager. A hard worker.

All I knew was that we were probably a little bit better off than some of the neighbors. Now, some of the neighbors done real well. But Tom Allen, for example, he'd raised a big family, he was a good guy. He lived in a two-room cabin—with a big family and no screen doors. They didn't even have an automobile.

I remember, we were middle class at that time. You didn't have very many neighbors doing better. Our storekeeper had a 1926 Grant Touring—it was a big automobile, you know.

Do you remember any folktales from your grandfather?

A folktale that I have is entitled "Lorenzo Dow." Lorenzo Dow was supposed to have been a famous Methodist minister, and one evening a lady was entertaining an amorous admirer. Her husband was away from home. Suddenly there come a stomp on the door—and it was snowing—and a knock. She went to the door. And it was Lorenzo Dow seeking shelter from the inclement weather. So he was admitted. He had soon taken in what was going on but he didn't say anything. He took off his outer clothes and sat down by the fireplace to dry out. Little bit came a man stomping on the front porch. And the wife jumped up and said, "Oh, my God, my husband."

The suitor paled. Said, "What in the world am I going to do?"

Well, over by the staircase sat a barrel of cotton—probably a staple in the pioneer homes. So Lorenzo Dow grabbed the lid off the barrel and told the suitor, "You jump in here." He jumped in, and he put the lid back on him.

And in a minute, in came the husband, drunk. He looked over at Lorenzo Dow and said, "Who are you?"

"Oh," he said. "I'm the great Lorenzo Dow, the Methodist minister." And he drew himself up to full height. The husband said, "Ah ha." He said, "I remember you." Said, "You can raise the devil, can't you?"

"Oh no," Lorenzo said, "I don't have that power."

"Well," he says, "You *will* raise him." And he pulled out his trusty 45 revolver. Said, "You'll raise him or else."

Well Lorenzo Dow saw that further remonstration was useless, so he just jerked the lid off the barrel of cotton and tossed in a match. Up jumped the suitor and ran out the door with great trails of streams of fire stringing along behind.

And Lorenzo Dow said, "There goes the devil."

Would your grandfather just every night be telling stories?

See, my grandfather wouldn't tell me many of these folk stories. My dad was repeating them from what he heard from him. My grandfather never told me the story of "Poor Old Henry Cobb." My father told it to me. But he had told it to my father.

Now, there was another country store about a half a mile toward the south, Ed Gilliatt operated it. I was not in it very many times. Had a one-room store building. Bert Weeks lived in his store and had one big room for the store and the rest of it he used, well, he had one room in the back he used to test cream in. They had a machine to crank by hand, and they spun the bottles that put sulfuric acid on the top for the test and creamed them. And they spun these, then they got it out. They'd take the calipers and see how much percent of butterfat they had. That's the way farmers got paid for the cream they sold.

He bought that. And he bought rabbits. They gave a nickel apiece. People'd snare rabbits and let them freeze. Bring them up and he'd thaw them on the floor and they'd haul them to Louisville and sell them. Bert said the "niggers" love them. Can you imagine the Pure Food and Drug Laws condoning something like that today?

Bert had a Model T truck and then he bought a '27 Chevrolet ton-truck that he used to haul his produce and get his groceries and things and bring back to the store. I can remember being in the store on Saturday. Billy Allen, a local man—he'd never married, lived with his sister and her husband, Tom Riley—across the road from the store. Well, he decided to put in a gristmill—to grind people's corn into cornmeal. Well, what he'd done—taken toll, certain percentage of the corn—for grinding their meal. Well, he got a Model T Ford and put it on the hind wheel and jacked it up. And then pulled the gristmill with this Model T Ford. Well, on Saturdays there was a steady stream of traffic. The spring wagons run all day, going to get their feed ground, their meal ground, and get their groceries.

One cold—I remember this so well—one cold winter morning, he was grinding the daylights out on this Model T car and he couldn't get it started. Well, Elmer Apple lived just down the road further, and Elmer was a horse of a man. He stood about 6'2" and weighed about two hundred pounds and was *extremely* strong. I've seen him take a one hundred-pound bag of wheat bran, outstretch his arms, and carry on his arms—outstretched—one hundred pounds in either hand, into a building. He was *extremely* strong. He come along, saw Billy Allen trying to crank his Model T, said, "Let me give it a try."

Well, Billy stepped back and Elmer stepped up, and he put his forefinger and thumb over that crank. He spun it like you'd spin a coffee mill. And in a minute or two he got the thing to running.

What did the women think of all this kind of stuff? Did they think, "Oh, those men just . . ."

When I first started to Moores Ridge Church—this as a child—of course, it was a very common practice to see all the women nursing their babies. That's something you don't see today. But you could look all over the church and see the women nursing their babies. But the women sat on one side of the church, and the men sat on the opposite.

And when they built the new church in 1925, that stopped, that practice stopped. People began to be like everybody, like they do today. My grandfather helped build that.

Back then people would go to church twice in one day?

Yes. That oftentimes happened. They don't much any more; but at that time they did. There's more entertainment now than there was in those days. About the only entertainment you had was the church, or school programs of some kind. And you never saw anybody unless you went to a neighbor's house or, once in a while, a traveling salesman would come through.

Nowadays people get their entertainment some other way, but if you had a debate or somebody special would come through, well it was very unusual, very different.

My Grandfather Seybold had a sister that married an Allen—Levi Allen. Well, they moved to Kansas. Well then, his son, Harmon Allen, became a famous minister. He got to be chaplain of Leavenworth Penitentiary, and he got to come on a lecture tour.

He came back in 1929 to Moores Ridge Church—just came back here on a visit. And he sang—he was a wonderful singer. He sang a song, "Life's Railway to Heaven." I thought that was one of the most wonderful songs—I was thirteen years old, twelve years old at the time. And I thought that was a wonderful song. And he was down at Helix then and had his pictures taken. I'm in the photo, and my grandfather, and he and others were, quite a group of them. He talked about the futility of crime and told personal anecdotes about federal prisoners. Of course, he was chaplain of Leavenworth Penitentiary. Very interesting stories he gave.

I remember you saying you only came to town just a few times before you started high school. So were you basically just out there?

Yes. There was no telephones in the country. When I first grew up—just a real small chap—there were some local telephones. They were battery operated. But by the time I was in common school, all the telephones had been eliminated. Not a one. You couldn't get a telephone. There just wasn't a telephone. Nobody had it. A kind of few still hung on the wall, but none of them were in operation. The lines were all down and people quit telephones completely.

Did you move here into town, into Paoli?

I bought an acre—it's just out of town, about a mile out of town. And I didn't like it; cooped up on an acre of land. So we just sold it and moved back and got someone to build us a new home.

Has there been an increase—or decrease—in farming?

Decrease. There is not very many true farmers any more.

When you say "true farmer," what do you mean?

That's all their occupation; that's their sole livelihood. There's a lot of part-time farmers. And there's less of those than there once was.

But the true farmer has to have hundreds of acres—if he's going to make a success out [of] it. A lot of machinery, a lot of equipment. And there's not very many of them. Some of them are still successful, because they don't owe any money—and they've had their farms for years. They're getting up in years and they can operate on a small scale and not worry too much about it. Your debts are all paid.

But as those people retire and die and quit, it's going to become more and more a tremendous, corporation-type thing. Big, big business.

The Paoli town square, you were saying that it really hadn't changed much?

Most of the buildings and a lot of the people are

still here that were here when I started business. And the Orange County Bank, of course, I insure them. One reason I insure the Orange County Bank—I didn't at first insure them—Pete Miller was a heavy stockholder in the Orange County Bank and was on the board of directors. Pete owned a little insurance agency—an old, old, old agency. Probably the oldest agency in the county—or in the township, or town—I expect, at the time. He had some old-time, old-line companies, London and Lancashire, and Ohio Casualty Insurance Company, and Merchant's Property; two or three other old-line companies.

Well, I seen Pete one day, going up the street, and stopped and talked to him a little bit. I said, "Pete, how about buying your agency?"

He said, "Hrump." Up the street he went, never said a word. And two or three days later he came in one day, said, "I'll take three thousand dollars for my agency."

I said, "OK." I just went in and wrote him a check, didn't ask any further questions. Just wrote him a check, went and picked up his supplies.

When you opened up, were the Saturday nights still big? You know, for the farmers?

Oh, real big. Saturday was our biggest day when we first opened up. We worked till five o'clock just as hard-as-it-goes. That's the biggest day we had. Of course, it's changed completely now. Paoli's no longer a Saturday town. We're just open until noon on Saturdays now, and very little business.

Oh, the bank closes Wednesday, and just all the businesses close up on Wednesday.

The A&P Store was here when I moved in here on the square. It's, of course, gone. And then, I guess, at that time too, there was still the theater, I guess, the pharmacy, two pharmacies.

You have three living children?

I have a daughter, and my daughter spent five years at Purdue. Got her master's degree in education and social work and married. She married a boy from Purdue who had a four-year degree in business administration. They came back here, and they wanted to work for me. Well, I was going to have too many in at one time in one business in one building. So I decided I was going to have too much conflict, so I helped them buy a home in Crawford County, the adjoining county, at Leavenworth. I set them up in business—from my agency, as a subagency at Leavenworth. Got them licensed then with United, and they were doing real well. And then Bob, he was selling a lot of property. Then Bob decided that he'd like to go back to school and become a CPA.

So they came in and broke the news to me that they were leaving and going to Tempe, Arizona, for a year. And I had thought—Roberts' Agency in English, and for this agency, give them the share of *it* to work at over at Crawford County. Well then, of course, I had to bring it back up here—all the material stored up here, to handle a lot of this business. But then he went to Tempe, Arizona, and got his CPA license, and then he and my daughter got a divorce.

So, they live in California—but they don't live together.

Is your daughter working out there?

She operates a flower shop. She sells flowers to weddings, and sells them to bars. She's got about, I think, seventy or seventy-five bars in Long Beach, California, that buy flowers from her. She makes good money. I wouldn't want the job. For no way would I want what she does, but it gives her free time. She's a music fan; she's in the folk music. She's gone, first, to West Virginia to a folk music festival. And a local man, Lotus Dickey, was on stage out there with her right recently; they had their picture taken together.

I knew Lotus Dickey.[2] I worked at the old basket factory with Lotus Dickey—years and years ago. Oh, he was a nice—it's been so long ago. It's been fifty years ago, I suspect.

What was the factory like?

They made baskets for . . . peck baskets, half bushel

[2] In his retirement in the 1980s, Lotus Dickey performed at numerous folk music festivals. His work was collected in *The Lotus Dickey Songbook*, eds. Nancy C. McEntire, Grey Larsen, and Janne Henshaw, introduction by Dillon Bustin (Bloomington: Lotus Dickey Music in association with Indiana University Press, 1995).

and bushel. It was a hard place to work, but you had a lot of fun.

You were mentioning about how, you know, the Saturday business has changed. Why do you think it has changed? Have you ever stopped to think about it?

It's a different society. I don't know why. I can't tell you. Of course, the people watch television, they have more entertainment, and they don't work as hard. They have more to do, I think, than they had back when I was growing up. When I was a young man, you walked to a lot of your church functions and one thing and another. And then you got a car.

And they went to the movies. Well, now you've got television. You've got everything imaginable. People go to different cities. They go to restaurants so much more. It's just a different society. I can't tell you why. I don't know.

I've had a tremendous change. I've got pictures of myself when I was about a year or two old, and a buggy with my parents.

I was just thinking about the stories . . .

I didn't tell you about the man that made the bootleg whiskey right above my grandfather's house, did I? Fellow by the name of Jim Riley. I remember him so well. He was an old wizened-up man. And every time he talked, he had to shake his head. He'd shake it like this. He couldn't keep his head still.

Well, he had a whole mouth full of old teeth. Every tooth had been crowned with gold. Well, he chewed tobacco. When his gold teeth would shine up, tobacco juice would roll out of his mouth when he was talking. Pretty nice old gentleman. But he owned a distill. Well, back in the early twenties, when they was rebuilding 150—paving it. U.S. 150? Well, they had a detour that turned off at the railroad crossing, and you go towards the Paoli Peaks. Turned off and went there, and went up on top of the big hill on what they call Copeland Hill. Well, the road forks there. Go right and you go towards Moores Ridge and French Lick.

Well, through this hill lived this Jim Riley. Well, he had a distill and, of course, he was making bootleg whiskey. Well, Marvin Leonard was a neighbor. He was just a young teenage boy. His mother was a sister to Bill Marshall. Bill Marshall was a revenue man for the federal government. He lived in French Lick. Well, they were raiding these distilleries in one place and another, just people from making this whiskey. Well, Marvin was charging Jim Riley a little something to snitch on him. He would find out from his uncle when it was going to be ready and then he'd tell Jim he could have his saloon or his distill hid. Well, he got to holding out on Marvin. Marvin gets a big pasteboard—piece of pasteboard, piece of wood—goes up the road where it forks off. Puts a big sign up: GOOD BOOTLEG WHISKEY—GOOD MOONSHINE WHISKEY. SEE PAPPY JIM AT THE FOOT OF THE HILL.

He seen Jim the next day and put his hand across his chin like that. Said, "Never sold so much whiskey in my life." Said, "Sold fifty gallons."

Next day, he went to the mailbox—and found that sign [both laugh]. He was a little put out.

They finally did catch him and put him out of business.

Owen Stout was born in 1903 and grew up on a farm in Greenfield Township.[3]

Stout: I was born here in Greenfield Township, the southern part of Orange County, on a neighboring farm. The farm, at that time, belonged to a minister. His name was Moses Ed Apple. Everybody called him M. E. Apple or Ed Apple. The place where I was born has long since gone. It was a log cabin. I can't remember the log cabin. But the ruins were there when I was younger. And I went back there when I was about twenty years old, about the time I was married, and I got a cedar tree that stood in the yard there—it had fallen over—and we cut it up and made a cedar chest out of it—just in memory.

My dad and mother were married thirteen months before I was born and that was in February of 1902. And they lived just for a short while—a very short while—with my grandfather and grandmother, and then they found this place that could be rented. My dad didn't own it—as I told you it belonged to Mr. Apple—but it was what they called in those days a "tenant house." And most of the farmers, if they could afford to

[3] Interviewed by Catherine A. Jones, 14 October 1987, Paoli.

do so, they would provide a house or a home for someone to tend land for them on what they called the "shares," which was really a rental plan. And they paid the rent by providing the landlord with goods from the land. Crops and garden produce and animals—whatever it might be.

So my dad was a farmer. He'd grown up as a farmer, and he'd worked for seven years for a neighbor whose name was also Apple—Alfred Apple—over north of us here. And he was very much interested in horses. And he took a course in horse training, and my dad was very good at handling horses and colts.

So he enjoyed farming. In fact, that was practically the only industry—if you might call it an industry—occupation, rather, of everyone in the country about here. The towns—and that's what you're interested in primarily, of course—had businesses and some manufacturing plants. In the country out here, almost invariably, everybody was a farmer. And that meant that, not that he was a professional farmer but he could raise enough to provide for himself and family without an outlay in cash.

Things could be traded or bartered and . . . for instance, you could go to a country store—and there were two or three country stores in this immediate area that you could walk; it wasn't too far. So you could take a basket of eggs, for instance, and walk to the country store and exchange those eggs for such things as you could not produce like salt, coffee, sugar. And those were the necessities. The farmers, practically everyone, had animals such as cattle, sometimes sheep; they had hogs, and they also had chickens—sometimes other fowl. They also raised geese and guineas and turkeys and all sorts of things.

Where had your mother and father come from?

They were both raised right here in this locality. My mother came from over in French Lick Township, and my father grew up right here at this very place because this belonged to my grandfather.

Well, this house actually sits on two acres that I purchased from Mr. Apple adjoining my father's and grandfather's farm. And the reason for that was, I bought the two acres immediately after I was married in 1924 because at that time the estate of my grandfather had not been legally settled. So there was some remote possibility that I might never get it, although I was in the line to inherit it, because I was the only child. But rather than take a chance at having any legal problems, I bought the two acres adjoining my dad's farm, and we built a house here in 1924.

Then in 1947 I moved away. I attempted to rent the house which I did for a short while, but that was unsatisfactory so I sold it. And the fellow that bought it lived here a year or two and the house burned.

So that was the situation when I decided to retire in 1970. So we finally decided that we would buy land back, my wife and I. That was my second wife—my first wife had died. So we bought the land back, which was just two acres right here and we built *this* house. So that's the history, briefly, up to that point.

The second farm that your father moved to when you were very young, how big was that?

The farms locally here would range from a minimum of sixty to eighty acres up to several hundred acres. The farm that my dad worked *on* before he was married, that I mentioned, belonged to Alfred Apple. Mr. Apple was increasing it almost every year and at the time of his death there was about between twelve and fifteen hundred acres. It was an enormous thing. But my granddad only had sixty acres and that's what I have now. Well, sixty-four acres actually. And so my dad inherited that because my dad took care of grandfather and grandmother when they were old. There were no such things as nursing homes. That was unknown in those days. So it was customary for the children to take care of their parents. There was no welfare. There was no help of any kind except the neighbors. And the neighbors then were very cooperative and very helpful, and there was never an exchange of money. Neighbors would help with anything that needed to be done.

Can you give me some examples so I can get a better idea?

First of all, the farmers that came in here to tend the land, they had to first clear the forest. And they had what they called "log rollings," which meant the neighbors would all come in—the men—and they would cut the timber, and roll the logs in heaps and burn them, and clear the land so the farmer could . . . that was one example. If the farmer had a house or a barn to build, they would have a log—I mean, a house raising or a barn raising and they would all come to it. And I remember some of those things. I attended a few of them. My dad, down here, was ill—he had been injured in an accident after he had a barn "pattern," they called it—which was the framework—all out and ready to build. Well, he couldn't build his barn so the neighbors gathered in and in one day, they set up that barn. That was 1912.

That was almost invariably done. The ladies would come and they would visit and sometimes they would have quiltings—various types of work. They even met together to take care of crops because quite often—for instance, I remember, a kraut making. That would seem to you, maybe, as being a very small thing, but some of the people including our neighbors here, raised cabbage enough that they could sell wagon loads of it. And quite often, instead of selling cabbage, they would all get together and they'd have a "kraut cutting." They did it all by hand, but they had these boards that you moved the cabbage back and forth, the heads over the board, and it sliced it up into big jars. And those jars were made of crockery. They would hold all the way from twenty to fifty gallons, some of them. So, I know my mother and I, as a youngster, would go with my mother to this type of thing. And, so, it was my pleasure to get the stalk of the cabbage, which was a delicacy. So they'd shave the cabbage off and I remember, as a kid, they'd give me the stalk so—that's what they called it, the center of the head. And I put a little salt on it. Boy, that was delicious.

So, the whole families would gather for meetings of that sort. And as I mentioned, of course quiltings where they worked. And there were many other things of that sort. Hog killing time was also an occasion for the women to "render," they called it, which was merely cooking out or frying out the fat in the parts of the meat that they wanted to preserve. So the menfolk would meet and they would kill the hog. They would shoot it, usually, with a muzzle-loading gun and then they would hang it up, head down, over a trestlelike affair and they would bleed the hog. They would cut its throat so the blood would run out, otherwise the meat's not good.

And they let that hog hang there over the noon hour usually because it had to cool. And then they'd wash it out and get it down on a platform and cut it up into parts: the hams and the legs and all. And then the internal parts of the hog, for the most part, were rendered into what they called "lard." They still use that term, of course. And the womenfolks did that. Then the parts that were suitable, they made into sausage and they had a hand-turned mill—which was very common—that they ground the meat. And they used sage and a few other spices—but sage primarily—along with salt and pepper to preserve the meat. And it was packed away. Usually the sausage was made into little patties, and they would put those in one of these jars similar to the one I described with the kraut making. And they would embed it in the lard. They'd melt the lard and then put those patties in. And they'd keep all through the winter. So, if you wanted sausage, you'd merely go and dig those patties out, melt the lard off them, and they're ready to fry. And they were pretty good.

Then it was also customary for all of the people that came to help, which sometimes was as many as maybe four or five families, to take home with them—free of charge—the choice cuts and parts of the meat. Because you couldn't preserve all of the meat all the time—according to Abraham Lincoln [laughs] so those parts of meat that needed to be cared for, they would divide and that includes such things as what they called it, "tenderloin." They had other names for a lot of the parts of the meat, which would not be intelligible. That's one of the projects I have considered doing—I might someday be able to do it—is to compile a dictionary of the words and their meanings that have changed over the years.

How many brothers and sisters did you have?

I was the only child. My mother had another child after I was born, that was born dead. It didn't survive. But both of my ancestors, my father came from a family of eight. My mother came from a family of twelve. So they were large families prior to my generation. In my generation, most of the people had begun to see and understand that a large family was, rather than being an asset—which at one time they were—they were really a liability because it begins to take money to do things.

I have a friend was asking me to help in locating some land deeds and there's a place out in Orange County here called Stout's Chapel. Well, Stout's Chapel was named after one of my ancestors. I'm not positive which one. But the Stouts came up here about 1815. They came immediately after the initial Quaker trek in 1811 and '12.[4] And, well, the first Stouts—about 1815—then my great-grandfather came in 1836. So there was several different times that they made these pilgrimages or changed their locations.

Now, let me ask you—just background information on your family. Is this something you grew up knowing or have you had to dig around to get this information about your own past?

I had to dig, yes. First of all, my Grandfather Stout was in the Civil War. And he enlisted and they sent him to Indianapolis. He was what they called in those days "bullheaded." He was the type of fellow that was going to have his way with everything and *did*. So he told the authorities, when they took him to Indianapolis, that he was going to come home when his first child was born, because he had just married my grandmother who was Lavina Willard. And they had a child on the way. Well, in the Civil War they needed men pretty badly, of course. So it was strictly against the rules. They wouldn't grant passes. That was in December of that year, early December—which was 18 and 63 I believe, or '2—I'm not sure. '63 I think it was. My grandfather along with another old man—he wasn't an old man, he was a young man *then*—had told the authorities that he expected to be home when his first child was born and that came up, it so happened, in December.

So in the early part of December my grandfather along with one of his buddies at Camp Morton—because at that time of the Civil War, there was a camp in Indianapolis named after Governor [Oliver P.] Morton—well, they deserted. And they walked from Indianapolis down here to Orange County. A hundred miles. And they walked, of course, by night. And they hid by day.

Well, he was here when Uncle Joe—that was my oldest uncle—when he was born. Well, my granddad, I guess, decided it was pretty easy that far, so he didn't go back. And naturally, of course, they sent out the militia police for him. They came down here and they couldn't find him [laughs]. He had gone to one of his uncles who lived over at Patoka and he was staying over there. So he evaded them. But anyway, after things cleared up and all was well, my granddad decided to go back to his army [regiment] because he felt an obligation to it. He knew, of course, there'd be a penalty. So he willfully went back. By that time the regiment, which was Company E—I could give you numbers if you wanted them, but that's not necessary—was down near Vicksburg, Mississippi, or rather Tennessee. And they'd been fighting up and down the Mississippi River because that's where the heat of the battle was.

So he went back down there; walked of course, that's about the only way they had going. And well, when he got down along the Mississippi—somewhere down along there, I'm not just sure where—he got sick. And they found him and they took him in to a military hospital in Arkansas—which was right across the river. So he came out of it, but they found out he had deserted so they put a charge of desertion against him, and they threw him in a prison up in Alton, Illinois. And he spent quite some time there.

But he went back and helped fight throughout the campaign in the South and, believe it or not, when he was discharged in 1865, I guess it must have been—again I have his discharge upstairs—they gave him an honorable discharge. And the result was, after he came home and years later, he drew a pension—very small. In those days, of course, the dollar was worth ten dollars today, or more. But eventually, after several years, the War Department caught up with him and they discovered that he had this charge of desertion. See, they took the pension away.

And your father, would he get money for helping farm, or goods or something for helping the farmers?

Almost never. After the depression our country went from this way of life that we had at that time. Once that was over, we became more or less an industrial nation. We left agriculture for industry—then the dollars came in. And again, I'm giving an opinion now.

Our country got in a very bad way and I can't tell you why. People began to lose confidence in govern-

[4] Quakers from North Carolina settled in Orange County beginning in the early 1810s. McEntire, Larsen, and Henshaw, eds., *Lotus Dickey Songbook*, 8.

ment. And the result was, when Roosevelt—FDR—was elected in the thirties, it was a landslide. Because everybody felt that we were going down the wrong road, that we were going so fast, it was going to be the ruination of the country.

But they forgot two or three things. First of all, we left our standards behind. The one that's most noticeable, of course, is the standard—the monetary standard. We left the gold standard. And our money is actually, today even, merely a note. And no backing. And again, this is my opinion and you may detect my politics, which I don't attempt to hide or I don't attempt to reveal. But anyway, from that day on, everything had a money value to it. And the chief reason for that, as I see it—again, an opinion—government can tax for money. You can't tax from people. In other words, if I want to give somebody something, if I want to trade a farmer an hour's work for a bushel of corn—or whatever may be—the government can't get their hands on money that way. So, I think it's primarily because of the tax system, and Roosevelt was an expert at that. First of all, he had studied the Keynesian Theory [John Maynard Keynes], which you probably know about, from England—and it's good. So, from that time on, everything had a money value. Sorry to say that, because before that time a man was as good a[s] his bond.

And a man's life meant more—and most of them were religious people. They read the Bible, they studied it. And they read in there: "What profiteth Man to gain the whole world and lose his own soul?"

Then you think most of these changes were around the thirties, after the depression?

In southern Indiana, yes. The majority of people here was affected as much by the depression as they were by the years leading up to the depression. Because the farmers, for the most part, as I said, they were not into it to make money in the first place. They never made much. They never *had* made much and they didn't *care* to make much—they didn't *have* to because you didn't have to have money to survive. So for the most part, the farmers I'd say in general came out of it about as they went in. There wasn't much change.

But immediately after the depression set in and especially when the taxes began to come, farmers went broke rapidly. And they decided that there was not much to be made and to be had by staying on the farm, so the result was they left in flocks and droves.

And by that time, the farmers first attempted to live on the farm and do their work in the town. So here, for instance, in Paoli there were two or three factories. One of them that I mentioned up there the other day was—they called it the Basket Factory which was—the correct name was the Edgerton Manufacturing Company. And they employed as many farmers as they could get—and some of the wives, though not too many women worked there, but there were a number—making baskets from the local timber. But they lived back here on the farm. They'd drive into Paoli. By that time they had Model Ts.

So most of the farmers worked other places. My dad worked up there some. I did too. I got thirty-five cents an hour. And my dad drew the same thing. That was the prevailing wage for labor. *Thirty-five cents*! And we had to go to Paoli and back, of course. And in order to do that, you had to have a car—even this far out. So I bought a car. I bought a Model T Ford in 1923, the first year I taught school. My first money went for a car. It didn't cost very much.

And when did electricity first come out this way?

Nineteen forty-seven, that's what I mentioned, I think, briefly. That's the reason I went to town. I had established a printing business down here, and it required power. And I had to generate what little power we could *myself*. So there was a company—Delco, that still makes automobile parts—came out with a plant that you put in a farmhouse or in the basement of the farmhouse, and generate electricity.

It was driven by a gasoline engine. So I first tried to drive—and did drive—some of my machinery directly from a gasoline engine. The gasoline engine is one of those little horizontal types that had two flywheels, you cranked it up and it pop, pop, popped and away it went. But they were inefficient. They were hard to start on a cold morning. You had to have water for cooling—which would freeze. There were problems.

So this Delco Company, in particular—there were several others, but Delco was one of the leaders—built a small farm-lighting plant. It was thirty-two volts, which is much less than these modern ones, and it was DC, which meant you could not transform it. There-

Opened as Paoli Normal School in 1871, this building later contained Paoli's grade school and high school classes. It was torn down in 1970.
Paoli News-Republican

fore, you had to carry the current with big wires, took a lot of copper. So they were fairly expensive. Well anyway, I bought a small Delco plant to run my press.

We got to the point where we drove two of them. And every cold morning you had to get out there and start those things up and it was a nuisance. So, when another one of Roosevelt's programs—that was Rural Electric Administration, REA—there were a few, very few, progressive people, farmers mostly, out here on these ridges, that wanted electric power. But do you know what most of the farmers said?

What?

They said, "We can't afford it." The minimum charge was $2.50 a month and the farmers said, "We can have our kerosene lamps for light for less than two dollars and a half a month."

So they wouldn't sign that. Well, I was one that did, because I needed it badly.

For your work?

Yes. My buddy out here next door, Albert Apple, had a little woodworking shop—he signed up. Out here at Wildwood Lake there was another family named Apple—Elmer Apple—he signed up. We three was all there was along this whole ridge out here for just about ten miles.

So when you were growing up as a boy, what did the word "community" mean to you then? What kind of area was that?

Two things: the school and the church.

In school, do you remember your first teacher?

Her name was Nola Breeden. And she was a young girl—I don't know but I would assume at that time she was about twenty. And all of those young teachers that I had, the younger ones, were girls. And they were very adept with the primary grades. And I always felt—as a teacher and as an administrator—a woman should be in that position. Because, well, I've tried to do that. In a one-room country school, I had to be . . . teach the first grade as well as the eighth grade. I *never* felt that I was adept at it. I never felt that I was adequate. I never felt that I made a success with those little kids.

What advantage would a woman have? These are kids, first through eighth grade?

They have a motherly instinct. And to deal with children, as you well know or you will find out, that means everything. That's all of it. If you have the goodwill of the child, he will do whatever you want him to do and the way you want him to do it. If you don't, you're just barking up the wrong tree [laughs]. That's what they used to say.

The school, in that day, and I know from firsthand experience—not only did I *go*, I taught under those conditions. The first years I taught, the schoolteacher was looked up to with respect and honor as much, and sometimes even more, than the minister was. And my dad told me many times, and I've heard other parents say the same thing, "You go to school and get in trouble and come home—there'll be no questions asked, but you're going to be punished again when you get home!"

Most of the farming class, which were the majority of the people, thought education was, first of all, unnecessary. They thought, if you had what they called "horse sense," that you could get by. And you could. But get by was all. And that's the reason my dad and my mother, I think, were head and shoulders above most of them, because they saw, my dad always told me, he said, "I want you to get an education so you won't have to work as hard as I did."

And little by little I became interested in printing and several other things. I wanted to be a chemist when I was growing up in school and there was no chemistry taught in the local high school at that time. So I took a course in chemistry by correspondence, and I gained enough proficiency [that] I did get a job as a chemist in South Bend. And so I went to South Bend, worked up there immediately prior to the depression; 1929, that's when the Stock Market Crash was. And I worked through that until work got so slow that I was only working about two days a week. And by that time I had these two little boys of mine—I have three children but my family's divided—my two boys were fifteen months apart and almost like twins. And I decided South Bend was not a good place to raise children. I don't like the city for the type of life that's there. And I had this place I'd bought, as I said, these two acres. I had a house here, it was all paid for. I came through the depression with flying colors, I guess you'd have to say, because I didn't owe anybody a dime when I came out.

So we came back down here. I had to renew my license because, at that time, a teacher's license in Indiana was for a period of two years. And I had, of course, lost that period. So I went back to Terre Haute—Indiana State Teacher's College—and did some more work there and got my license renewed and then I taught either two or three years—I forget. But anyway, a total of eight. And during that period then, I became interested, among other things, in printing.

Where did you teach school? Did you teach here in Paoli?

I taught in this township, seven of the years. One year I taught in West Baden over there in Northwest Township. And the reason for that was political. The teachers were hired, in that day, by the township trustee who was elected by the people. And we had a fellow that was elected trustee, named William Grimes, and he had, I think—I'm using my opinion—I think William Grimes was very biased. He was a politician more than anything else. So he and I didn't agree too well on a lot of things. And one of the things that caused me to have trouble with him, he was a great friend to the mother of one my pupils. And this pupil had bad eyes and in those days you couldn't go and buy glasses and get them fixed like you do now. So they were using that as an excuse—and that's the way I saw it, and that's what the superintendent said—to get him out of school. They didn't want him to go to school, but legally he had to. They passed a law you had to go till you were sixteen, unless you graduated.

So, I had a letter from the superintendent explaining that this boy had been out of school too much and that legally he would just have to go and he wanted me to notify the parents. So I did. And this old lady, the boy's mother, she told the trustee that I had, that I said that I got a letter from *him*, on the boy in school. Well, if I said that, it was a mistake; I don't think I did. But I could have said *trustee* instead of *superintendent*. But anyways, she tried to make me a liar and he came up and Mr. Grimes took her side. So it came time for the next school, I asked him about a school and he said, "You didn't support me [in] the election, did you?"

And I said, "No, sir, I didn't." Because I didn't believe in that.

Then he said, "Then I can't use you" [laughs]. So I lost my school. So that's when I went to West Baden.

Of your generation, how many years did kids go to school?

Eight grades. Out of those three in my class when I was in the eighth grade, I was the only one that went on to high school. The other two quit. And that came about gradually because it wasn't too many years following that till almost everyone, at least, started into high school. Not too many graduated for a long while. Now, then, nearly all of them do graduate.

First of all they have the buses—they don't have to walk or depend on parents. When I went to high school, my mother or my dad—usually my mother—took me with two horses hitched to a buggy from here to Paoli on Monday morning. And they rented a room up there for me and I "bached." I cooked what little I could, till Friday. Then they came on Friday evening and got me and brought me home. I stayed down here over the weekend, they brought me back on Monday morning. And with a horse and buggy to get from here to Paoli on a cold winter day—when the days were short—we had to start sometime at five o'clock. It was dark. So that's the way I got my high school.

So when you started high school, what were your main aspirations?

My aspiration, first of all—as I mentioned—was to be like Tom Edison. I liked science, and I like invention and especially, I was wild about chemistry. And they didn't teach chemistry, but I did take physics and general science and everything I could. So, I wanted to be a chemist and, like Tom Edison, I wanted to have a laboratory. I'll tell you another little kiddish thing. It's so kiddish I'm almost ashamed to tell you. But when I was in grade school—fifth and sixth grade, I'd say—I used to get the Sears-Roebuck catalog down. They had that big catalog then. And Sears, at that time, carried a lot of things that you don't see in the catalog anymore. For instance, they had a long list of books. You could buy nearly all the classics out of Sears-Roebuck. You could get the *Iliad* and the *Odyssey*; you could get James Oliver Curwood's *Zane Grey*, Gene Stratton-Porter—all of them. And they had all kinds of things in the way of electrical devices, as far as they were known: telephones, electrical bells, batteries. I used to take my notebook—like this—I'd made an order, which I knew I couldn't—I didn't have a dime. I'd make an order, out there, for a library. I was going to have a library that had all these classics in it. It was going to have an encyclopedia and a big dictionary—because we did have a big dictionary in school. And so, I was going to have a library. Then, when I got into music—oh boy!

I had to have a concert home for that orchestra. 'Cause I was going to have an orchestra, no question about it [laughs]. So, in my kid's mind . . . I wish I'd have kept some of them. I had that list of books that [I] was going to have in my library. And I had the list of music that I wanted, if I had the instruments. Because the kids couldn't furnish the instruments, a lot of times. And, even like Edison and some of the others, I was going to have an observatory up there on that top floor, with a telescope that I could study those constellations they used to tell me about. I had to know *their* names, too. So, I dreamed in my childish fancy that that was going to be on top of the high hill, right over here on my granddad's farm.

Louanne Rutherford was born in Paoli in 1947 and has worked as a bookkeeper, clothing store clerk, school aide, and deputy treasurer for Orange County.[5]

Rutherford: When I was a kid—of course, you could see things differently from the time you were a child from when you're an adult. But the smell of summer was really great. It's like no other smell I can even begin to compare with, right now. Maybe that has something to do with my innocence with what's going

[5] Interviewed by Maria Green, 21 April 1989, Paoli.

on, but in the summer my cousins came from Tennessee, and they came from New York. And we'd swim down at the pool, and my grandmother had a swimming pool in her backyard too. I mean, at the time we thought it was huge, but now [laughs] it looks like a little birdbath. But anyway, we'd swim, and then in the evening we'd play cards. And we'd play cards until, I don't know, one or two o'clock in the morning. I was a big kid at this time, but you don't keep track of time when you're with family, so it's no big deal. We played canasta and crazy eights, and I think we played a little poker maybe, and lots of gin rummy. But that's the best memories I have: the family thing.

We used to also—my aunt would drive up from Tennessee, and my grandmother had this great big old '55 or '58 Buick. I mean, you talk about tanker: baby, this is one tanker. But anyway, my aunt, one aunt would drive us to the drive-in, and they'd leave us, and they'd visit with friends or whatever [laughs]. And there were all these kids, six of us, grandchildren, we were all over that car.

And we'd take blankets; we'd lay on the grass and we'd watch the movie. Now, they'd come back and get us, but I mean, you could do things like that then, and you can't do those types of things now. No, you can't.

How come?

Well, the town has changed a lot. For one thing, kids aren't as well behaved as they used to be. And I don't think you could leave that many kids, at the varied phases we were in at that time, alone and not have them destruct something, or get in a lot of trouble. Also, the movies aren't quite the same, and I don't know if you'd want to take the kids—the ages that we were—to some of the shows that they put on at the local drive-in now. They're more—they're not pornographic but, you know, they're just—the language is different, the scenes are different. And, I mean, I'm talking about movies when I was a kid that were really home entertainment. Family-oriented. So I don't think you'd want to take kids to do that now, and I don't think you could leave them and not tear up everything.

Paoli's still a hometown. OK? And it's still real comfortable to me. But . . . 'course a lot of what I perceive is because I've gotten older. I mean, I'm thinking of when I was seven, eight, nine years old, and I'm almost forty-two. So you look at things differently. And as a mother I see things differently. But . . . no, it's just times have changed.

Paoli has changed. We have a lot more people in here from the city. Names that we don't recognize. That's something else. When you were a kid, in Paoli, *everybody* knew everybody else. People didn't even lock their doors; they didn't have to. They didn't feel the need. The biggest crime epidemic we've had in Paoli was Peeping Toms [laughs].

Well, I mean, it wasn't just me, but in the neighborhood we lived in, there was a little old fellow. And he was not quite, as my mother-in-law would say: He didn't stand too tall. It didn't have anything to do with his physical height; it had to do with his mental capacity. OK? But anyway, I loved the way she put it: He didn't stand too tall. But anyway, he was always doing things like that: peeking in people's windows, you know, at night or. . . . He was notorious for being a Peeping Tom. And everybody who knew him just knew he could be *naughty* at times [laughs]. So . . . but he was harmless.

So you kept your shades down?

Yes. And a lot of times you could see his reflection. That's the one thing I remember. I woke up one night, and the shade was down, and there was a streetlight right next to my house, on the corner. And it was just a perfect silhouette of his head. And I can remember lying there thinking: "Gosh, *scream*." And I was, gosh, I don't know, maybe I was ten, eleven, twelve, thirteen, someplace in there. I don't remember. "I've got to scream," or, "I've got to get up and move." I *couldn't*. I was *so* scared, I couldn't move. And I finally let out this *really loud* scream, and even my dad came running. And he went outside and found the concrete block where he stood up on that, trying to peek in. But, well, *whoever* he was, we assumed he was that person. I don't know who it was. But anyway, that was . . . [laughs].

And now, I mean, Paoli's got the only woman on death row.[6] Woman's name is Lois Thacker, and she

[6] Lois Ann Thacker received the death sentence after being convicted of hiring a group of six people to kill her husband. John Thacker was shot in an ambush near their home on 3 November 1984. "Regional News: Indiana," in Lexis-Nexis database, 18 May, 27 June 1985, available from web.lexis-nexis.com.

had her husband killed. He was coming home, I don't know, from work or whatever one night, and she had a cousin or a lover or somebody. . . . I don't remember the details; it's been a few years back. But . . . put a big tree in the road, or a tree that they could handle. You know, these huge things. But anyway, he got out to check it out, and they shot him. With a deer slug. And it was proven; it was traced back to her. And also one of the boys turned evidence against her. So Paoli had the only woman on death row. The sentence has since been commuted to life in prison.

We have a lot more crime now; you don't want to leave your door unlocked. I don't know, when I was younger, you just always felt secure.

I can remember a time in high school; I was in the band. And we were leaving for a particular concert engagement. And the bus was leaving at three o'clock in the morning. So I got up at two and walked to a friend's house, which was two blocks away at the most. And I wasn't scared. Well now, I wouldn't let one of my kids do that.

One night we saw a boy out to Chat and Snack, and he was in pretty bad shape. And I told my husband, I said, "We should take him home to his parents." But his brother came, so we didn't. And he was involved in a really bad wreck later on, and I felt *real* bad about that for a very long time. The brother did try to help him, to get him home, but he got the keys and left again. He's a good boy and a good family. It was a bad situation.

Nowadays there are dances. They're not scheduled as routinely, I think, as what *we* had. I mean, they have a lot of them, but I think we had more, at that time. And basketball has really picked up here in the area since we went to semistate. We had a great team this year that we can be proud of. But the movie theater provided a lot of entertainment for kids from the time they were little until they were older. That's something else. I could walk to the movie theater of an evening and come out, as a kid, seven, eight, nine years old, my parents lived across the highway, and walk home. And they felt real comfortable about that. You couldn't do that now and feel real safe.

There aren't a lot of things for kids to do here. For a lot of entertainment, you have to go to other places. You have to go to Bedford or Jasper or Bloomington or Louisville. There's just not a whole lot of an organized program here for kids. And what there is, comes through the school system. They've done a *lot* of really good things. I mean, our sports program is very good; and our band program is very good. I think we have some of the best facilities and a very good school system for the state of Indiana, I think.

You said you invented your own games. What kinds of things did you do?

Oh, you know, like climbing trees, and we played baseball—I said that. And we'd swim. And you'd sit there and play with your dolls. Gosh, I can remember a Jenny doll I had. It was *great*. I loved that doll; had clothes to match. I even had a little—not real, but a little fur cape. Not a genuine fur, but it was fur to me. And I loved her. I had a canopy bed for her, and a beautiful dresser set. Oh gosh, if I didn't think I wasn't Queen Isabella, I don't know.

We played dolls. We did a lot more playing dolls. I mean, I'm talking about girls [laughs]. I don't know how many boys played dolls. But we had a lot of fun with that.

I did *paper* dolls. That was a big—oh gosh, I can remember buying paper dolls probably every week and cutting them out, you know, and playing with and. . . . I don't know, just stuff like that.

So, your kids don't do things like that?

Not paper dolls. And now my girls like dolls. Barbie dolls are a big thing with them, you know, but. . . . Now, there I go again, and I'm as much responsible for this as anybody. My kids watch too much television. They watch a lot more television than I did. I mean, we read, and we colored, and we did things like that. But they really enjoy TV. You know, like *The Brady Bunch* [laughs]. Whereas I grew up on Howdy Doody and Clarabell the Clown, and these guys, you know. They watch *The Brady Bunch* and *The Flintstones* and stuff like that, but. . . . Yes, they watch a lot of television, and I fear that they get more easily bored than what I *remember* that I was.

I have to tell you something. When I was growing up, my grandfather, Raymond Stout, was a banker here in Orange County. He and his family. And he died May 21, 1955. He had Parkinson's disease, and he did not die a pretty death. But he was well loved by so many people, and he did so many really good things for Paoli, as a community, OK?, for the *future* people of Paoli, that in his memory, the community built a swimming pool and dedicated it to his memory.

Now, it took a lot of money, and it took, oh, I don't know, I think about two or three years. When I look back now, I don't think that was so long for a community of our size, with the amount of money they had to raise. But it was dedicated to his memory. And that's the *pool* that used to be—I don't know if you've seen it or not.

But I *love* Paoli; I really do. And when I think back, I think about that. That was a neat memory to have. The people felt so much love for my grandfather, and so much gratitude for what he had done for them, that they wanted to give something back in his memory. So I don't have any ill feelings about Paoli at all. It's home, and I love it a great deal. Yes, I really do; I love it a great deal. I'm glad I raised my kids here. I've been aggravated at times that there isn't as much for them. . . . Like, my daughter takes gymnastics, and we had to go to Jasper to do that. And when the girls want to take dance, we had to drive to Bedford to do that. So, you know, I get a little aggravated and put out about things like that.

I think we're all pretty friendly people here. I don't see us as being a restricted community or rigid or unfriendly or cold. I see us as being pretty friendly. And I think people who come in from the city that aren't used to that, you know, I think it takes them . . . I think it's probably a little bit overwhelming. I don't know; they just are more reserved and more guarded. They're not as trusting, I think, as Paoli people are who have lived here a long time. And I'm not saying that we're all that trusting; I think we're all a little bit guarded, you know, with all the stuff you see on television, and the things that are happening all over the world now. And with a few things that have happened in and around Paoli, I think everybody's more guarded, but I think people coming from the city are even more so.

OK, an example. My sister and her husband moved down here, from Indianapolis, about three years ago. Well, everything they do, they lock their doors in the car. Well, I don't know too many people that live here in Paoli that lock their doors [laughs] in the *car* when they go to the grocery store and stuff. Now I think they're getting more haphazard about that, but it was just a habit of precaution they had learned from the city. And I think things like that carry over with people who have lived in the city for very long.

So I have to think that it was in the last five or six years people have become a little more guarded. And I think a lot of that has to do with the things that they see that are going on in television, that are happening all over. You know, people opening up, in McDonald's or the school yard with a gun, or people putting bombs around. In the Loogootee school system, a good friend of ours, and neighbor, moved to Loogootee. He's the principal there at the high school. And right before he moved down there, somebody had a pipe bomb on the high school door. I mean, things like that are happening all over, and that wouldn't have happened twenty years ago, or twenty-five years ago; it just wouldn't have happened.

I guess the media has made it *so* easy—I mean, everybody's blaming the media for everything. But the media has made it *so* easy, and so fast, to hear about everything that's going on all over that, I think, because we have such accessibility to all that now, that people are more guarded.

Paoli doesn't have industry like it used to have, either. I mean, we used to have a factory called Cornwell's that employed a lot of people. And they still have reunions. It was a big factory down the hill as you go towards French Lick too. We've got a lot of industry, but we're not a real wealthy or prosperous community. We have a lot of unemployed people.

And that's something else. When I was a kid, I'm *sure* there were unemployed people, but I don't remember there being as many. There were poor kids in school that I went to school with when I was a little girl, but I don't remember them being *that* many. And now . . . there are *so* many on welfare, and so many who get free lunches and reduced lunches. And so many who get welfare checks and food stamps. There are just *so* many here in the community. So many. And I don't remember seeing that many "quote/unquote" poor kids when I was a kid. There were a few, and you knew *who* they were, but I don't remember there being as *many*.

So there has—is it my child's memory, there had to be more employment than what there is now? Or then again, maybe people were more willing to work. And now there are a lot of kids whose parents have a real hard time making it.

Max and I were married in July of 1966, and before we were married, a friend of mine, the boy she was going to marry, he was killed right before he was to come home and they were to be married. I mean *right* before, maybe within two weeks. So, you know, when you know somebody who died in *Vietnam* and you know what a good person they were, it puts it on a different basis than to see numbers and totals on the television screen. Or you hear things. It makes it more personal.

And I'm just real sorry I didn't do more to help out. Maybe it wasn't necessarily in that field, just to make a difference. Not that we were so . . . any of us were so cold and callous that we didn't notice or didn't hear, or *didn't* care. We did. But we were having a good time. We were sixteen, seventeen, eighteen, nineteen years old. We were carefree, we were out of school or we were going to school, we were free for the first time. We were married. You know, we just didn't pay enough attention. Or *I* didn't; I can't speak for everybody else.

How did you meet your husband?

Max was seeing my best friend. And she was having trouble with him: "Lover's problem." Would I go out and talk to him for her?

"Sure. Why not?"

And, I got to tell you: I think I *really* believed I loved him from the first minute I saw him.

So, you didn't go to high school with him?

Well, no, he's older than I am. I remember him: he graduated in 1962, and I graduated in '65. And I remember him. But he was going steady with somebody else and so was I. I went with a boy for four and a half years, and it was just a general assumption that we would marry. And the summer I graduated, I spent the summer in Memphis taking care of my aunt's kids—my aunt and uncle's children—while she went to Europe. And while I was gone, he strayed and . . . you just didn't do that.

And I came back, and I was getting ready to start college at Terre Haute . . . and he had the most gorgeous set of biceps on him you have *ever* seen in your life. He was a country boy, and he put up hay, and it's like working out, you know. You develop those things. Oh, God. And he's dark; he's *real* dark, real dark—it's Indian blood but . . . anyway, I went out there to talk to him for her. And like I said, he lived in the country. OK? It was a beautiful, *beautiful* fall day. It was October the second of 1965, to tell you the truth. And he was getting ready to hitch up his dad's pony to a pony cart. . . .

Was there a problem deciding whether you'd live in the country or town?

We lived in town. We didn't have the money to buy land. He didn't have any money. He didn't have that great a job, and here I was—I'd just quit school, you know. So, we lived in town.

What did you do? You were able to find jobs?

Yes, I worked. I was working in a bank. The day I quit college, my dad, he was devastated because he had never been—his parents had never had the money to send him to school, and he always wanted to go. And a lot of his dreams and hopes were put in *me* to go and get that education first, you know. Accomplish what he was never allowed to accomplish. And I wasn't happy at Terre Haute, and I wasn't doing that well. So I quit—before I flunked out—thinking that I would go back.

But anyway, he told me the day I came home. "You have to go out, and get a job right now. Otherwise I'll take you back." So I got a job that day.

I worked at the hotel in French Lick as a cashier. So, you know, I had a job when Max and I got married, and he worked at the chair factory when we got married. So we both had jobs, *but*, you know, we weren't by any means, although money—you know, we had enough money to pay the bills and eat and have a good time; that's all that really mattered. We weren't about saving; Lord no. We were having too much fun. We partied every weekend. I mean, we ran around with a group of kids that he had gone to school with and we partied every weekend. That's *all* we did [laughs]. We partied from Friday till Sunday, *every* weekend.

People that we partied so hard with for so long—say, for years—we don't even see any more. We have contact with at Christmas but we don't see very many of them. Life has changed—lives have changed and—

you know, divorces, change in occupation, getting religion, so-to-speak.

Max started driving a truck about sixteen years ago. We'll be married twenty-three years in July. Up until that point, he'd always been there with me, and I depended too much on *him*. When he started driving a truck, the first winter, I thought: "Oh, my God, I'm going to die." Every time the phone rang, I thought: "Oh, he's been killed." You know, you kind of think. . . . So I had two choices: I could either sit on my duff and watch the world go by, or I could get up *off* my duff, and make the world alive for me and the kids.

OK. So that's what I decided to do. And for a long time, he'd be gone sometimes two and three weeks at a time. Well, he's home a lot more often now; he's only gone two nights a week. And because we missed out on being with one another for so long, we really enjoy being just the two of us a lot of times. Not *all* the time, but a lot of the times.

But then again, now that I'm working, I love it that Max helps me out with the house [laughs]. He does dishes, and he does laundry, and he can cook. And I love *that* [laughs]. And I think that's great. But I think it should be that way, you know. If two people work out, then they should both share the responsibilities of house and kids. That's just fair. Because it's *really* hard being mother, wife, chauffeur, friend, sister, doctor, nurse, aunt, uncle, brother, you know, neighbor—all these things.

Would you say that your life is a lot different than your mother's life?

Oh, most definitely. Most definitely. Oh, my God. I don't remember my mother *ever* coming to school for a party. I don't remember . . . my mother didn't drive. I don't remember my mom and dad *ever* participating in anything I did, or even being there when I did participate in something. And my kids have been my life. Whatever they were involved in, *I* was involved in.

And I still am that way to a certain degree. I don't think I missed a party that they . . . growing up with, and even though I've been working for the last five, five and a half years, I've still been able to attend a lot of parties for, you know, for my kids.

I drive. I'm active. Yes, my mother . . . I mean, it's like day and night. My mom, bless her heart, she doesn't know how to balance a checkbook. Her whole life—no, I shouldn't say her whole life; that's not fair. A lot of her life revolves around soap operas right now. You know what I mean? She and my dad, both, get really into those. And I just don't have time for that.

Do you remember . . . I've heard a lot about Saturday nights on the square?

Oh gosh, yes. That was . . . the square on Saturday night was *packed*. I mean, there wasn't a parking place. It wasn't like it is now, you know. But there were *more* parking places then. It was something else. People would come to town, and they'd bring cheese and crackers and Coke, you know. And would sit there and visit.

You know, the square would be *packed* on Saturday night. Country people would come early just to get a parking place [laughs]. It was great. 'Course there were more stores on the square. There wasn't TV, or not as many people had TV. People didn't drive out of the county to get their entertainment; they made their own entertainment in visiting with one another up on the square. *That* was the place to meet. And it was something else.

And there again, I can remember a smell, in the summer. We had . . . [pause] mercy, forgive me . . . a *bandstand*. And we used to have music concerts on Wednesday—was it Wednesday night? On Thursday night. Thursday nights in the summer, the band would perform. On Thursday nights. From the time I was a little girl, listening to it, up until I was a big girl and got to play in it.

And even after I married, I still did it for a while. Now, the bandstand has since been torn down, which is a dirty shame. It was on the lower south side of the square, kind of southwest. Oh, it was great. People used to come, and when the band was done playing a song, they all blew their horn. Instead of applauding, they blew their horns. Beep, beep, beep, beep. That was great.

Why do you think it stopped?

Oh, it was television. You know, everybody got

Paoli courthouse and square, early twentieth century
Orange County Historical Society

Paoli courthouse and square, 1930s. The bandstand is in the lower right corner of the photo.
Orange County Historical Society

TVs, and people started going to Bedford, you know. And you can drive to Bedford to go shopping; you didn't have to stay here in Paoli. It wasn't such a big deal to travel twenty-one miles. But you know, we still have a lot of people in Orange County who have never been out of Orange County.

We had a place here in town called Andy's. It was tough, man. We would walk past it, and that was something else—kids *walked*. We walked home from school. We walked *to* school; we walked home for lunch. We walked. Nowadays, if they can't drive, they don't go.

Anyway, you walked past Andy's—and *only* certain kinds of people hung out there [laughs]. And when you were sixteen, you think there's certain kinds of people that hang out there. They've got a name, and they are tough. You don't mess with those people.

Now, it was just called Andy's. And it was right here on the corner where this building is now, where the parking lot is right here. It came down this way a little bit; it was called Andy's Restaurant. And we walked past it every day going to school, or coming home from school, whatever the case may be.

And that's something else. Boys carried girls' books home from school then. They talked; they communicated. Nowadays they drive or they don't do anything. I mean, I just am lost. We've lost a lot. We've gained a lot and we've lost a lot.

Did you go to church much when you were growing up?

Yes. I did a lot. But as much as I went to church, Grandmom had a ritual every night where we always read from the Bible. Always. She read a book called *The Upper Room*, which is published in Nashville, Tennessee. It was then, and it still is now; I still get it. And there was always a story and a Bible verse and a prayer. Things to read and discuss. And we did that *every* night. Every night.

And just because you *do* go to church doesn't mean that you are a Christian. I like my religion a lot. I'm not as knowledgeable about it as I used to be. I've slid a *lot*; I've slid a lot. But I've learned a lot [of] things too. It's just a real laid-back kind of thing.

The Mennonites here in Paoli are a terrific group. They're energetic and enthusiastic, and they're a *great* bunch of people. They're very loving and giving, and they're very business oriented, and community and civic oriented. I mean, they have been—a lot of people will not agree, but I think they've been a great asset to the community. A *few* people feel like they've tried to take over.

Born in Washington County in 1918, Lucy Deckard relocated often with her husband, a construction worker. They returned to Paoli in 1965.[7]

What year was this that you were born in?

Deckard: Nineteen eighteen. I was born, oh, three weeks at least before the Armistice was signed. And I had an uncle there at the same time, in Belgium, at the same time. My daddy had been wounded actually about a month before I was born, but we didn't know it, you know, my family didn't know it yet. And the same day my dad was wounded, my uncle, my mother's brother, was killed, in Belgium, the same day, and they say at about the same time.

What a story. Where was your mother from?

She had grown up in this little community on the other side of Borden. It was called Swayback, was the nearest place to it.

What county was that?

That's in Washington. I think I may have told you this, but my mother's brother was drafted from Washington County and sent to Camp Taylor, Kentucky. Her name was Owens. So my daddy was drafted from Orange County and sent to the same camp and *his* name was Owens, but they were not related—oh, I think probably three or four hundred years ago they may have been—but I have traced it back to the Revolutionary War and we haven't found where they're related. And Mother goes down to Camp Taylor to visit her brother, and Frank is in the bed, in the bunk next

[7] Interviewed by Catherine A. Jones, 11 August 1988, Paoli. Name changed to preserve individual's identity.

to him see? And that's how she met him and married him before he went overseas.

What kind of work did your father do before the war?

Before he went to the army he worked at the chair factory here; it was called the Paoli Cabinet Factory then. He *had* worked for the railroad. But he worked in the cabinet factory, and when he went to leave, to go to the army, he had a big round old-fashioned oak table halfway, and they scooted it over in the corner and left it. And when he came back from the army, a year and a half later, that table was still there, and he and Mother ate off packing boxes until he finished that table and bought it.

And he took government training as a mechanic, which was a brand-new thing then you know, we had very few cars in those days. And Dad was one of the better mechanics around here up until—oh, when they came out with the new Model A and Dad said he would've had to gone back to school to learn more and he wouldn't do it. But after that he worked more as a machinist, I think.

Still at the factory?

No, no, not at the factory at all, he went to work—well, and then in the twenties, oh, say in the mid to the latter twenties, Dad and two other guys here in town owned a string of quarries all, oh, there was Palmyra, White Cloud—I don't know all the places, around the southern part of the state. And Dad used to go from one to the other every day.

Mother never worked. Well, her—the thing that she did—Mother sewed all her life. And her mother had the first sewing machine in that part of the country. And they thought they were great sewers. They actually were very crude [laughs]! But they thought they were great sewers. And, when she was, during the war, my mother, her mother, and mother's two sisters—that would have been four of them in the family—all made shirts for the government, and they made two bundles, that was sixteen shirts a piece a week. That everyone of them made. And the day that I was born, my mother had finished her sixteen shirts and her mother had finished her's and made a big barrel of sauerkraut, the same day I was born [both laugh]. I said, they couldn't take time out for me to be born, I was

Political parade on the square, 1912. The boy on the calf, Roy Padgett, later served as Orange County sheriff.
Paoli News-Republican

A 1916 parade on the square
Paoli News-Republican

born at midnight that night!

Did your dad talk very much about the war?

He would *not* discuss [the war] with anything. . . . He just—he didn't want us to know, and then one night while my mother was really bad before she died, my brother and I sat up out at the hospital, and Earl and I talked *all* night long about where Dad was during the war and about where Earl was in World War II. I think I learned more war history that one night than I have in . . .

Do you remember, as a kid, did people talk about the war that had just happened?

No, except—I think people in general were more—well, they *honored* our soldiers more from World War I than from what we've—maybe because we had so *many* in World War II. But I can't remember, or maybe I've grown and more a part of that generation, but I do not remember people making as much of an issue over World War II soldiers as they did of World War I. And, of course, when *I* was little, we still had about, oh, maybe ten Civil War veterans here and, like, Memorial Day, we always honored them and everything.

Oh, on Armistice Day especially and Memorial Day, we used to have this bandstand here that Edith Stipp had a fit to get torn down. I suppose you've heard about that.

I didn't hear why it was torn down.

Edith Stipp always had this . . . antipathy toward this bandstand, and it *did* mess up the—I have to admit the courthouse is prettier without it. But I have wondered if maybe she had this thought for one reason. Her husband, we used to have band concerts every Thursday night in town, and everybody in town came, and listened, you know, and they sat on the square and would walk around and get an ice-cream cone and talk and everything. I think all the older generation looked back with pleasure on those Thursday nights. Well, Edith's husband was a dentist and he used to *play* in the band every week. And I wonder if she resented maybe

"Welcome Home" celebration, Indianapolis, 1919
Indiana Historical Society,
Bass Photo Company Collection, 66384F

one night of practice and one night band concert every week. Because she wanted that bandstand torn down worse than anything.

But to see what we used to do on Armistice Day and on Memorial Day, we would have these speakers, would gather up there on the bandstand, and all the school kids would march from the school downtown and fill the courtyard. And different kids, you know, one or two from each class would get up and make speeches and things like that. And then on Memorial Day, why, everybody in town brought their flowers, and they were all divided up into bunches, and the kids carried those and marched to the cemetery and put them on the soldiers' graves. Whatever flowers you had in your yard. Of course, peonies were *always* good on Memorial Day, and whatever other things happened to be in bloom, but everybody brought their flowers, and then they were divided into little bunches and tied up in bunches, and all the kids marched to the cemetery and put those on the soldiers' graves, which were marked.

What other kinds of things were special events?

Well, all holidays were special at our house. Mother was a great traditionalist [laughs]. And we always, you know, we celebrated them *at home*. But my sister and I always got a new dress for every holiday, that was because, I think, *because* maybe Mother didn't have the clothes she wanted growing up in the country.

And we always got a new dress for every holiday that came along. And we got fifteen cents apiece to spend, that was a fortune in those days. We got a nickel for a bottle of Orange Crush or grape or whatever we wanted, a nickel for a candy bar, and a nickel for Cracker Jacks. On the holidays. Each one of us. And that was our great day. And of course when the carnival came to town it used to be on the square instead of out in the hills like it is now. And we got to go—most kids went every night, but we got to one or two nights when the folks would take us.

I don't think I was ever young. I think I was born an old woman [laughs]. When I was three years old, my mother was putting pillows around my brother on the bed and leaving him and my little sister for me to watch while she carried water twice a day from, oh, all the way from three blocks to five blocks depending on what well was broken. That was until we moved over to the other house.

Did you have a lot of responsibilities?

Absolutely! I said I never was a *child*. I mean, Mother would leave me to watch the two of them while she went to town. I was from October until December past three when my brother was born. And I know Mother and I talked about it before she died. She said, "Well, I had to do it." Well, I don't think she had to. I think I would've found another way. Because she "had to," you know, she "had to" have somebody to leave her kids with. But I can't see it that way. Because a three year old, you won't think of leaving a three year old without a baby-sitter much less to watch two others.

And I *think* I remember this. At least I've been told it many times. My little sister, one time Mother had gone to town and my little sister decided to go run off and go *after* Mother. And, see, at the time, that street we lived, it wasn't even gravel. It was big rough rocks. And down the street she ran and here I was carrying this baby and running after her. We got to the corner and my neighbors came out and one grabbed her and was trying to take the baby from me and I won't let her have him! And when Mother got back there was one, the girl was holding my sister, and her mother was holding her arms under me trying to keep that baby from falling [both laugh]. Well, there was no *way* I would've let her have that baby!

I've been told that at that time, people in the town had a certain kind of attitude toward people from the country.

Now, I have had some friends, you know, well, almost exemplify the country way that we used to talk about. But nowadays, well, now I remember, when I was in school, one boy who came from the country who was always nicely dressed at school and everything. But most of the country kids, you know, came in overalls and, as my dad said, barefoot and stuff like that. And in those days, country . . . well, it just—farming wasn't what it *is* now. And so people also didn't think as much of the people who farmed. They were the poor people. Weren't we *all* poor?

Especially, see, I would've been eleven years old when the depression, when the stock market crashed. But we were not that poor. We were always taught how poor we were, but my mother drew half of her brother's insurance every month. And my daddy was getting a pension from being wounded. Besides, this sounds small to you, but in those days it was a fortune. I've known Dad to make a hundred dollars a week because he was a darn good mechanic. So we were not—I remember right, oh, I would say it was '30 or '31, Dad bought the last new car he had. And I remember when he brought it home, it was a new Pontiac, and we, we were all walking around that, you know, and looking at it and ohhhing and ahhhing and Dad says, "I don't want a *one* of you going to school and saying a thing about this in the morning."

You mentioned your dad drinking with his buddies. Was that one of the things that the men, that just the men did?

Home brew was a great thing when I was young. It was during Prohibition and every family that drank made home brew and, you know, you made it on the kitchen stove in this great big crock stone jar. And then, when it got to a certain stage, you bottled. And then they put it in the attic to cure or age or whatever they called it and this is the common thing that's happened at *every* family sooner or later. That is, it only happened like when the preacher came to call or Lady's Aid was there or something like that. These bottles would start blowing up in the attic going bang, bang, bang!

But I can remember now my mother never went out with Dad drinking. But she did have his beer parties for him there when it was his turn to have one, they all came to our house.

I think he must have drunk a lot when he was young. And when he first came back from the war, he only drank on weekends. And eventually by the time I was in high school, he was drinking, instead of working most of the time. But the fact is that we always had enough income to live on. It never kept us from—I *really* believe that my dad thought enough of family life that if they didn't have the money to live on, I don't think he would've used it.

That must have been hard. Is that something that you tried to keep in the family?

No, it isn't; it should've been. I think, you know, with most families it wouldn't have been known. But my mother was one who wanted everyone to know how bad he was and how good she was. I can't quite forgive my mother for it. Because when I came back down and helped take care of my dad that last summer, I think I grew up hating my dad. I was taught to. And we were taught, you know, that Dad was mean to us and things. He wasn't mean to us, he never, you know, people that come in, you know, and beat the family and stuff—Dad wasn't like that. When he came in he was a nuisance when he was drunk. But—[sighs] I'm sorry, my mind does go sometimes.

What were some of the advantages and disadvantages of living in a small town?

Well, the big advantage that I can think of is this: I lived here practically my entire life except those first three months until after I was married, we lived away from here for about twenty-five years and came back and it was just like I had never left town. I still had *all* the friends I'd always had. And when my husband died I would not have been anywhere else but right here where I had all the people I've known my entire life support me. *That* is something you do not have in the city and I *have* lived in the city and I *worked* there.

See, my husband was doing construction. And I've lived in thirty-nine different houses in my life. And I had never lived in but three until I was married. He worked with these great big buildings, see? He was a plumber and steamfitter.

How did you meet him?

Just during the war. He was a plumber then, but he went and got his steamfitter's license. And, of course, it paid well and that's where we went. Wherever the work was. The first year we were married, why, we were only married three months when he was in the hospital for three weeks. They told me he couldn't live with stomach ulcers, he kept having one hemorrhage after another.

I was married the first day of 1941, I was twenty-two in October before I was married.

You knew what you were getting into and everything?

No! I did not know that he was going to go into that. He had a filling station when we were married. But then after all those hospital bills we needed *money*. I think that's partly why he went into steam fitting.

[Lucy recalls when women got the right to vote.]

One day while Dad was at work and this lady that came around to register people was the wife of one of Dad's partners where he was working at the time. And of course Mother talked with Leota Hoke and she told Mother that, you know, that they would need to be registered, that they wouldn't ever be able to do this or that unless they were registered. So she registered. And Leota explained that it didn't mean she had to go vote, that just if she would be registered. And when Dad came home and Mother told him I think he didn't speak to Mother for about three days over that.

And she said, "I will never vote." And *all* those years she never voted till I think it was maybe in the mid-thirties. One time there was a man that Dad especially wanted elected. And he wanted every vote he could get. And he asked Mom if she would register and go vote that year and that's when she started voting again.

But that would be my guess, because I would guess that many of my dad's friends probably felt the same way. That their wives never voted. And then, too, a good portion of this town to this *day*, they vote the way they are *paid to vote*. I'm not kidding you a bit! I mean, maybe I don't hear about quite as much as I did even ten years ago. Now I used to go work at Democratic headquarters and I *never* saw anything out of the way, but I knew what was going on. But this guy who was county chairman had gone to school with me and I think he *knew* better than to let me see anything. Because I never saw a bottle of whiskey, I never saw any votes paid for or anything, but I knew it was being done by both parties. But my neighbors over there, where I said where Mother lived? "I told you! Whoever pays the most!" Listen, they didn't pull any bones about it. They would say, "Well, what did *you* get with your election money? I bought a new dress, I bought me a new dishpan."

They were poor people?

It was the poor people, you know, that if they got paid two dollars for voting and it wasn't all—I know they paid as much as twenty dollars, I don't know more than that.

Now how about your husband, was he . . .

My husband was so, his parents were so Republican, or his daddy was, that Mr. Deckard would not have wanted to go to heaven if he thought that there was a Democrat there. But that, he didn't worry about it, because he knew Democrats couldn't get into heaven [laughs]. Does that tell you anything?

Did his son share those sentiments?

No, we changed after his dad was dead, but I'm sure we would never have told him, any more than we told my parents, if he'd been alive. We talked it over, we were just sitting talking one night and we said we're being foolish, that we've been thinking *like* Democrats but we've been voting like Republicans and so we decided it was time to change. So I went down to Democrat headquarters and asked them what they needed done and from that day on I worked. And then when we came back down here the county chairman was the guy I'd gone to school with, and he knew I could write and stuff and I said he kept me busy. I wrote all the Democrat stuff for years here, stuff for the papers here. Well, advertisements too. Like, you know, things that came over that radio at election time and stuff like that.

What was different in the way you were thinking versus how the Republican people were thinking?

When Democrats were in, there was more money, we had better jobs, nicer places to live, you know, and then we would get a Republican. You remember we had a recession, we don't call them depressions, they're recessions nowadays, just the big one. But we did have during Eisenhower's term, you know, and I think that's when we decided that—and then, of course, you said, "That's John Kennedy's bust" [indicating sculpture in the room]. I think everybody sort of worshiped John Kennedy. He wasn't just a Democrat, he was John Kennedy. And those are Eisenhower prints on my wall. And I've had them for years.

How old were you when Lupus started to stop you from doing these things? Were you confined to a wheelchair at that point?

No. No, I worked. Before my husband died, I went to work for three years after he was having heart attacks. And then after he died, I didn't go to work for six months. And then I went to work and I worked for three years and that's when I had the first stroke. But even then, I was walking with a cane then, and the girls would have to help me in and out at night. And many times my boss—not just the little boss, you know, in factories it's like a caste system, there's bosses all the way up, his was the boss of the whole upholstery department—would come to me in the middle of the afternoon, "Give me your car keys," and he would go walk to the parking lot and get my car and bring it and park it right in the front of the door so that I didn't have to walk to the parking lot.

You know, that was the only job I'd take. Honestly, I worked at Beta [factory in another town] for three years before he died. And I have to tell you I had to pull to get on both places. They do not hire somebody that's near fifty or sixty years old to work in a factory with no experience, I'd never worked in one. But my husband had a cousin who was a boss that worked at Beta and when he started having those heart attacks, why, I went over there and I told her, and she talked to them, and by the time I got home from putting in an application there was a call for me to come to work the next morning. I know, however, three days after I worked there why I wouldn't of had any troubles getting a job. And then after he died, I told them I would come back, and they said that whenever I got ready to come back, just give them one day's notice, that maybe they couldn't hire me that day, they would the next.

Beta was a hard place to work. I told my boss once if they hired ten people one day that half of them would be gone by break and three more would be gone by that night when you come back the next day. And he says, "If they had to, the other three might make good workers!"

Were you not able to get something here in town?

Well, I really don't know. I said, they don't hire you at a factory—I did try a, there was one bookkeeping job and it didn't pay nearly as much as factories did. See, I'd always been a bookkeeper. And it didn't pay nearly as much as factories did. Well, I'd wanted work and it seemed ideal. But then, after he died, I had planned to go back to Beta, but I told myself I was going to take six months to rest. The week he'd been dead six months, I told a friend of mine, I said, "Well, I'm going back to Beta this week." And she said, "Don't go there. Give them a chance to hire you at the chair factory."

I said, "They're not going to hire me without any, you know. . . ." And she picked up the phone and called Irwin Vest who was boss out there, and I went up there that afternoon and the personnel manager already had a blank filled out for me on the desk. 'Course he had a few things that I had to tell him after I got there, and then he told me, "Well, I would like to hire you." But he says I had told him that I won't take anything but *sewing*, see? He says, "I can't—we've got all the sewing machines full right now but let me go talk to the upholstery foreman," whatever they called him, and he came back with this—Dale Kendall was that then. And when he came back into the room with Dale, they had gone in and taken a girl off a sewing machine and put her off in the upholstery department so that I could have a sewing machine the next morning and go to work.

And then—oh, that one chair that I told you that I did so many of—and then, they got an order from the Minnesota legislature. I think it was more than 450 of them. It was an enormous bunch of chairs. So they call me into the office, "Do you think you can get that many done?" Well, we didn't *any* of us know whether I could sew that many because there was a penalty clause—if they didn't have them finished by a certain time, why, they had to pay for every chair that wasn't done. On the other hand, if they put girls that didn't know how to sew them and they had to do them over, they would've been worse off. So the last week that I worked on those, there was a steady stream of *bosses* come in, "Are you going to make it? Are you going to make it?" And I just felt like saying, "Just leave me alone. Just leave me alone."

When you were working at the chair factory, was it piecework that way?

Well, piecework essentially—I'm not sure that it's good. Because I said you can make more money that way but there is also the temptation to do a poor job to get more done. But that's what they told me when I went there, they didn't care if I ever made piecework, what they wanted was a good job. But we had a couple that did, that probably made more money than I did. But they were, you know, they weren't that careful with it. And then we had a couple of girls who, poor things, couldn't have sewed if their life depended on it. They did lousy work and, of course, they didn't stay very long too.

I was thinking about your daughters. I was remembering what you said when you were young and you wondered why anyone wanted a little boy . . .

When we were first married, I wanted the first one to be a boy and then a girl, because I'd always wanted a big brother. But he had two sisters—both died of cancer in their twenties—and I think that's the reason he wanted a girl. Oh, when Mary Lou was born—see, people with Lupus notoriously have a hard time with babies. I was unconscious four days when she was born and in the hospital three weeks.

And when we started out of the hospital that morning, he was carrying the baby and I was still in an ambulance. I still was in bed three more weeks. I think it was six weeks before they let me up and, of course, they wouldn't even let me feed myself. My heart quit beating while I was unconscious all that time.

Anyhow, here comes some old woman as we were going down to the ambulance entrance and she was like I am now, and she stopped right in front of us with her arms like that on both hips and she says, "Oh, what a darling big boy."

My husband says, "It's not a boy. It's a girl."

"Oh, what a pity."

But he says, "We wanted a girl."

And she says, "Oh, well, maybe you'll—" No, she went ahead and talked to him while they stood there and held, you know, pushing me and him holding that baby for about ten minutes while she talked. The last thing she says is, "Maybe you'll have better luck next time." And we knew there wasn't going to be a next time and that didn't help. But . . . "maybe you'll have better luck next time." See people really have that idea—well, I think they still do! Because, I said the last five babies in our family have been boys. Well, I know my granddaughter had a baby last year, she wanted a boy. My two nieces have, and they wanted boys. But I'm looking for another girl. I'm getting tired of boys.

Do you think things are different now, in terms of how little girls are raised and little boys are raised?

Yes. I can remember when I was about six years old, probably. It was after we moved to the new house. Mother had taken my sister to town with her, and my brother and I were there. And the little boy who was my age and lived in the next block came over to play with us; we were allowed to play with him. And my brother had his wagon and Russell and I, and we were all three playing, you know, riding the wagon out in the yard. And my daddy happened to come from work in the middle of the day. And boy, did he haul me in the house right then, he told me *little girls* didn't go out and play with little boys that way. Can you imagine that having happened now?

How do you think World War II affected Paoli? Were a lot of men from Paoli . . .

In the war? Yes. I lost a *lot* of friends. See, I was at the age, I said I was twenty-three when we declared war and, and I was right at the age where, you know, they were *prime*. And then, before the war was over, they were taking up until thirty-nine or something like that, and I even had a few, you know, friends that were older than I was that was there.

But, I think the whole world has been different, because I remember during the war they kept telling us about this new material called *plastic* and how everything was going to be made out of plastic after the World War. The nearest thing we knew to plastic was using glass before the war. And, and just think that plastic has just really changed the world. But, then something else that changed then, and this is a little thing, but if you ever had to wash with soap, you'd know what I meant, because all we had to wash our clothes with was soap. And you remember few of us had washers either. And you washed and you rubbed it on a *board*. I got my first washer during World War II, what I had ordered about two years before I got it. And they kept telling us about this new thing called detergent that we were going to be able to get, and I remember the first box of Tide I *ever* used. That was the most marvelous thing I've ever seen in my life. It was so different from making water with your soap and then in a few minutes all you'd have left is a curd around edge and all that.

Just a little thing, but it sure has modernized our world, just about everything, be it cleaning house and keeping house and things. For another thing, when I was married, you couldn't buy tomatoes or anything like that in the winter because there was no transportation for them. They had to have refrigerated trucks to get those things here. And in that year that we moved to Alabama, and you could get tomatoes in the stores down there, you know, and I thought it was marvelous, because I like to live on tomatoes.

The night that the first man landed on the moon, oh, my grandkids would've been about seven years old, I gave them a quarter a piece to sit down and write, "Today, I saw a man land on the moon." Because we got them out of bed, you know, it was in the middle of the night when they landed. But the night that John Kennedy was killed, I sat down and wrote what was going on. And the day, oh, that big blowup over in Russia, the nuclear plant over there, I've got it all written down, how I felt about it. And this might seem silly to you, but I think if I had something that my grandmother had written the day that the Civil War was over, she was four years old, when the Civil War was over. And the day, if I had something that she had written then and that she was 'specting her papa to come from the war, 'cause that's what they called him, is "Poppy," why, won't that be something? That is the kind of thing I can leave to my great-grandkids, and they probably won't give a darn.

If you could, well, in this biography of mine, I keep saying that Mother's prime thing in her life was that a girl grew up to get married and have a husband and that she couldn't understand when we would bring awards home from school, what good those were going to do us about getting a *husband*. Because as far as she was concerned, that was the only thing for a girl to do. Even in *my* generation, it was, really. I mean, we might go out and get jobs, but girls didn't go out for a career.

If I were going to school *now*, I don't think I'd want to be a lawyer, I won't want to be a doctor, but I know what I would be. I'd be a writer or a schoolteacher. And if I were teaching, I would teach English and journalism. Yes. That's what I would go out for if I were in school now. But, in my day, women didn't go out for things. That's what I was telling you that nobody in our class was anybody great. We were just lucky we got through school, and you worked and like I said. Just imagine living day after day and never having any fun happen to you. Anything different. And I think about factories because most of those people, you know, they get up and they go to work every morning and they work through the day, the same job, the same motions, the same thing. They go home that night and they eat the same things for supper. And they go back to work the next morning and same thing over day after-day for maybe fifty years of their life. How would you live?

Well, I used to tell everybody, you know, that I did not believe in women's lib, because I liked being treated like a lady. And then suddenly it occurred to me that you take two people, one man and one woman, on the same job and he's making half again as much as she is, not doing a bit better work. And that galls. So now I've gotten to the place that I *do* believe in a certain amount of women's lib and now, you know, that I'm getting old, I'm not so sure that I don't believe in it after all.

Lotus Dickey was born in 1911 in Muncie, Indiana, and moved to Orange County as an infant. He worked in factories, in construction, and as a carpenter and in retirement gained recognition as a folk musician. He died in November 1989.[8]

Dickey: I was born at Muncie, Indiana. And I landed down there [in Orange County] May the 4th, 1912. I was four months and six days old, to be exact. I was born December the 28th, 1911.

I grew up out in the sticks, about six miles southeast, in a place called Little Africa. During the Civil War, they had the Underground Railroad, and they settled some of the runaway slaves out in that district. And there's a graveyard three-fourths of a mile due east of me yet. And there was a church, but not in my time.

And the colored people were settled back in there and right on the place, right on a rough, little forty acres there. But it was settled, I think, first, from the government by a black man by the name of Thomas Roberts. And the man that brought him there and settled him on it was the first settler of Orange County, Jonathan Lindley. Orange County used to include what is known as Lawrence County now, too. He had property in both counties and, they said, maybe a little bit in Monroe.

But, of course, that's getting away from what you asked; only I'm just getting my way around there.

So I grew up going to little one-room schoolhouses in the country; walked about two miles each way. Then, I really didn't get to Paoli a lot; oh, I went a few times. Still, I did go to high school, which was in the fall of 1925. However, my next oldest sister—Avis Dickey, that married Bob Hilliard—Avis Dickey Hilliard started teaching school in '23. She went for four years to high school; she was about ten years older than I. Then my younger sister, four years older than I, graduated the first year I went to high school. She graduated in '26 and I started the fall of '25. And then I graduated in '29. So then I began to see more of Paoli. And I stayed the first season with friends where both of my sisters had stayed about most of the four years going to high school: Albert and Effie Doherty. They're right near the school. So, I stayed that first year there. Their youngest boy was about a year and a half older than I, and we slept together.

Cars were pretty scarce at that time. Once in a great while, somebody'd pick me up, but at that time I could walk to town or walk home and, maybe, never meet a car going or coming. That's how scant the traffic was. Now you pull up, you have to watch, there'll be something coming when I pull up to the intersection, there's something coming from one direction or the other without fail, or in sight. But they had built this new road, 150, and they had made an asphalt road of it and, boy, that was a well-built road. George Teitel, back in the twenties, was the superintendent over the roads from Palmyra, I believe, to, well, maybe, to Loogootee. Then later on his son, Ray Teitel, took it over, and my brother worked for them for eight years as a truck driver. And that was my first connection to Paoli, pretty well.

[8] Interviewed by Maria Green, 18 April 1989, Paoli.

Then, of course, as I got older, I worked at home for a couple of years; I got to working at the basket factory in the summer of 1931. I was about nineteen and a half. Well, I worked there for ten years; it was seasonal. Average six months; maybe another few weeks extra around through the wintertime. They'd get a run for baskets.

It was a cheap industry but as I think about it, Paoli needed that factory really. It was cheap, but wasn't much available at that time.

I started at twenty-four cents an hour. Ten hours a day, six days a week. In '31. In '32 they cut me to twenty-two cents—along with others. Thirty-three they cut me to seventeen cents. Some got as low as fifteen, and the women got ten cents an hour—if they were on hour work. Ten hours a day for a dollar. They put them on piecework. And if they knew a person, they let them try their hand at making at webs sometimes. They'd let them come in. And it took years to acquire that skill. And away back after World War I, that paid pretty good money.

But a new person come in then, it took a while. I remember I counted. . . . I knew what the rate was, and that lady stood there not ten hours one day, and she made forty-five cents—in ten hours. She didn't stay long, you know; she hadn't developed the skill. While the others more skillful could, with their speed, make somewhat above hour work. That's just the way the whole setup was.

And they hauled logs in, largely big beech trees they cut. And they cooked them in vats. And they put them in big wood lathes and peeled them down to where they rounded up right, and then they cut it into veneer. It turned around there and sliced it off into just a continuous—oh, I'd say about a sixteenth of an inch thick. Come out on a big long table, the fellow stripped to the waist, and they'd run back with that as it comes out and it pretty well runs the length of the table. And then run back here as it's coming again, and just fold it and fold it.

So you worked there ten years?

Ten seasons. Started in '31, about July of '31. I didn't start quite at the end of spring, but got out a crop there at home. We farmed just a little bit, for a while.

Stagecoach of the Rhodes Livery Stable, early twentieth century. The coach made weekly trips to New Albany, Louisville, and Vincennes.
Paoli News-Republican

What did you do the other parts of the year? What kind of work did you do the other part?

Well, we patched around the farm a little, and I'd help get the crop in in the fall. And cut wood and tend the stock; we had a little stock.

This was your family's farm?

Well, yes, it was. Well, that's where I lived; it was my father's and mother's. I was the youngest of the family, and I was the last to leave home. I didn't marry . . . I married about four months under thirty-two, and the folks were old. My father was born March the 16th, 1860. Mom was almost thirteen years younger; she was born January the 5th, 1873. And they were from Darke County, Ohio. Darke County is in west-central Ohio.

My father's folks were Dunkers. Sort of like . . . oh, they say that they were . . . they called them the Brethren now, I believe, but they were a branch off of the German Baptist, my father said years ago.

He was baptized in a Dunker church. And his first wife—his first wife died before he met Mom. He had bad luck. And I have two half sisters. Well, the first one died when she was three; she was born in 1883. The other was born in 1886, and she died when she was sixteen, when my oldest sister, Bernie, was six years old.

So your father was almost fifty when you were born?

He was almost fifty-two when I was born. And he had a memory also, and his Grandfather Dickey, Alexander Dickey, that came from Kentucky in a covered wagon to Ohio, and I don't think it was to Darke County. Of course, he lived there with my grandfather, Michael Dickey, but he was born around 1790, and my father was seventeen before he died. So I have the word of mouth what happened way back. And then *his* father, my great-grandfather's father, had come from England and settled in Kentucky. And rode with Lighthorse Harry Lee in the Revolutionary War; Henry Lee, Robert E. Lee's father, with his Lighthorse Brigade.

What are some of your memories of growing up in Paoli?

We'd go barefoot until frost got pretty heavy and at home my feet was tough. Not just me; a lot of kids did. We'd go to school in the fall barefoot until it got too cold, you know, to walk through. And somehow I stubbed my toe in the fall. This was in 1921; I was a little short of ten then. So I started to school. I started to wear my shoes and couldn't do it. Used to once in a while wear overshoes, and that was a mistake. I wore that overshoe on that; I got it infected somehow, on that toe. I finally got down sick and, [pause] oh, that toe just about . . . I had an awful time with that. Had Doc Merris out, which I never went to a doctor them days. That about drove me up the wall. Finally, it wouldn't get well, and my neighbor, Matt Longwith and his son Harry, they came by. They brought about the salve. I think it was Border B, it might have been ten cents then. Well, we started using it, and my toes just started getting . . . just got . . . well, if that did it or if it was ready to go, I don't know. That was quite a setback.

But, actually, we kind of grew up with a pretty close family. Kind of "All for one and one for all," you know. And back at that time, you didn't have radio or television, or we didn't have a phonograph—ourselves. The neighbors, Spencers, that came down, had a phonograph. A "Talking Machine" they called it. An Edison. Good playing; just a little cabinet. Had some old records on there that was interesting. Good Hawaiian music.

But we made our own music. My father taught himself to read the notes way back. He learned on the shape notes which probably might have been in the *Sacred Harp* [songbook]. I can't remember him saying so, but his father before him learned the shape notes. Back then was when that *Sacred Harp* was in vogue, way back there.[9]

Dad had an excellent memory. Well, Mom did too. Mom taught a little school, way back, before she was married. But Mom was almost thirteen years younger,

[9] The *Sacred Harp* songbook, using a system of shape notes in its musical notation, first appeared in 1844 and is still in use among many rural folk hymn and gospel singers. "Sacred Harp Singing" and "Shape-Note Hymnody," in Stanley Sadie, ed., *The New Grove Dictionary of Music and Musicians* (London: Macmillan Publishers, 1980).

and she lived another eight years till March the 9th, 1961.

And we . . . well, they taught us to mind. What I mean, there's no child perfect, you know, needing no looking after. But they'd get after us, you know: "Here, here, don't do this," and stop us and teach us and . . . when we went to school, they said, "Now you behave yourself," and told us to be respectable to the teacher. Like Mabel Wells—we called her Miss Mabel. Mr. Burford. They said, "Now you go there and behave yourself and get your lessons," and said, "Now, if you get a licking at school, you'll get another one when you get home."

How was it different back then? What were the changes?

Well, of course, the change is the fact that when I grew up there weren't as many people and we walked to school. Now, they did have a stagecoach; a fellow drove a stagecoach. Rode a few times with that. But we moved, and we walked it. We hated the bus; it was too mobbed, too full, you know.

Well, the teacher'd have a bell or speak to you: "Eighth-grade arithmetic arise. Come up front. Be seated." Or tap the bells sometime. I think when my sister taught some, she had a bell. Some of them did.

And they had order; they would have order then. They didn't have—oh, I don't mean—they didn't whip us, but they kept it down. And literally, when Mabel Wells taught later—she passed away not too many years ago—she was twenty-one and, boy, she had order. I mean, you could literally hear the pin drop. I mean, she would have order. That's the way it was, and they just didn't tolerate. . . . I've seen in later years, of course, the teacher had a whole class full. They have a lot more students, see.

When you were in high school, you lived in town, did you say?

Well, I *stayed* in town. But I went home on weekends. No, we never did live in town. We were poor people. My dad was honest and wanted to pay everything he owed. Boys didn't believe in taking advantage of anybody, you know. Now, Sherman Bosley was a big farmer there. Sherman owned a lot of ground. He set his two boys and his daughter up and their grandchildren live there. And they had a good bit of land; I mean, compared to us. We just had a little forty. And he farmed pretty big back then; he had mules, you know, and horses and cattle and sheep and hogs. Well, he liked my dad's work; he told me one time—after he got old, of course, my dad got old he couldn't work like that. But he said, "Marion Dickey's back is always reared up," he said. Just like a mule, you know. "That hard work . . ."

That's why people . . . it's just survival; you didn't have unemployment. And once in a while, you know, people *have* had to get stuff from the county. They got real hard up, you know, but my people hated to do that. I mean, you know, you just . . . we never . . . we'd raise our living largely on that forty acres. Mom would can and dry fruit. We had seedling peaches then. Some apples and grapes, and we raised raspberries, strawberries. Picked wild blackberries and dewberries, always busy. And stood over a wood stove the whole summer. That heat, you know.

We didn't even have an icebox. No electric, just the old way. That's the way a lot of people had it. It wasn't just us. A lot of . . . of course, in town, now, they had electric long before, you know. I think, yes, they had electric in town. When I went to high school, they had it before that. But I don't, if I remember right—they had electric then. I *believe* they did, if I remember right. We had oil lamps.

I thought, "My land." You know, we didn't drive much then, in depression time. I had a car. Money was scarce. If you went around the road, it was three miles to Chambersburg. But I could walk through—two miles—and Wilson Danner's store, then John Coulter and old Stevenson. And I traded with all them some; I went to Wilson's a lot. He was . . . he didn't marry until he was older too, like myself. But back then, that car'd sit there, and the battery'd run down. And I'd just go through and carry groceries home on my shoulder, a couple of miles. Or I'd ride the mare around the road three miles and carry them on her. When I had the car . . . it was standing right there, but I . . . money was scarce and I didn't want to run up a bill for gas, and just save that little money. A dollar'd buy a lot of things, you know.

There was [a] fruit stand, on the square there in Paoli, there used to be a fruit stand way back—might have been the twenties too—but in the early thirties for a while. Well, I called him Poppa Gandolpho, but he was . . . well, I don't know if he was Spanish or Italian. I think they had a stand down in Louisville too; him and his two sons. They'd come up there and bring stuff. They had produce. Oh, they'd have the best baked bananas, you know, just . . .

I remember one . . . well, I walked into town, if I remember right. We worked six days, ten hours a day, and walked to town on Saturday night, you know. They had what they called Handy Andy's Restaurant there. He started it. He made his own ice cream; he had a big dairy, he and his brother. His name was Andrew J. Leonard—and his brother Thurman. And back in the twenties, then in the thirties, *two* big dips of ice cream on the cone for a nickel. I don't mean little dips, but great big ones. You know, just stack it on there for a nickel. Or a malted milk, or a milk shake actually—a full quart of it—fifteen cents. He poured that in the other, little smaller vessel there, twice. I remember one night, after supper, I'd eaten good at home, I walked into town. I bought my two malted milks, two dishes of ice cream, and either a cake or a pie. A nickel—used to get them for a nickel, and they don't . . . felt just fine.

Do you remember much about World War I?

Well, I was six years old that December the 28th in 1917. The main thing I remember about . . . we had cracklings and corn bread three times a day. Flour was kind of scarce and, well, I don't know if you know what cracklings are or not. You butcher hogs and cut your fat into . . . boil that in a big pot and watch that it doesn't stick to anything. And then you put it in a lard press and press it out. It's cooked fat after the lard's squeezed out of it. It makes it like a rind, but they're good. They're like bacon, I mean; crisp, you know.

Well, Momma used to put that in corn bread a lot of times. And usually crackling—you didn't waste much of anything back then. I remember one time, that was that winter, we had that front room, and up-

The Mineral Springs Hotel on the south side of the square, early 1950s
Paoli News-Republican

stairs was a shed kitchen. That shed kitchen gets so cold, you know, your water bucket freezes solid. It got so rough there, it got, oh, twenty, twenty-five below zero that winter, you know. The big snow—two foot on the level that year. I was just six; they didn't let me out much. I know I'd go out once in a while and my dad would shovel paths out to the barn. 'Course you know how tall a six year old would be. I'd worry through that bank way above my head, you know; big, deep snow. And then it'd come three-inch high on top of that, to hold a horse up.

And I remember I was sitting at the table one evening and, oh, my folks were great on canned stuff. And they'd bury potatoes, turnips, cabbage, parsnips. But, you know, it's more of a dry diet. You know, I kind of burned out on corn bread, and I was kind of bucking at the table. Oh, Mom had said something to me and I guess I was kind of pouty, I guess. My dad just looked across the table. I think he was standing up. "Now, you just sit up and eat," he said. I mean, he just said it once. I mean, I got my head in my plate and [laughs] . . . I mean, you paid attention then when your parents spoke; you paid attention. I mean . . .

My folks would [play music] too, you know. Well, them was nice times. And then his cousin, old Alan Downey, came along about 1920. He was a fiddler. I learned a lot for my fiddling.

And what the conglomeration of the fiddlers I've learned of it, and Alan Downey's one of them. I think I learned . . . yes, either seven or eight tunes. Well, I learned more than that, but I mean I recorded. And old Albert Garder, worked at the high school, six of his tunes. Old Eck Ainsworth, a man that came up from Arkansas, six of his tunes. Then three . . . 'course I knew more tunes than *that* from all of them, see. But thems the ones that Paul Tyler, he especial liked some of them ones that we recorded.

Then John Coulter, a storekeeper there at Chambersburg, who I spoke of before, he used to peddle up second for him. I think I recorded four I got of him. Then odds and ends of others. I recorded thirty-two in all.

Gerald Stout—oh, he could play; oh, sing too. Oh, they were beautiful. Had two boys and then a girl. He was a lot younger. And we'd go down to learn, you know. Owen Stout had a little orchestra. And Morgan, Doc Albert. Then he'd be playing it; he might be playing a fiddle along here. He'd lay down the fiddle and pick up a trombone, or a trumpet. He'd just play them, all of them, you know. Arrange them parts. YCO, the Youngs Creek Orchestra. Way back to the twenties. And they said YCO stands for: "Yonder Comes Owen." But it was the Youngs Creek Orchestra. Yes, I call him here once in a while. We had a sing last fall. He was eighty-five last December the 24th.

Where did you work after you left the basket factory?

In December, and on January the 3d, of '41, I went down to Charleston. They were starting that powder plant at Charleston, Indiana. Let's see, DuPont du Nemours, I believe they called it. Largest munition makers in the world, say they're running that plant. And I took my brother and five other fellows; seven of us. I had a '36 Chevrolet. Five of us got on. My brother said, "You work here," if they'd give him a job; other fellow didn't make it. Well, the five of us, the next morning, we went to work. I hauled all of them; it was the fourth of January. Well, I worked nine months on construction labor. Sixty cents an hour. See, I'd been getting twelve- to fifteen-dollars a week on piecework. I put in *forty* hours, but we worked forty-eight hours down there. 'Course we got four-times the salary.

And that was . . . when I first drove it, it was sixty-seven miles each way. I stayed two months, in New Albany. But aside of that, I made that trip all the time. And, oh, I got wore out; I didn't need to make so . . . I give them a week's notice and left. Farmed a little. Then I got working of Cornwell. In '45, a woodworking place here in Paoli. They first made "whatnots" and "wallmarts." I run the saws. Oh, they'd give me bunch of wood and I'd just saw them up for things. And then they finally got to making television cabinets and they got in a bigger machine. Stickers and fingers machine. But I run the saw there for years. Well, I worked there about [pause] oh, about six years and a half straight, and then I went back about three times; I expect about eight years all together. But I got onto construction; I joined the carpenters union in New Albany and worked *some* jobs. And the pipeline came along and I joined this 741 labor local up here. Ever hear of it?

And ever since then I've worked construction. Oh, a lot of times, oh, I'd do anything. I'd cut wood. Worked for a farmer, you know, if I didn't have anything to do. I had a big family; had to keep doing something.

The former basket factory, later owned by the Cornwell Company, mid-1960s.
Paoli News-Republican

How would your life be different from your father's, and how is it different from your son's and grandson's?

Well, like I said, I lived throughout the transition. What I mean, I can remember the *old* way. Then after the First World War, the beginning of things changing, and much more after World War II.

Well, we got into this firepower age, you see, as it came along. Then we begin to get radio, way back in . . . my sister got the folks a battery set, Emerson radio, in '37, for Christmas. Of course, the neighbors had some before; my brother-in-law and I heard the Grand Old Opry and a few things, you know. Now and then but not all the time. And the neighbors, in 1925, got their first one. Big speaker and all you could hear was static on it, unless you put the earphones on, which I didn't get to do much. But that was Spencers. And, well, the thing of it is, my dad never drove an automobile and Mom didn't either. No, I got to driving a car; started driving when I was sixteen—just barely. They'd let me drive, my brother-in-law and my brother. Just a little on the road. And then I started driving *real* slow and real careful, you know.

And, well, 'course the thing of it is, I got into the machine age. I'm not dealing with horses now. What I mean: my dad, who had a horse, you know, and a cow or two. I think the most we had was five; and raised a few hogs for meat sometimes. And had, oh, maybe fifty hens, maybe a hundred. I think one time two hundred hens.

Benjamin Minton was born in Paoli in 1906 and worked for most of his career at the Handle Company, a wood products factory.[10]

When you were growing up, what did your father do?

Minton: He hauled logs and cut wood, and just one thing and then another. He hauled logs for different people and he cut . . . a fellow by the name of Stout gave him, I think it was forty acres of that, after he cut the timber off of it. And he give him the, oh, everything on it. Needed to hew, crossties you hew with a broadax. He give him everything down in that wood

[10]Interviewed by Catherine A. Jones, 9 December 1987, Paoli.

Oxen team on the square, early twentieth century
Orange County Historical Society

and everything. And he would go in there and cut pole wood and everything. And he would go in there and cut pole wood and pile up enough for about a hundred cord, and then he'd hire somebody to come and cut it for him, then he'd hauled that and sold it.

[Benjamin recalls his young adulthood.]

Well, my wife worked, done a little housework for different people before so—you know, it wasn't like it is. So we got married, and, you see, I got laid off up there at the refrigerator plant, icebox plant, and I came home, and I went and started work up there in Bloomington in the box factory. When we got married, why, I wrote up there to a boss of mine, and asked him about a job, and he told me to be there the next Wednesday, ready to go to work. Kelvinator owned it then. They bought him out, and I went to work for them, and I asked how my job was there. We was just a-staying with a couple up there that I'd stayed with before, and she'd—this lady, she was a cripple; had one leg was, oh, about that much shorter than the other—and she didn't charge my wife no board, all I did was pay my board, and she just helped her. She had, well, she had three boarders. And I went and asked this company how my job was, or whether I was, you know, suited. They said, "Well, as long as you do what you're doing now, why, you have a job here as long as we run." So, we went and bought us a home up there. And in a year's time, they went bust—well, in 1930, they went bankrupt. I lost everything I had, about two thousand dollars back then. Two thousand dollars was a lot of money. And I never left my address to where I was a-going. And if I'd a had a forwarding address, why, they'd probably called me back, but I didn't, and we just lived hand to mouth for about two years, just kept jobs.

We came back home. You see, I got the jump there at the Handle factory. And I knowed what I was going to make every week. I worked there thirty-six years, and I was off three days on account of being sick.

Yes, I was glad to be back home. 'Cause we knowed everybody down in here and in a city, you don't know your next-door neighbor.

I worked the tomato factory, too, before I started the Handle factory, and those tomatoes, sometimes you'd work twenty-four hours. You see, your tomatoes, that's something—they don't keep, you had to get rid of them. That was an interesting place to work.

When did things start changing a bit more?

Well, in World War II, then things just started to . . . well, there was just more work, you know, was available, and then people just got, well, they got cars. That's when the cars got, you know—a lot of cars. People didn't visit other people, you had someplace to go. They'd just go to Bedford or Bloomington or Indianapolis or Louisville or. . . . They was, you might say, on the road all the time. But back when they was horse-and-buggy days, why, it was either walk or. . . . And they didn't go like they did and they visited. When we first moved on the Cy Jones place over there, we took—well, they did it before, too—when they thrash wheat, see, they cut their wheat, chopped it, and then the thrashing machine come along, and thrash your wheat or oats, whatever there was, and all the farmers, all the neighborhood around here, would join in and come in and help you thrash. Then, when you got done there, you'd go to the next neighbor till you got the whole neighborhood done. And then, in the fall, you come in and you cut your corn and chopped it, and they come in and shred your corn, and they done the same thing, they went around and all of them helped till everybody's crops was in and they don't do that anymore.

Bethel Elizabeth Cornwell was born in 1915 and worked as a schoolteacher.[11]

Cornwell: My dad was reared up there in that home, north of Livonia. As he grew up, his father was a Baptist minister. Well, they went [to] different church areas, and my mother belonged to Pleasant Grove Baptist Church, so they met at the church. Then when they married, they first lived there near my great-grandfather, but they later moved into this area, and that was where she of course grew up. So I spent most of my life in this area.

He was a farmer, and he was also [in] construction engineer work. Back in those days, they used the old steam engines, and he operated one of those. So did his father. They both did that as well as some farming.

We always had milk cows, and she [mother] did a lot [of] milking, but I have seen her go into the woods to help Dad get wood, so he could go on back to work, you know. Whatever needed to be done. She also worked in the hay field. She worked in the cornfield to help. And so have I.

Would women living on a farm usually help out like that?

Yes, that was quite common. They did things of that nature, but I've often thought and heard said that my mother probably did more of that than anyone else in the community, because my father was gone so much.

But you know, back then, money was scarce. I grew up during the depression, and it took money to keep the family going, so he worked away, and that helped then to supply our needs. We were very poor during the depression. They did have a little money in the bank when the depression started, but when the bank closed, why, they lost all that money. There was no money anywhere for anybody—that had any connections with the bank.

And we would sell eggs maybe for three cents a dozen, that's all they paid anywhere. And often if you had a veal calf to sell.

Well, we didn't have a car until—oh, I was probably twelve years old, and then we had a Model T Ford. But before that, we had a horse and buggy. We always had that. And that's the way we went to church or went to visit my family. We went in the horse and buggy.

It was a close-knit neighborhood. We weren't all exactly relations, but we lived more like people that were related as a family. Our neighbors were important. Oftentimes, at night, when supper was over—that was our night meal—Dad would pick up the lantern and say, "Let's go visit George and Florence," which was up on the hill. Or let's go the other way and visit Charlie and Kora, which was down the other way. And we'd go visit for an hour or so before bedtime, because there were no TVs in those days. And so you had more association with your neighbors, and if there was any sickness or anything of that nature, your neighbors were there, you might say, from day to day to see how you were, and to see if you needed anything. And it was very common for them to come in carrying a pie, or something like that to help out. And we did likewise.

[11] Interviewed by Catherine A. Jones, 1 March 1988 and 22 March 1989, Millersburg.

Can you remember any examples of neighbors helping out that way?

Yes I can. During the depression, we had gotten down to where we had no hogs on the farm which, you know, about every farm did have. And we were in school, my brother and I, we walked about a mile and a half to school. And one night we were walking home past these people I mentioned, Charlie and Kora's, and he had some little pigs in the bunch and one that wasn't as big, we called it the runt. So, he said, "Would you and William E."—that was my brother—"like to have this little pig?" And we, of course . . . that thrilled us. So we took the little pig home—I don't remember exactly—I think Dad came and got us maybe. And it grew up to be a big, fat, nice hog. And we had meat, so Dad said, "Let's butcher your hog, and then when I get the money, I'll pay you for it." So that's the way we got our meat for that winter.

What kind of chores did you have growing up?

Well, me myself, I did most of the housework. I learned to cook early in my [life]—and I liked the housework well enough. And I also loved the outdoors. And then I did the gardening as I got older. We raised chickens, and I also raised chickens of my own, as well as help mother with hers. And sometimes I could sell—back then, you could take chickens to a poultry building in Paoli, also one in Livonia—so you could sell them that way, and make some money on them. Because you raised your own corn, your own feed.

At the time you went to high school, was there a bus to go in?

There was no bus until my last year, my senior year we had a bus most of that year. And when I started high school, it was necessary to rent a room, and you stayed in that particular place. And went to school, then, all week, and then on Friday, why, Dad would come to get us, or get me, and I also roomed with three neighbor girls, over here.

What was it like being a kid? What did you do for playing?

You made your own way to play. You didn't have things that children have nowadays. You would, for instance, in a big summer rain, you would enjoy going out and wading in the creek, puddles, and so forth, of that nature. And my mother would unravel an old sock of Dad's and make us a ball. And we would maybe use a big stick for a bat, and she made that ball, and, why, then we could play ball.

Now when you say "we," is this just you and your brother?

Right. We, well, we had one family up on the hill that had some children that was our age, and sometimes they'd be here. And then over the ridge, so to speak, were some more children. And we would sometime visit with them, and they would visit back and forth, and it got to be a custom that they would come and stay all night with us.

Did your parents encourage your education?

As we got farther and farther along, and it took more and more money, why, my mother said, "We simply don't have the money for you to go to college," because when I was in the fourth grade, I said I wanted to be a schoolteacher. And she said, "We just can't ever do that, I don't think. So will you take a commercial course? And when you get out of high school, why, then you can get a job"—in those days—"as bookkeeper or whatever." Well, I did that to please *her*, not—but I did enjoy it, I particularly enjoyed my shorthand, I wasn't too good at typing, I guess, probably nerves more than anything.

I enjoyed everything else. But when I finished high school, I said, "I still want to be a schoolteacher."

So she said, "I don't see how." But we had a neighbor that was a schoolteacher, and he talked to Dad and Mother, and he knew a place that I could stay in Terre Haute, for my room and board, and it wouldn't cost me anything, only I'd do some housework.

I just enjoyed things about school. I enjoyed seeing children learn, and we had one in my class that, he had a hard time learning. And I more or less taught him, and I think that's what maybe did it. Because as I stated, my grandfather, he lived close by. And at night, he'd come for me to help him to get his lesson, almost every night. He just couldn't do it without help. So that's probably why, you know, that I wanted to teach.

And your mother, was she—what religion was she?

She was Baptist. Mother was always ready to go to church, and did, as long as she could walk to church. We walked through fields. So, I wouldn't say that she went every time. Sometimes, she didn't go because Dad didn't want to go. I've seen her almost in tears, you know, wanting to go to church, and he didn't want to go, and sometimes she'd stay home with him, and we children—my brother and I—would go alone to church. And grandfather lived—her dad—just down from the church a little ways, so we'd go early and go to Granddad's. And my grandparents always went to church. They never missed. So then we went with the grandparents.

Why wouldn't she go anyway, even if your dad didn't go, if you kids were going?

Well, she had this feeling, and I don't blame her, I probably feel somewhat the same way: that a family should go together. And a wife should do what the man says, or wants. And that's why I think that she stayed home.

Did women have anything in the sense of a chance for women to get together? Do you know what I mean? To talk?

Yes, we had—well, I was little at the time, of course—but we had what they called quilting bees back then. And sometimes instead of quilting, why, they would do what [they] call "tack a comforter." It'd be thicker than a quilt, and it would be faster work. And there would be several of them get together to do that. And of course, then in the fall of the year, and in the summertime too, there was always the wheat to be got in the summer, and all of the neighbor women would come in to help prepare the meal, because there would be, maybe fifteen men to get dinner for—the noon meal. So they'd come to help do that, but maybe half of them or more would come to socialize, visit and all that.

And the same thing in the fall, when you got the corn in. And they enjoyed, you know, the visitation at that time. Just being there together and getting that meal done.

Would each woman bring a dish?

Some would, and then some didn't. And it depended, I guess, on who could and who couldn't. But sometimes, they did. And there would be at least, maybe six women there, doing things like that. And back in those days, we didn't have club organizations, like we do now.

It was really a shame. If she could've lived like people live nowadays, my mother was exceptionally strong. I think she blamed her father for not letting her go to high school. There never was very much said about it, but he had a cousin that lived in Orleans, and he offered to keep Mother, and it wouldn't cost her anything, and she could go to high school. And my grandfather thought that that was letting her go too loose, too far from home. Of course, Orleans then would have been quite a distance. So he didn't want her to leave. So then, of course, after she met Dad, and she got married, she was—let's see—she was almost eighteen, I guess, when she got married.

It wasn't that he was against the education. It wasn't that part of it. And it might be, that he also inspired *me* to be a schoolteacher—I didn't mention that a while ago—and he might have had a guilty feeling there, because he'd take me on his lap when I was in the third, fourth grade, like I was a little child, and help me with my lessons. When we got through, he'd say, "You're going to be my little schoolteacher." And I think that, you know, helped me and maybe made him feel better.

Does it seem to you that something has been lost?

I think because people have drifted apart in those

areas somewhat, they have found very little to hold them together in love and bondage, and it has created the fact for young people. What do I do with my time? And they have resorted to more drugs and things of that nature. When I was growing up and, say, even twenty years or twenty-five years back, in this area we never heard tell of drugs—cocaine and things of that nature. Alcohol, yes. And beer, but that was the extent of it. And the older people spent more time with their child or with their children, teaching them the sins and the wrongs of partaking in alcohol or any kind of beverage like that. Whereas nowadays, they seldom have the time, or at least they don't take the time to teach children the difference. They're beginning to; that is coming back, and I'm very glad to see that.

And even in the schools, they are teaching them more now than a few years previously because it wasn't spoken of; it was an untold or unheard of word in schools. You didn't mention things of that nature. Neither was sex taught. When sex first began to be entered in the school system, why, many, many parents were not in favor of that at all.

When did that start?

That has started in the last fifteen or twenty years. And, of course, actually we taught sex back farther than that, because you teach it, for instance, how the baby chick was born from the embryo on up.

Of the girls you knew, when you were a girl yourself, would your mothers say something? I mean, how would girls find out?

Very, very little did they ever find out. Most of their knowledge that they gained, they gained from each other. And that was a very bad way because no child could explain that in the right form in those days, because they hadn't been taught how to explain it. So some of them learned wisely and some didn't.

Well, now that we're talking about it, was premarital sex very . . . ?

Oh, no, that was looked down upon very, *very* much. You were counted an outcast, you know, in the community—if that became publicized in any way. That was a very ugly thing. . . .

And I often wonder if teaching girls how to prevent pregnancy *in* high school now is a good idea. I know it's going to happen *either* way, if they teach it or if they don't. But if they teach them what they can do to prevent pregnancy, to go ahead and have premarital sex, what is that really doing to the individual?

I think it would be more appropriately taught by the parents and the minister; whatever the minister can offer. I know they can't, you know, necessarily go into detail with the daughter or a girl, but I think that the parents, if they would put forth the information in the right form instead of it being taught as a general thing in a high school class because, as you say . . . in a general manner, why, they're going to say: "Well, it's been taught to us, and we can do this because everybody else can."

It's the modern, fast way of life. Almost every parent, man and woman in this area, both of them work to make a living to live by the standards that they want to live by. Used to, people were content to have one car. Now they have to have two or three in the family, as well as many other things. They want at least one TV, and sometimes two or three. And that demands that they have more income in order to live like that.

Evansville

Evansville

Evansville sits alongside the Ohio River in southwestern Indiana. In this chapter three residents offer not only vivid accounts of life during the middle decades of the twentieth century but also stories of their ancestors. Stories told by people like Alice Hottenstein prove that many citizens thought extensively about their ancestors and located themselves somewhere in time and in American history. Ralph Dorris even allows us to observe the inner workings of families. He tells us about family debates over whether women should vote and how a son measured the improvement in his life by comparing it to his father's. Dorris also explains the precariousness of family finances in the days before Social Security and unemployment benefits. In such situations, sons, as Dorris explains, also took menial jobs to help "put food on the table" of their parents.

Alice Hottenstein was born in 1918 and grew up on a farm in Vanderburgh County. She has lived in Evansville since her marriage in 1941.[1]

Hottenstein: Some of my family, James Martin and two sons from South Carolina, came here in 1805 and settled out in Armstrong Township. He came as a Baptist preacher, ran a tavern, and sold whiskey and took in boarders for four and five, six people sleeping one room at night at the little town of Armstrong. Well, it was just basically their home that they settled out there. And there was quite a settlement: that's real good farmland out in there. And that's why they probably came. I have been told that they sort of knew George Rogers Clark. Whether they did, I don't know. But, of course, all the land here was bought early, bought in Vincennes.

And then my other side of the family came from Scotland, England, France, and Germany. One was named William Olmstead, my great-great-grandfather, from Connecticut. And he came here in 1816, bought land out on Pigeon Creek, which became much more important than Evansville, Indiana, because the people had to go north and they had to cross this creek so they ran ferries and everything else to get across with their animals, plows, everything. Interesting stories. And he became judge of Vanderburgh County in 1822 and held that judgeship until '44.

My grandfather, Matthew Olmstead, used horses and mules in a progressive way to farm. Got up at four o'clock in the morning to go to the fields to work. And his ten children all were, a lot them didn't get married, of the girls, because they didn't want more big families, but they all made their way in this world. And my mother said they all knew how to paddle their pound of butter. And that's what the world should all be about today.

My dad—that's where my Scotch blood comes in. My dad was half Scotch and half English. He went to a business college in Evansville Business School which was—there were people here who went to Indiana University and DePauw and got better educations—but my

[1] Interviewed by Barbara Truesdell, 18 August 1996, Evansville.

Alice Hottenstein's father, Tom Jarvis, shoveling corn into a crib
Alice Hottenstein

Tom and Amelia Jarvis drawing water, 1908
Alice Hottenstein

dad went to a business school here in town and learned math and beautiful handwriting.

But it was my grandparents on the Jarvis side, my dad's mother and father, had two farms and they wanted one for each one of their sons. So my father, Tom Jarvis, worked in town, but my grandmother was a very cautious person and she took him, brought him out to the country, and he farmed until the depression came along.

And we were sort of helping keep up my grandparents' farm and ours and there wasn't the money there that we needed. And my dad took a test and became the county attendance officer in Vanderburgh County and traveled the whole county. He made five dollars a day [laughs], and then they gave [him] ten cents a mile for gasoline. He furnished his own car. My dad was a very warm and caring person. He did with very little money—I mean, people would laugh at that money now—but he did many nice things for people and it was the conditions people were living in then.

And, at that time, they didn't have clothes, they couldn't buy books, and all those kinds of things. And the teachers, at that time, were *dedicated people*. And they pitched in and helped kids who were having a hard time. And when my father died in 1952, a procession of teachers that came through to see him, and all of them had such wonderful stories to tell of my father.

So your parents were farmers?

They were farmers. My mother, well, my mother was trained to be a dressmaker. I mean, she came to town, and you could go and learn to sew. Today, it would be a technical school. And she worked for a lady, Wallenmeyer was her name. My mom was a beautiful seamstress. And to make that story go a little bit further, my aunts went down to Miami Beach, Florida, when it was just being pumped out of the ocean [laughs] and they started a dress shop and they did real well on Lincoln Road. They made beautiful clothes, and it was when women's golf clothes came in, and so they made golfing dresses.

I think that takes care of my family. I'm not bragging about any of them. They were just good. They were the people that made America what it is today.

And when were you born?

I was born May the twenty-sixth—I better get the right century—1918. And when I was born, I had hair down to my shoulders and my mother—you didn't get out of bed at that time—my mother got up at seven o'clock in the morning. I was born at five, and she got up at seven and had my hair cut in a Dutch bob. And I wore it that way until I got through the eighth grade [laughs]. And she cut it until I was sixteen.

You said that you grew up on a dairy farm?

My parents had a separator that stood in our kitchen, and we had an old pitcher pump that we pumped water with. And my mother made butter and cottage cheese and we'd take whipping cream into town, and they would take vegetables if they had them. And they had regular customers, and they were some of the nicest and richest people in Evansville.

What values did your parents stress at home?

Honesty, truthfulness, caring, sharing, always thinking of the other person first. If you could do anything for him that will help him, help him get along in this world, to do it.

We were raised among—there was still "slavery" going on, as far as I'm concerned, when I was a kid in our neighborhood. We had people that, the black people hadn't had a place to live. And I'm not going to call them African, Afro-Americans: they were blacks when I was a young kid growing up. And my mother taught them how to make hominy out of corn. Dip the corn in lye and take that outside husk off of it, and every so often Mom would take them chicken. And I don't know how they survived. I really don't. They would come over and borrow a yard of thread from Mom to

Anne and Stella Olmstead, Alice Hottenstein's aunts
Alice Hottenstein

Left to right: Florence Olmstead, Gertrude Skeels, and Amelia Jarvis at work on threshing day
Alice Hottenstein

sew something up and things like that. And I don't even know where they got their groceries. I don't know how they got their groceries home because they had no horses or anything like that.

And Mom, we had a lot of skim milk, and Mom would give them skim milk, and such as that, to feed their kids daily, so their kids would have milk to drink. But there were about six black families, yes, there was six black families that lived within a mile of us. In fact, one family lived right besides my grandparents.

When you were a child, when did children in your family start to work?

I never can remember Mom fussing at us. My nickname was Billy, and she would say, "Billy, take that food out to the chickens." Well, I think when I was four years old, I was doing it. I knew how to milk a cow at six years of age. And I milked cows through high school. I would get up early in the morning, caught a school bus at seven o'clock and drove, rode thirty miles to Reitz High School. Because we had to go up and down all the roads in a bus and we were the first ones to be picked up.

My dad was the quiet person but was quite a jokester. I was the boy that he didn't have. And Mom ruled the roost. I never knew that she ruled the roost, or anything like that, but Mom called the shots as far as the way we behaved when we were out and so on and so forth. And we knew how to behave when we went to my grandparents over at the Olmsteads where all the big family was. And we knew how to sit up and eat. We were not special, like the kids today.

My family also made friends of wonderful people. There was a doctor that came out to our house every Thursday night. Well, he and Dad were sort of in the cow or bull business together. He furnished the bulls, and he had money but didn't have any common sense about dairying. And Dad would get up at four o'clock in the morning and help a cow have a calf, or when Dr. Tweedall would call, his hired hand would call. And Dad would go over there and help bring calves into the world and such as that.

And Mom was the same kind of person. On the

farm back of us was a lawyer and his wife, before I was in high school, that bought a farm and put a house up. You know everybody was moving out to the country at that time. They thought they could make a million out in the country. And the Peckinpaughs were wonderful neighbors.

And Mom, it was a two-way street, between Mom and Dad. My dad was a musician, played the violin, or fiddle. We had many people come with their violins, and it was always the violins, which I just thought was awful when I got up in high school. But now I realize what a talented person my dad really was. I don't think my dad would have ever gotten married because he liked to hunt and fish and be a sportsman.

What religion did your parents belong to?

Absolutely nothing. But I'm not saying that they didn't have a basis of religious thoughts. My husband, Carl, was raised very religiously. And Carl said that of all the people he ever knew, my mom and dad lived the most religious life. But they saw that we got to go to Sunday school every Sunday, to McCutchanville Methodist. And there's a picture of it, there's a book there with pictures of it. It's just a little brick church, then there was some little back rooms. And the small kids got to sit back there and play around sand tables. I am very sorry that I didn't read the Bible more and so on and so forth. I don't want it to become ingrained that I know nothing of the Bible. But I think, and I didn't know, but my mom had many sayings that were biblical verses, that came out of the Bible. My grandfather, Matthew Olmstead, neither of my Jarvis grandparents were Bible people either. And it's just real funny that they could come out so well. I almost say you don't have to go to church to be a good person.

Carl and I have got along very good together and Carl was overly religious. Overly religious when I married him. I mean his folks went to Pilgrim Holiness Church at that time.

What denomination did you and Mr. Hottenstein end up going to?

Well, Carl's brother was a pilot during World War II and was killed over in England in an air accident, not in combat, and he's buried over in Cambridge Cemetery in Cambridge, England. And he had a wife and a baby that was just three months old when he was killed. And they were at Central Methodist Church so it just fit in with me.

The Methodist minister at McCutchanville married Carl and I. And Carl didn't, you know, didn't push his Pilgrim Holiness on me [laughs]. But we liked the preacher that was at Central Methodist then, not an elderly man but an older one. And Dr. Horace Sprague was just a wonderful man. Carl believed in the philosophy of changing ministers, I mean, you know, moving them around, not stay until they wear their welcome out.

What political party did your parents support?

I can't tell you that they supported any political party until my dad became attendance officer, and at that time, the trustees were Democrats here in the county. He had to be a Democrat to get the job. He had to say, "I'm a Democrat," to get these, because he didn't know all the trustees. It was when I was—I guess I was a freshman in high school, so it was 1931 or '32.

Well, the depression was so terrible at that time, but I didn't know there was a depression going on, because we had food; we had food to give away. And we cut corners. Mom ordered all of our material for our dresses from Sears and Roebuck, or Sears, as now it is. And she made my grandparents' shirts and dresses. In fact, she made both of their dresses for their burials, and—I mean, they were made beforehand—and everything was in place. And I didn't really notice that there was a depression going on.

Did your school friends feel that you were a rich kid because you had enough to eat?

Oh, no, no. Because they were as poor, some of them were much poorer than we were. There were kids that didn't have shoes that went to McCutchanville School. You wouldn't go out there and find that now in McCutchanville because it is a very affluent neighborhood.

Mom and Dad were both more industrious. My mom, I guess, was the leader. My mom and dad were more industrious than a lot [of] people were at that time and with us. They were just that kind of people. My mother sold registered Jersey cattle. Dad would talk to them and get them in the mood. Mom always sold them, but Dad was the one that took care of them all out in the barn. And then my mom had Rhode Island Red chickens, and she sold settings of eggs, settings of eggs of fifteen. And she sold settings of eggs for five dollars and then you had to pay the shipping charge on them. And, well, that goes back to when I was just a baby, because she was packing some, and I fell off of the stove where she had me laying on a pillow, and I fell in a coal bucket.

Did your dad feel conflicted about having to say he was a Democrat when he was really more of an independent?

No, because politics then, the news media has run the political situation in our country. And Dad had friends, I can tell you, Dad had friends that were Republicans, and he had friends were Democrats. There was Jim Einsley that lived out there that, I know they were Republicans. Now, I didn't know it at that time, and Dad would go over and talk to him. Well, doctors and lawyers were handled different then than they are now. You were a friend and you could go and ask, "What do you think about this situation?" and a lawyer would tell you, "Now, Tom, you should do it this way," or, you know. And they never charged you, because then you would turn around and do something for them.

Well, right now, I'm a red-hot Republican. I can't stand Clinton much longer. I can't stand liars and I can't stand cheaters and I like educated people. I don't like, I don't want to see our country going down the drain. I am proud of my heritage.

Have you ever heard anything about shady politics in Evansville?

Carl Hottenstein with the first truck of the American Dairy, 1934
Alice Hottenstein

Oh, yes. See, Evansville was a big Ku Klux Klan town, and I'm not saying that that caused any trouble whatsoever. Carl's mother and dad were Ku Klux Klan. But people lost their jobs, if you were a Ku Klux Klan. And the Ku Klux Klan wasn't then in Evansville like it is now. I remember when Carl came home and had hired his first Catholic on the milk route. And Carl says, "Don't ever let Mom and Dad know that I hired this"—well, he was a real nice guy. And I don't want to give names. And I don't think the Hottensteins ever knew that he was Catholic.

And the same thing happened when he hired the first young black man to work in the dairy. That was during World War II. And he says, "I hope Dad doesn't come over and see that." Now, wasn't that foolish? But I think I helped liberalize Carl, or my family helped liberalize Carl, you know, of those ways.

Did politics change when the depression came?

Well, I'll tell you. When Roosevelt came in, it changed. And Roosevelt changed our country for the worse in many ways, because he ruined the dairy business. I would like someone to write a book on dairying. That was your beginning of entitlements.

And Eleanor Roosevelt came up here on this side of Vincennes and up above Princeton, and they bought some of the richest land in Knox County that's along the Wabash River. She was the head of, she was in to getting these farms that were co-oped, farms like the Russians had at that time. I'll send you the story on this farm. They paid thousands and some politically activated Democrats took advantage of the sale when it was sold.

[It was] Communism. I would say there's two to three thousand acres in that plot. They bought, they built little houses for the people that were going to work there, and I think there were about maybe eight houses. And they had the people to communal farm and so on and so forth. It never did work out. It never did work out.[2]

[2] Deshee Farm was a federal agricultural project started in 1938, twelve miles south of Vincennes, as an experiment in cooperative farm production. Participants were mostly young families with little agricultural production experience. It disbanded by 1945 because of a decline in government support and cooperative spirit. See J. Rebecca Thompson, "Deshee Farm: A New Deal Experiment with Cooperative Farming," *Indiana Magazine of History* 91 (December 1995): 380–406.

How does your family life differ than that of your parents?

We've given our children, kids, entirely too much. Carl was a great person to travel and he was all for his business trips. He included them. He would take them out of school. Yes, we took them out of school to take them to Eisenhower's inauguration. But if it wasn't, you know, real important, we had baby-sitters. But I'll tell you something else in a minute. Carl never went on a trip by himself that he didn't bring the kids something.

Did your parents feel a woman should work outside of the home?

My mother never had to, other than volunteer work. When I got right out of high school, we didn't have money for me to go to college. I wanted to be a nurse and I wanted to go to Johns Hopkins Hospital School of Nursing. We knew a woman that was up there as one of the teachers at Johns Hopkins, and that's the reason I wanted to go because I'd heard her tell so many wonderful stories. And Mom says, "OK, you can go, and we'll get the money together, but you can't come home and you can't call home. Just every time something happens it will be that you're there, and we will furnish your books and your education, but beyond that, we haven't the money."

And my sister had no desire, but we both took college preparatory courses. And we both were prepared. And OK, at that time, University of Evansville was Methodist and a lot of preachers' kids got educations free of charge, but it did keep the college open for today. So, I mean, it wasn't all bad. But Mom didn't believe in freebies in education, "Pay your way after you got through school," and that was it. So there was just no money for us to go, because then my grandparents were dying, the depression was on, and we just had a hard time keeping our heads above water. Dad would say, "Tomorrow will be better" [laughs]. The kids of today are given too much in education. We shouldn't be giving all this education money away without them being responsible for what we're putting out.

School wagon to McCutchanville School, about 1919
Alice Hottenstein

What did you do, working out at Servel? [3]

I worked in the purchasing department as a teenager, wrote out a whole lot of purchase orders in a day, but I learned a lot. I didn't know there was left-handed screws and right-handed screws and things like that. We had to call and get prices on things, and it was a liberal education. It taught you business.

And they were very up and coming. I mean, Servel was really the place to work at that time. Well, I shouldn't say that because Mead Johnson—baby food products—they were very respected. And the kids from Reitz that got to go to Bristol Meyers were really honored. They didn't make any more than I made at Servel, but it was more respected. But the Johnson family were a wonderful family in a supportive way to Evansville. They were too good to their employees. They were too good.

Do you think? Why is that?

Well, if anybody would have a catastrophe, like if somebody was killed in a wreck they'd just go out and pick up the bill. But when unions come in, you can't do that. Because if you do it for one person, you have to do it for everyone and that's an impossibility. Carl learned that in the dairy business he owned, American Dairy, that you, when the union takes over, you just don't hand out things. Up until that time, he had paid for operations and catastrophes and loaned money. Sad! Sad! Sad!

What did you like and dislike about school when you were growing up?

When I got to high school, I really turned loose, and I took newswriting, I took debating, I was in plays, I

[3] From its origins in the 1920s, Servel was a leading producer of refrigerators; during the Second World War, the plant also made aircraft wings. At its peak during the Korean War, the plant employed twelve thousand people; however, the company began to sell off its divisions shortly thereafter. Robert P. Paltry, *City of the Four Freedoms: A History of Evansville, Indiana* (Evansville: Friends of the Willard Library, 1996), 196–98, 206–7.

was in—God bless my dad. He would come up to Reitz High School and get me to take me home. And everybody knew that I had to leave at around five o'clock, and I was just in everything I could get in school.

What's your favorite memory of your young adulthood?

I could shock you with this. This would be my favorite: I went to dances when I was thirteen years old. But they were real fun. The people that ran the dance hall were real good friends of my mother and dad. There was nothing for country kids to do that was really recreational. We didn't have money to come in and swim or even buy gasoline. We didn't have money to do anything. And they started this dance hall, and it was a quarter to go there every Saturday night and dance, and it was called Lake Grove. And that furnished my recreation basically all through high school. And the reason I got to go was because one of the gallant people of McCutchanville slapped the preacher's son in our house. We had something called Sunday Night Singing, and we were the choir in the church. And this woman—she was sort of the choir director—she slapped the preacher's son. And Mom says, "You don't have to associate with those kind of people." And the Angermeiers, who were Catholic, started a dance hall and told us about the dance hall and everything. So Mom started taking us to dances, and that caused us to be, we weren't really respected in McCutchanville after that time because *Methodists didn't dance*.

And your worst memory?

When I was in grade school, a very good friend of mine who I liked very much, and her mother was a schoolteacher, not in McCutchanville School, she was in a little one-room school down on Oakhill Road. And nobody ever knew what happened, but her father went, well, he had had a family argument with his family, not with the wife or the kids, but his family. And they were Germans, sort of stubborn and greedy, I'd say, and he shot himself, and they didn't find him until the next morning.

And I think that I grieved as much over his death. I used to get to go on errands with Dad; Dad would take me over there when he was getting the car fixed. There was a garage across the street from my friend, across the road from their house. And I played with this girl and I just loved to go over there. And I just loved to see her lunch box at school, because she had baloney sandwiches and baker's bread, and I had nothing but homemade bread and ham, and that was upsetting to me [laughs].

But she took it so hard, and I think I mourned his death as much I did if it was my dad—no, not as much as if it would have been Dad because that would have been a catastrophe—but it really hurt me. It was my first experience with death.

And then everybody gossiped and everything. And poor little Mary Frances just had a hard time over the whole thing. Then when my grandmother died, the second death, she died when I was twelve years old. And I was helping Dad wash our old Ford and I said, "Why isn't anybody crying for Grandma?" And he says, "Well, Bill, you just grow up."

And that was a shock to me. And I grieved her death, because they lived across the road and I'd carry their food to them every night and so on and so forth. So that was sort of . . .

When did you leave your parents' home?

When I was married, and that was in April of 1941.

How did you meet your husband?

Well, I was in love with a guy that went to high school with Carl. And he, Charlie Mann, had the first number that was on the draft to get into the army in World War II. So he was settling some things. Well, he and some more guys from Central High School had bought some oil wells stock. Oil wells were big at that time here in southern Indiana, and they had bought, I guess, one share of stock. I know it was not more than a hundred dollars for all of them. And we went to the dairy. Now I had double dated with Carl's brother that was killed over in England in World War II, but we went to the dairy to get this thing settled, and I had on red fingernail polish, high heel shoes, probably enough—I looked like a streetwalker or something, because I had money when I worked at Servel. And we went up there, and Carl looked at me, and all with his eyes, "What is this?"

And he hadn't even heard about me, or me about him. Never had met me. Never seen me. Now, I knew where they lived, and being in the dairy business and us having cows and such as that, I knew the Hottensteins, knew about the Hottenstein family. And so when Charlie left, Carl said, later on, "Does she always wear that much lipstick and all that much rouge?"

So Charlie says, "Well, you know, she's really a nice gal. Now, I'm going to marry her, but you call her up. She'll have a date with you." And about two weeks later, he called me up and asked me to go to a football game out at Reitz Stadium. When he came to the front door here, he had his face all bandaged, his arm was in a sling, and I didn't even know whether it was him or not. He was taking some milk out to an army colonel that was over in Evansville inspecting American Dairy, and he fell because he was running in his haste with these bottles of milk. He fell and had cut himself on these bottles. So it wasn't a gushing love affair or anything like that, you know, but seven months later we were married. And the day before I got married, Charlie Mann called from an army base down in Mississippi and said, "Please don't marry Carl."

So I cried all that day, the day before I got married, because I didn't know whether I was doing right or not. And Carl and I did a lot of giving and taking in our life, but we were a real good team in the end.

You had quit your job or you were still working at Servel?

Oh, no. Women didn't work in Carl's family. Ha! Ha! His mother killed herself working in the dairy, picking up ten-gallon milk cans, so he didn't want his wife to ever work and make money.

So we rented a house. It was a new house. A man and his wife were going, he was going into the army, and she couldn't afford to stay there. Well, we rented that, but for some reason, he was discharged within one year, and came back, and we had to get out.

So then we lived in Carl's great-aunt's house in—not a slum area. It's a slum area now, but it wasn't then. And I painted all the walls. I did everything in that house to make it livable looking. And when I married Carl, he only made five dollars a week.

When and why did you join the DAR?

In 1955. Oh, my mom wanted me to. And it was all done for me. I didn't have do any research, and I don't [know] why I've done so much on it, but research just intrigued me. And I've spent many hours down in the courthouse. I know more about our courthouse . . . [laughs] I tell people I can go down there and find your will and all that kind of stuff. "You can't, why, that's private."

I was on the Evansville Museum Board, and when they did the Lincoln area downstairs—I'm a Lincoln fan, I love Lincoln, the history of him, because he was born and bred, I mean, he was raised right up here, you know, in Spencer County. And I did an awful lot. It's a real pretty village, and I completely did the kitchen, helped other people do theirs.

I've given book reviews. I was the project's chairman for the DAR in 1976 when Barbara Alexander, my good friend, was the regent. And they told me I couldn't get a marker put up for all the Revolutionary War soldiers buried in Vanderburgh County on the post office property. You know, in front [of] the Federal Building. And I said, "Well, yes I can."

Well, I'm a collector of books. I'm a collector of the poet, the Indiana poet, James Whitcomb Riley. And I'm a big collector of Abraham Lincoln. And, well, I tell you, during the bicentennial year, I also took on quilts as an American women's hobby. And quilting was just coming back at that time for young women. Well, I went around and I gave these talks, and everybody wanted to call me. "So, how do [you] think [about] this kind of quilt—? Do you have that kind of a pattern? How much do you get for an old quilt that's two hundred years old? How do you date a quilt?" And all those kind of things.

And I thought, "Alice, you better get with it." So then I started making quilts of my own and I started talking about them, you know, going up as far as Jeffersonville and Vincennes, and took quilts, and so on and so forth. It was fun. And then I had people to bring their quilts. And they liked to talk about their quilts. So that took up a lot of the time [laughs]. But that's what I like.

Do you belong to any kind of a quilting guild?

Yes. We have one here in town. I belong to Raintree Quilter Guild in Tri-State. But I'm not that interested, I mean. I've made about ten quilts now, and I want to make more if I live long enough. But I've done enough quilts. My kids will never wear all of those out, because I bought quilts, for one thing.

We talked a little about the neighborhood you grew up in.

Well, it was Catholic, Lutheran, United Church of Christ, and Methodist. Now, my dad was in a threshing machine company that was Catholic. And we were sort of ostracized because we weren't in with the Methodists' threshing group.

Now the Catholics, they made home brew, and the old men would come up and drink home brew in a big sauce pan, mustaches would go down in it. And I just thought that was the dirtiest thing I'd ever seen [laughs]. But they were all real nice, real nice Catholic families. They were sort of on the border of Warrick County and Vanderburgh.

And we were closer to them, that's the reason that Dad was in the threshing company. They had these threshing companies all over Vanderburgh County. Every place had threshing companies. People now have shows of older farm mechanical machines.

Why has the community changed?

Why has the community changed? There's just nobody downtown. Now this has happened in other towns, too, all over the country, not just Evansville, but they didn't improve anything. You go downtown and there will be a few people out sitting watching a water fountain while they eat their sandwich, but that isn't what a town should be. Now, out here, go out to our Green River Road, you can't get up and down and across it. Just one atrocious building after, one neon sign after another—just honky tonk.

When I was growing up, we went downtown to shop, and, you know, if Mom had to get buttons for a certain dress or something like that we could go downtown to a nice textile shop or go to Sears and Roebuck. When Sears and Roebuck came to town, that was a wonderful thing. Now, nothing is downtown but the banks and the office buildings, the lawyers and so on and so forth. And, you know, what do they have really to promote? Then there was Smith Barney and those kind of companies. Well, how many people go downtown to Smith Barney to shop? But when I was in high school, you did the drag after football games and such on Main Street. And that was something to go up and down Main Street and see who all was down there and wave at them and stop and talk to them and all that, just driving up and down. Our Main Street runs into the river, and then you wind around and go out to Garvin Park.

When did it start to change?

Well, when the WPA left. I don't even know what they called the government committee, but they decided that they were going to tear all of the old United States down. And the government came in to condemn wonderful old storefront buildings and so on and so forth. Every place. You know, they just tore them down and left big holes in the ground for a long time.

Now, right now we're tearing down our inner city, and we're getting a lot of houses by Habitat. And I often wonder what they're going to look like in thirty years from now. But the people seem to be very proud. Our church has built three of them. And I think it's for a good cause. I wouldn't want to live in a roach-, rat-infested building.

However, I sold my aunt's home over here on Lincoln Avenue at a very good address. It was one of those Lustron houses that's metal and they set them on concrete. There was only two thousand seemingly made, or around two thousand, and the concrete underneath it had gotten infested with roaches, and I bug bombed [it]. And the roaches would fill a half a bucket full, and so there's roaches in every place. And my aunts, they were old, you know, they're ninety and ninety-four now, and they didn't realize it was infested.

But this end of our block is coming down right now. And the type of people that are moving in—couples that aren't married. Right there, people next door, they never sweep their sidewalk. They never do, they think the city's suppose to do it. And I get out, well, Jan before she left, she cleaned the gutter out all the way to the sewer. I don't know, people aren't what they used to be.

Do you have any poignant memories of the Great Depression and World War II?

I've had so many of my friends killed during the war. Like when we went around the world, we stopped by a few of the government cemeteries. And you could go to these big, you know, where they didn't even find the boys, and we had memories of it. See, we built the B-47s here in Evansville out here on Highway 41. And it brought a boon to Evansville, that's all I can say. I still think wars are going on to make people money.

I mean, I guess Hitler had to be stopped. But it wasn't all necessary what we did, I don't think. And I don't hold it against Harry Truman for stopping the Japanese. I think he had to do something. And I know a lot of my friends, we've discussed it in Sunday school classes, said that no Christian should have ever done anything like that. But, to me, I think some people have to get that kind of treatment, to wake up and know that they're wrong. I think that *Schindler's List*, that was on TV, I think that was very awakening.

Going back to the Ku Klux Klan. I think I touched on this, that it wasn't just against black people, it was against Jews, it was against Catholics. But, nevertheless, that was just people's hatred and that's just hatred. Why should you hate your fellow man in a country that gives you so much?

Now, you asked me about World War II. Well, that was just a devastating war because too many people were killed that didn't need to be killed. And they were some of the best people that were shot up and then, well, I guess it had to happen. We have to have a war every so often to satisfy greed and jealousy.

What is the most important historical event that has happened in your lifetime?

Now, I did not vote for Kennedy. But when Kennedy was killed, I can remember the exact spot I was on the street, and the time radio announced it. It made me realize there was a lot needed to change in America.

I was driving. I was down on Main Street. I never pulled over and stopped but I cried because he was around my age. I mean, you know, near enough to it that I felt, to just have a . . . and then when I got home and saw all the pictures it was even worse.

Ralph F. Dorris was born in Evansville in 1929 and worked as a journeyman electrician and superintendent at power plants in Indiana, Ohio, West Virginia, and South America. He is a retired member of International Brotherhood of Electrical Workers Local 16.[4]

Would you tell me about the history of your family?

Dorris: Well, my father was born down in Kentucky, below Providence, Kentucky, in 1906—May 30, 1906. And they were raised on a farm. He was the oldest boy of seven children. He had one sister who was older than him, two years older.

My mother was born here in Evansville. She was born in 1908 and she is still living. In fact, she lives right up the road here. And she worked at the Fendrich Cigar Factory for several years. And then after I was born she still worked for a while. And then, I think, when my sister was getting ready to be born, and she was pregnant with her she quit. My father came to Evansville, he worked at timber cutting down in Mt. Vernon. And then finally, in 1930 he got into the electrical trade at Howard Electric, and he got to be a journeyman. And then he worked for Swanson and Nunn in the sign department. He worked there for thirteen or fourteen years.

Do you know why your father left Kentucky?

Well he couldn't make a living down there, for one thing, especially in those days. And he worked at cutting timber in Kentucky for a while, and he finally moved over into the Mt. Vernon bottoms and worked in that area for a long time. And that's back when before they had any gasoline saws and so forth and he

[4] Interviewed by Samuel White, 11 May 1995, Newburgh.

Frank Dorris (far right) puts up a sign for the Indiana Fur Company in Indianapolis about 1940.
Ralph Dorris

done all this cutting [and] sawing with another guy. But they worked cutting wood. Then he went to work for Mathis Electric Company. He worked there about a year. He got hurt, got hurt awful bad, nearly got killed. And he was in the hospital several weeks.

He was on a fourteen-foot ladder. He fell, his back over a ladder rack on the truck that was right under him. Broke his back, and it almost scalped him—cut all the hide off the top of his head. And Earl Angermeier, even though he was an apprentice, kept his head and called the police. And they came out, and in those days, they didn't have these emergency ambulances. They came out in a police car and took my dad to St. Mary's Hospital. He laid there unconscious for about three days before he came to. And in the meantime, they found out that he had a fractured skull, he had a broken back. After he got out, he, he never was exactly right after that. His back was always stiff and his one leg, it shortened a half an inch. And from then on, he worked as a journeyman electrician. He died then in 1970, August the 6th, I believe. But he had a heart attack, he died, and that was it. He was sixty-four years old when he died.

Can you tell me about the values your parents stressed growing up?

My dad led the procession of the values. He always stressed that you had to work hard, and regardless of whatever your position was, you had to work hard. And save your money. He was, he wasn't tight, but he was very thrifty. And he wanted to make sure that you got the idea of hard work. And he thought that by implementing hard work you would do a whole lot better in life. And that's what he stressed on me, that I could start in a trade. And I started in a trade when I was fifteen years old.

This was back during World War II, and I had to get a special working permit. I could work in the sign shop. And I worked in Swanson and Nunn's Sign Shop for two years, in the summer. And then I worked for Mathis Electric the third year and the fourth year. And I worked there two summers. But that was the extent of me working. He wouldn't let me work during the school year unless it was a holiday or something like that. I remember we worked all night at the old National Bank downtown on a remodel job.

I tried to save as much as I could during the summer so that I would have money during the school year to spend. But I always ran out. I'd run out right after Christmas.

Do you share your parents' values?

Yes, I do. At the time, I guess, that they were teaching me I didn't share them very much. But I've found that, since then, I am sure that they were teaching me the right thing.

What political party did your parents support?

I know my dad at times, he'd vote Democrat and my mother would vote Republican or vice versa. And that would always make him so mad because she wouldn't tell him how she was going to vote and he wouldn't tell her. And then when they, after the election was over, he'd finally wheedle it out of her or she'd wheedle it out of him. He'd say, "Well, there's no reason for us even to vote," he says, "You're canceling my vote out." And that's, that's the way it went all of their lives.

I always favored the Democratic party up until the last election, and that time I didn't vote for the Democrats, I didn't vote for the Republicans. I did vote for Perot. And the reason I did is because he was protesting the way the country's been run. And I'm not sure I'm voting this time, but I can't see voting for, either way right now. I just don't agree with either side.

How do you think your family life differs from that of your parents?

I've been a lot luckier than my dad. I would say it was plain luck. In the first place, after 1965, there was better jobs to be had. My father was hampered by his education. He only went to the third or fourth grade. However, in his station in life, he could outfigure me in math, just right out of his head. By the time I would put a math problem on a piece of paper, he could tell me the answer before I could come up with the same thing and it would be right. So, that's one thing.

Electricians preparing to pull cable at General Electric's Tell City plant, 1957
Ralph Dorris

The next thing is I worked as a journeyman from 1951 until 1964.[5] Well, in 1956, I had one foreman's job at Fulton Square Housing Project, and it was about a four- to five-month job. Then I didn't get to do another one until 1964 and I was foreman on the road for Borman Electric. Well, based on that, then I went to Swan[son] and Nunn and I was foreman up there from '64 through October of '65. And Lester Drapela came down from Pittsburgh and came over to the Kiln Building. I had the Kiln Building operation. And he came over there and wanted to hire me to go to work for ALCOA as a supervisor. And in 1970, as a foreman, the job superintendent and I got together and he hired me as a superintendent for E. C. Ernst. That time I went down to Charleston, West Virginia, and the next five years I made a lot of money. And it wasn't like my dad's. He worked hard, always worked with tools. He was a foreman a couple of times but not for any long duration. And I was able to accomplish a lot more than he was in my lifetime. But it wasn't that I was smarter than him. The opportunities—I just took the chances, took the opportunities.

You mentioned your mother worked at the cigar factory before she was married. How did your parents feel about a woman working outside the house?

Well, in that day and age, my dad didn't work that much. He was just starting in the trade. And he would work part of the time, and the next part of the time he wouldn't work. When he wasn't working she was working. So, consequently, he didn't, I don't think he minded it too much because she didn't have enough money coming in, and there wasn't any Social Security in those days, you've got to remember that. And whatever she brought in is what put food on the table. And I think that's the main reason he didn't mind too much.

Who disciplined children in your parents' home?

Well, that's a great thing to bring up. My dad would be gone about, maybe two weeks at a time. My mother would make a list of everything I didn't do right or did wrong. When he'd come home, we'd have supper, and she'd start telling him everything I hadn't done right. Right after that, I got disciplined very harshly.

When did you leave your parents' home?

I was twenty-one years old, and I got married. My birthday was April 23, and I got married July the 14th, 1950, yes, 1950. That was the last day I was there.

How did you get your first job?

Through my father. I scraped paint off the signs. In those days, you couldn't get sheet metal because of the war. You would take old signs and clean them up. Then they would repaint them. Where the old electrodes stuck in, they'd seal those up and then punch in new ones, whatever configurations they needed. And then they would have a new sign. Then later on, I started in to going out on a service truck. And we'd hang small signs. Later on I graduated to the bigger signs.

What kind of work did you want at that time?

I didn't know. Anything that would make money. I started out at fifty cents an hour and worked two years at fifty cents an hour, and I went in and talked to John Ahl, who was the general manager of the sign shop. It was the beginning of the third year, and I asked for a nickel raise. "Well," John told me, he says, "business is so bad," then he says, "I just can't afford to hire you and keep you on." So he says, "You can go on home." He says, "If I need you, I'll call you."

Well, I went on home. And that Friday, my dad comes home from the road, he'd been there for thirteen, fourteen years. He was lead sign man in this whole part of the whole country. Then he come home, and he asked me, "Well, how you doing on your job?"

I told Dad, I told him, I said, "Well, I'm not working."

He said, "Well, I'll look into it Monday morning."

Monday morning he went to talk to John Ahl. John said, "No, I didn't hire him." Although, he had hired a couple of boys who were brand new, right off

[5] Skilled trades workers typically work as apprentices for a few years before becoming journeymen. During the apprenticeship period, the worker's salary increases each year to the journeyman's level.

the street. So my dad gave him a week's notice and quit that Friday night. But before he quit, he called on a Wednesday to Wilbur Knight at Mathis Electric. Of course, Wilbur, Bob Brown, and Max Mathis went together and formed Mathis Electric.

He says, "The only thing," he says, "I've got to know right now, could you use the boy?"

Wilbur says, "Why sure we could use him."

So, that's when my dad quit Swanson and Nunn Signs. After fourteen years he moved to Mathis Electric. I went to work about a week after my dad did, and I got started out at sixty cents an hour.

What are your favorite memories about your young adulthood?

Well, I just, more or less, grew up. I had, by the time I got up to thirteen years old, I started a paper route, or I bought a paper route. And it was just, I guess, about two miles long, kind of out in the country. Well, they used to, you paid a quarter a head for a paper route. You had a hundred customers, then you paid a quarter a head, that's twenty-five bucks. And then when you sold it you got a quarter a head. So, consequently, I bought my route and probably had about seventy or seventy-five customers. And after I had it about nine months, I sold it, and I had about 180 customers. But I kept extending my route all the time. I carried the *Evansville Press*, evening paper and the Sunday paper. And before it was over, my sister, she took part of the route, Pollack to Riverside, and then Riverside back to Weinbach. She took that part of the route. I took everything all the way out Riverside to Boeke Road and everything back in there. And then from that point north, I didn't carry anything. I carried everything on both sides of Riverside, all back in there. My route was, at the time, when I got rid of it, was about seven miles long. And I went up and down every street collecting.

How do you think your life differed from what you imagined it would be growing up?

Well, when I was in, even in high school, I always had a dream of being an electrical engineer, and I've always been around the electric trade. And there was a school in, I think it was Ohio, and I thought about going there. When my dad got hurt in January of '47, he was in bad shape until most of '47. It was about the next first of the year before he got back to work. Well, that pretty much wiped the family finances out. So, I quit looking at going to college and started looking at going to work.

At the time did you resent having to make a decision like that?

Well, I didn't really because my dad, he was really bad. And I was working, I worked at the grocery store during that time, part of the time. And I helped put food on the table. And I felt that it was not only my duty but my opportunity to do something for my dad.

I've had some very harsh disappointments. In 1958, I got to be assistant electrical inspector for the city of Evansville. I kept that job for about six months and quit it. In 1960, Frank MacDonald, Sr., first became mayor of Evansville. Through politics and pulling strings, I got to be chief electrical inspector. I was one of the youngest chiefs ever to be in that office. And I was chief from January 1st, 1960, until February 11th or 12th of 1961. And I got caught up in a, it wasn't a scandal, but it was a bunch of baloney. I was accused of being paid off, and the money I was making I couldn't have gotten paid off, and I know it. But, thank God, they had a big session in there and all the heads of the departments, and it was me and two or three other people. Anyhow, they finally decided they really didn't have enough on me, and I was cleared. But that afternoon, that day at noon, the mayor asked me for my resignation. I wrote out my resignation, took it down and put it on his desk, or on his secretary's, cleaned my desk out and left. That night in the *Evansville Press*, I read that I had been fired, and he had asked me for my resignation. I guess he could have said I was fired and it would have been all right, but he didn't. Then I thought, "Well, from now on I'm going to start making some money. I don't care what they say." Because at that time, the inspector's job paid less than $100 a week, about $98 or something like that. Anyhow, that was a letdown for me.

When did you join the union?

Well, I joined June 20, 1947. And although I'd worked '44, '45, and '46, I just was working as a temporary. And then in '47, after my dad had gotten hurt, I put my application in to become an apprentice, and I joined the local union in 1947. This is International Brotherhood of Electrical Workers Local 16. I came out in 1951 as a journeyman.

Your father was also a member of the same local?

Oh, yes, yes. And he was, in his earlier years, he was pretty dominant in the local. He was on the executive board. He was pretty much a good, hard-working union man.

Why did you decide to join the union?

Because of my father, I think. Because I didn't know anybody. In those days if you was a plumber's son, you would try to join the plumbers union or go to college. If you was a carpenter, you followed in your father's footsteps, sheet metal, the same way. I just followed my dad into the trade.

But my father was the first one in the union in the family as an electrician. Then his brother, he came in in 1940, or around 1940. He had gotten to be a journeyman. He got his two cousins in, Elmer Jordan and Clarence Jordan. And then in later years, he got Larry Bell, a cousin of mine.

How did you or other members feel about the international coming in at that time?[6]

We never did like them. Nobody in this local, that I know of, embraced the international in running the local's business, that we figured was the local's business. And although that was true, there were several times when I was on, well, I was always on the outs with someone.

How do you think your community has changed during your lifetime?

Well, in Evansville, back in the thirties, we had a lot of old brick buildings on First and Second Streets that I can remember. The main business district was up and down Main Street. And this remained so, at that time, up until 1952, when the fire, right after Christmas, about January of '52, it burned out nearly, probably about 75 percent or 80 percent of the downtown department stores and all of that. And '53, I came back here and went to work because everybody was working. At that time there wasn't any Eastland Mall, there wasn't any Washington Square, there wasn't any East Place—there wasn't a shopping mall. And everything stopped, well, all the business was downtown there, down on West Franklin Street, and that was it. Since that time, they've had Washington Square start up, and then Eastland Mall, it's just grown. Out on the west side, there's a new shopping center out there, Wal-Mart, and all that. I've seen it just expand and expand.

How do you think the country has changed during your lifetime?

The first president I can remember is Franklin Delano Roosevelt. He was controversial, but I think he was a pretty good president. And then you had Truman, I remember him. And he was, again, he was controversial, but he was another good president. And Eisenhower, Eisenhower I never could understand, really, but I suppose he was a war hero and all that. And then you go on up to Kennedy. And Kennedy wasn't in there but a couple of years and he got killed. Then Nixon, not Nixon, but Lyndon Johnson took over, then Nixon, and up to present.

It seems to me that when we went through the Vietnam War, which was a war I don't think anybody agreed on, that it was [not] any good for us. We shouldn't have been over there, probably, in the beginning. The Korean War, it was a bad war but we never did win it, and we haven't won it yet today. And

[6] As part of a general movement against organized labor in the postwar era, many United Electrical Workers (UE) locals came under attack for alleged ties to the Communist party. Some local union leaders were removed from office, while other locals confronted efforts by a competing union, the International Union of Electrical Workers (IUE), which was formed after the UE's expulsion by the Congress of Industrial Organizations (CIO) in 1949. Ronald W. Schatz, *The Electrical Workers: A History of Labor at General Electric and Westinghouse, 1923–1960* (Urbana: University of Illinois Press, 1983).

the other wars since then, the little wars, why, we've managed to get through. But I think that after World War II, we just didn't have in our souls to really get out and fight a war that we didn't have the legitimacy to. I think that's what happened in Korea, the U.N. war, the Vietnam War was the U.N. war. We didn't have a built-in legitimacy in Vietnam. You can't run a war from Washington, D.C. I think that was proven. It just doesn't work. You've got to put it in people's hands that are at the front. So consequently, I think, we came around to the fact that it's better now than what it was at that time.

Now, you mentioned Franklin Roosevelt and Truman, and thought they were good presidents. Why would you, why do you say that?

Well, Franklin Delano Roosevelt had done something that no other president's ever done. He started the Social Security program. And that, in itself, plus the labor movement grew under him at a rapid pace. I think those two things, in itself, is very, very good to this day. If we wouldn't have that we wouldn't have had nothing, the labor reform and Social Security.

What about World War II?

World War II, what I remember, is rationing—gas rationing, food rationing, and that sort of thing. That's what stands out in my mind. I know my first car, I could get an "A" sticker—that was about five gallons of gas a month, I think. It wasn't enough for you to blow your nose at. And that was it, that was all the gasoline I could have. You had to have your "A" sticker pasted on your windshield and all that. I had a '31 Chevrolet coupe.

Main Street between Fourth and Fifth Streets, about 1946
Willard Library, Evansville

Fourth Street, about 1946
Willard Library, Evansville

But anyhow, meat, it was rationed. My dad decided out there on Riverside that he was going to get around that so we started raising hogs—him and Florian Gable next door. It ended up that they had three hundred head of hogs and Jimmy Gable, who was Florian Gable's son, and myself, we ended up doing most of the work. We slopped the hogs. In that day you could slop the hogs. We watered them, day and night. Well, Dad would always give me fifty dollars or a hog, one hog out of every bunch in the process, and that was about fifty dollars. We had any kind of pork to eat.

***Marcella Massey was born in Evansville in 1921. She was a teacher for thirty-two years.*[7]**

Let's start with a history of your family, where your father came from, and your mother.

[7] Interviewed by Barbara Truesdell, 24 July 1996, Evansville.

Massey: Well, my father came to this country when he was sixteen and he came from Austria. When he came over, it was Austria. Then it became Czechoslovakia. He arrived here when he was sixteen and he worked, and then he had to go to school and learn how to speak English. And, of course, Central High School was here at that time.

And then in 1915 he married my mother who had taught school in Pike County but had come to Evansville to work. And then they were married in 1915 and then they opened a restaurant on the west side of Evansville in 1919 and kept their restaurant for forty-five years: Horny's Restaurant. My mother prepared the meals. My father worked out in front. And then they finally hired another cook, and another cook, and another waitress.

They were very busy. All the businessmen in the west side were from the small German community in Evansville. The dentist across the street, Dr. Ensminger, Charles Wolflin who owned the lumberyards, Will Stinson who owned a dry goods store, John Haas who owned a dry goods store, they accidentally would come at the

Inauguration Day parade at Sixth and Main Streets, 4 March 1933
Willard Library, Evansville

lunch hour and they got to know each other and talk to each other. And they had so much fun together.

They said, "You know, we ought to have some kind of an organization in this end of town to promote business," because it was a German settlement. And they got together and organized the West Side Nut Club. And if you never—I know it sounds silly, but they have done so many philanthropic things with their money.

Then my father died in 1931. And my mother, realizing that she was going to have to raise a child, figured she would stay in the restaurant business. And she did until 1964. She was in the business for forty-five years.

Upstairs, we had two bedrooms and a living room and a bath. We did not have a dining room because we ate all our meals downstairs in the big dining room in the restaurant.

I could carry a plate lunch out and set it down. And of course they'd only let me set it down to people that they knew. And they'd say, "Oh, here comes Marcella with my lunch today" [laughs]. But then, see, I would work after school. Well, most of the time during the noon hour rush.

And, you know, there's a place in there [the interview questionnaire], it says, "What do you resent?" When I was going to college, all my friends got to date. But on Saturday night, I had to stay home and work at the restaurant. Wasn't that something?

Do you share your parents' values?

Yes, because I taught school. And I could see in school where that was what worked. But you know when you have a working mother, you really do not spend all the time together because I was always in school. And if I was free, and I was waiting on customers. You don't have time. And she worked six days a week, closed on Sunday, and that was the day that

German Day parade, Main and Iowa Streets, 1908
Willard Library, Evansville

she did a lot of cleaning. Of course, I resented that too because I had to help clean on Sunday.

What religion did your parents belong to?

You know, my father came to this country as a Lutheran. My mother belonged to the Baptist Church, but neither of them attended. And as I grew up in the west side the closest church to us was a Methodist church. So that's where I went and that's where I was confirmed, baptized.

Are you still Methodist?

No, because we have a church in Evansville now called Christian Fellowship Church, two thousand members. People are leaving their other churches, Catholics are leaving their churches to go out to Christian Fellowship Church. And it's all biblical. I was rebaptized—completely immersed. Yes, right there in the church. And so I love that church because they don't stray from the Bible. Everything is strictly biblical. And I think that's what draws, I think people today are hungry for religion. When I went to college, I couldn't even study the Bible. I had to take philosophy because of being an education major. But when I became a junior, then I could take Bible, but that was an underclassman's subject. And so I never did. And I really never had much training in the Bible even in the Methodist Church. But I sure do out there.

Did you raise your daughter differently than your mom raised you?

I tried not to. I'm very proud of the way my daughter turned out. She graduated and went to IU. Got her degree from there to teach but she never taught because the fellow she married was a teacher. And they went to Louisville. He was in coaching and he really wanted to get into Indiana athletics so he took a job at New Castle. And when they were at New Castle they didn't want to employ somebody else in the family as a teacher. So consequently she went into real estate. And then they moved to Evansville.

And now we all own Premiere Video Superstores. We have four video stores with ten thousand movies in each store, getting ready to open a fifth one over in Henderson, Kentucky.

But values changing, no, not like it seems today. Our society has changed so much. And I know in her family. She has three children—seventeen, fifteen, and nine. And kids rule first. They do what their kids want. Their kids are so much into athletics. They go to every game. They are real, they are darling kids. They're all into softball. They're all into soccer.

So my daughter, they go to all the games. They don't care anything about the meals. They just go to the games. We used to, I always felt that a wife had to, at least supposed to have dinner on the table. Not anymore.

Let me ask you about the disciplining. How did your mother discipline you?

Oh, if I wanted to go somewhere, she'd say, "You can't go." That was it.

When my father was still living, one afternoon—I must have been about five, six—the little girl next door to the restaurant, we took off and walked out to Mesker Park, which was a zoo. My parents didn't know where I was. And when I got back, my father had a razor strap. Now, today we'd call it child abuse. But I was smacked with that razor strap and I never went anywhere after that without telling where I was.

What did you like and dislike about school?

I hear so many people say, "Oh, I liked recess." But, you know, I really did enjoy school. And I couldn't wait to go back to school and I'd always raise my hand in grade school because I knew the teacher. I mean, at first I'd wait and see if anybody else was going to answer it. And, of course, I had always studied. And I always knew the answer, but, of course, that's why I loved it so much. And I made real high grades. And I got a scholarship from the University of Evansville. So I just loved school.

I went to Centennial School, which was a block away. Then I went to Reitz High School. And then I went to University of Evansville. I did my student teaching partly at Centennial School plus some other schools. And when I got ready to teach, where do I get hired? Back at Centennial School.

So it's just like a bad penny. It always comes back.

Did your mother stress education as being important?

Well, see, she taught for two years up in Pike County before she came to Evansville. But when she came to Evansville she met my father, and then they were married and she stopped teaching. So of ten children in her family, almost all of them became teachers. So, see, teaching just ran in our family.

And then when I got to college, well, I guess in college, I was selected to be in *Who's Who among Students in American Universities and Colleges*. And that was a real nice thing. I was proud of that. And you were selected for that by your professors. Then we went to a Phi Zeta sweetheart dance and I was pulled out of line. Everybody was dressed in formals, and they pulled you out of line. And I was up for Phi Zeta sweetheart. And, of course, that wasn't important, but at that time in my life they were.

One of the most important things, I think, is becoming regent of the Daughters of the American Revolution. That is really important. I'm really proud of that. Of course, when you're two years as second vice and then two years as first vice, I think I'm ready.

Do you have a worst memory?

Well, I was married and my husband died. Then I was married again and my husband died. That's kind of, see, you don't have any control over something like that.

Can you tell me a little more about your work history? You said you taught.

I taught home economics. I started out—my license, in those days, was from all through elementary—kindergarten through eighth grade. And so when I first got out of the University of Evansville, I taught third grade for five years. And then we had so many in the third grade that somebody, the next year, was going to have to teach fourth grade. So I volunteered because, after five years teaching almost the same thing, I felt I needed to be promoted.

But the following year it was almost the same thing. Somebody was needed to teach the fifth. So I went to the fifth and the same thing. I went to the sixth. And while I was teaching sixth grade, a home ec teacher retired, and my principal called me into his office. And he says, "I want you to take that job next year in home ec."

And I say, "I can't. I don't have any special training."

He says, "Well, you could go back and pick up a couple courses." He says, "You're a wife, you know how to cook. You know how to sew." He says, "Go take some extra classes."

And so when I went back to school, I got my master's in home ec. And then I taught home ec for the next twenty-five years, and I loved it.

And home ec was wonderful. I loved it because I had all girls in my classes until about the last four years. Then, boys were integrated. Wasn't quite as much fun because, you know, the boys just kind of felt as though, why should they learn to sew? And I tried to try to show them that the best tailors in the world—Bill Blass, Halston—all these famous—Christian Dior—were men. And I said, "We need mechanics on these machines," these sewing machines that I had. Well, that was all right.

When I was teaching home ec in 1976, everybody was doing things for the bicentennial. So I thought, "What could we do in my classes?" And I said, "How would you girls like to make a long dress?"

And we put elastic up here at the top. And puffed sleeves and little mob caps and make it go all the way to the floor. "And you could wear it for a Halloween costume or you could wear it as a nightgown." Or, and then I said, "At the end of the school year, we'll have a program, and you can all wear your long dresses."

And we churned butter. Oh, we invited the different grades in one at a time, and we served hot Boston tea. And the girls that were in that particular class they would—I wouldn't get them out of class, but only the girls that I had that period—and the ones that were in there, they'd play the flute or the violin or something, perform chamber music when we invited the other rooms in to drink tea. And they had soda crackers and tea but it gave them the idea—like a scone and hot tea. Of course, some of the kids ate it just because it was free.

And they wore those long dresses. So before the thing was complete—oh, and then I had somebody from DAR come out in their costume. And I got pictures of that. But anyway, I said to the girls, "I would love one little scrap of your fabric." And so each girl in the class gave me a scrap of their fabric and made this United States [gestures to wall hanging].

Do you think people work harder today than they did a generation ago?

No. The kids that we hire are all college kids that go [to] University of Southern Illinois, or they go to University of Evansville, or they go to Ivy Tech. Some of our managers are graduates of IU, and most of our managers have college degrees. But the kids, you know, they might not show up. And if they don't show up and they don't show up without an excuse, we just fire them, because there are other people that want work.

We pay above minimum wage. And we pay a little more than McDonald's, a little bit more than Hardee's and some of these fast food places. And our place is a business where everybody wants to work for us.

People just don't work like they used to. People, a lot of people lived on a farm. My mother was born and raised on a farm. And yet, she didn't work as hard as her parents did because she'd talk about how they'd get up when the sun got up and go to bed when the sun went down. And they worked all day long. No time for naps.

When and why did you join the DAR?

You know, I always wanted to but I never had time to do any kind of research. And one of the ladies who was after me to, passed away. And she was outstanding. Well, she worked at University of Evansville, and I just made up my mind—I needed to do some work on that. And I had retired by then and I started working on papers.

And I did get a researcher. Dee Margardant knew a man who did research. And he helped me tremendously. He did a lot of my research for me, for which I was so thankful because I don't think I would have found nearly as much as he did.

And I have my relation, the original relation to

Parade in front of the M. J. Reising Feed Company, 1022 West Franklin Street, 1925
Willard Library, Evansville

1661, which makes me eligible, but I'm missing a hundred years in there from 1848 back. And I had it all figured out, sent it to the Colonial Dames in Washington, D.C.

See, I joined DAR in 1990. And then the next year I was eligible. So I was second vice for two years, first vice for two years. I will be the regent for another two years. So I said, "I'd better hurry up and get here because by the time I'm regent, I'll be seventy-five."

I feel proud that this one that's coming up in September [1996]. We are going to erect, we are going to mark a house in Evansville. That's close to twelve hundred dollars, but we're taking that out of the treasury. And the third president general of the United States lived in Evansville—her name was Mary Foster; it used to be Mary Park MacPherson Foster—she was the grandmother of John Foster Dulles. And she lived in Evansville. So they have a big granite marker that's going to be put on the house that she lived in which is the historic preservation area. And it's already been marked as an historic preservation house.

And we got permission from the historic preservation in Evansville and then we had to send a lot of papers to national and they had to OK. And, you know, you have so much back and forth and back and forth. And then, we're going to have the mayor there. And we're going to have our state regent, Margie Anne Souder will be there.

Can you tell me a little more about the neighborhood you grew up in?

Well, it was a business. And we were right on the main street. It was called Franklin Street. As I said before, the people that owned the furniture store lived upstairs. And their daughter and I were friends. Next door to me was a harness shop when I was real little. And when the farmers would come to town, they would park their wagons and their horses in our backyard because it was all cinders.

But as times began to change, he no longer had harnesses. He started selling tires. Rubber tires. You know for cars. And then, eventually, he went and had a liquor store [laughs]. And he lived upstairs also.

But there was enough kids in the neighborhood that I could play with. But it was always a business. And, you know, I kind of, I didn't really like living above a store because I didn't have a home like everybody else. But the kids loved to come visit me because it was a restaurant. We could have chocolate sundaes. Oh, they loved it.

And sometimes the kids would stay all night. And these tables, we would in high school, some of the girls lived in the country out in Union Township and really, I don't know how they got home, but anyway, they'd stay all night with me.

Out in front, on the sidewalk, gosh, the sidewalk was so far from here to here before you got to the street. And we would draw hopscotch on the sidewalk and we'd play out there. We'd play marbles. And jump—oh, my goodness, the jump rope, the kids would, you know, three or four of us, five of us. Two would turn the rope and the others would jump.

But it was still a business neighborhood. The theater was down in the next block. Drugstores were down in this block.

It was an interesting neighborhood.

It was different—you know what was strange? Like, during the depression, we always had plenty to eat. And I don't know we actually called it the depression because I was pretty young. But I remember my eighth-grade teacher would call each person in class and say, "What does your father do?"

"Owns a restaurant."

This one little girl was too embarrassed, and she walked up to the teacher's desk and whispered in her ear that her daddy worked for the WPA. Works Progress Administration. I don't know if you know what that is, but she was embarrassed.

And it wasn't until many, many, many years later, they'd say, after they got out of high school and college and came back—they'd always come back to the restaurant because they knew that the restaurant was always there—and they'd say, "Yeah, we always thought that you were a rich girl because your folks owned a restaurant." But we didn't. We just had a place to eat. And I never had ever thought of myself quite like that.

WPA workers laying water main along Allen's Lane, 1936
Willard Library, Evansville

USO dance, November 1943
Willard Library, Evansville

But they—we were merchants. And I guess they looked on merchants as people who made money.

How has Evansville changed in your lifetime?

Well, the horse that used to, don't park in the backyard anymore [laughs]. Eventually, we were able to sod the grass and we had a real nice backyard with flowers and things. There used to be a streetcar track down the center of Franklin Street. There used to be bricks, and now it's paved and the streetcar lines aren't there anymore. Everything changes because of technology.

Oh, naturally I wouldn't want to go back. I love it like it is. But, you know, I would not like to be a child right now. We didn't know about drugs or pot. And women didn't smoke then like they do now. I didn't smoke until I got to college but then my child was born. I didn't smoke after that.

I feel sorry for my grandkids. They have so many decisions to make. And they have so many more possibilities, vocations, decisions to make.

When we were in college—I was an only child—but we all belonged to the same sorority. And I loved all those girls in my sorority. And I just knew that once we graduated—I had heard too many other tales. People go and they work. You never see them anymore.

So we were—this was during the war. We were all dancing in an airplane hanger up at the airport. And I said, "Let's get, let's do something like a club. I don't care if it's a sewing club or a card club or—something to hold us together."

So we decided to make it a bridge club. It was in 1943. And we celebrated our fiftieth year two years ago. No, three years ago. This August, we'll be fifty-three years. Everybody got married. I went to everybody's wedding or was in the wedding. Everybody had a baby or two babies or three. Those children have grown and as those children graduated from high school we gave each one of them the same thing: a silver bonbon dish because at club we always served our candy in silver dishes. But we didn't give anything to the kids that went to college because not everybody could have gone, but everybody graduated from high school.

And then came the deaths. And then deaths of husbands. But no matter who died, the wife or the husband, the whole bridge club turned out. And out of those eight girls that started in '43, there's still five.

So I made a book, put the whole thing together, and passed it out. And we did something special. We all went down to New Harmony. And everybody read the book, their particular page to make sure everything was correct on it. And they couldn't believe that on that page was every place they had lived, when they moved. But they had given me that information. I had just compiled it.

Indianapolis

Indianapolis

Stories from the major urban area of Indiana concentrate mostly on the history of an African-American community. Five residents describe migration from the South to the city and activities in several neighborhoods. Willard Ransom, a leader in the city's black community who was interviewed in 1983, offers an extensive discussion of his family's history and of the civil rights activities undertaken by him and his father. Both Ransoms took an active role in pursuing democratic rights and integration for racial minorities. Willard, who became a lawyer in the city, described how he served his nation in World War II and then returned to his hometown to experience an improved climate in race relations. This chapter also offers an account of the Flanner House project, a self-help program that allowed African Americans to build homes for themselves in the 1950s and 1960s, and the issue of securing decent housing for minorities. In the Flanner project one could reduce the overall cost of a home purchase by laboring on the project himself.

Willard B. "Mike" Ransom was born in Indianapolis in 1916 and worked as an attorney for many years. He died in 1995. [1]

Ransom: My family history—my father was F. B. Ransom—Freeman B. Ransom was his name—and he was an attorney here in Indianapolis. My mother's name was Nettie L. Cox—maiden name—and became Nettie L. Ransom. There are six children in my family.

My brother Frank, who is the oldest son, spent most of his life working for the Department of Corrections in Indiana and just retired about a year ago from there. My brother Fred finished his career in housing. He was the manager at Lockefield Gardens project at one time, and then he was manager of Lugar Towers housing project. My brother Robert—Bob Ransom—he is a worker with the Madame Walker Company. And my brother Clifford is retired from the YMCA where he worked with YMCA as physical education director and with the Atterbury Job Corps for a few years and then the YMCA as physical director. My sister is a librarian at City College in New York.

My father's mother I'm very familiar with. My father's father—I didn't know anything about him. We never saw him. My father and mother both came to Indianapolis from Mississippi and I've heard him talk about his father, but his father must have died several years before he came here, to Indianapolis. But he brought his mother here from Mississippi, and she lived with us, my father's mother lived with us for years. And also my mother's mother, they brought her up to Indianapolis, and she lived for years.

Willard B. Ransom
Ransom family

Why did they come from Mississippi?

Well, you know, at that time—that was the time when there was a great exodus of blacks coming from the South. That was back—see, my dad came here in 1911 and that was back when things were pretty tough in Mississippi. He came north after he had gone to school—he and mother went to a school called Walden University in Nashville, Tennessee, which subsequently became part of Fisk University, which is now in Nashville, and he and mother they went to school there and decided to come north after that and they came up to seek their fortunes.

My mother's side—she came from a very large family—a prominent family in Jackson, Mississippi, and there were a lot of girls in her family—several boys and I think there was—let's see, one . . . two . . . there were three boys and about six girls, and most of them came north, practically the whole family came—those girls came north. One of her brothers lived in St. Louis—he was a pharmacist in St. Louis. One of her brothers came here and was a dentist here in Indianapolis and so on. They went various places, more or less moved ahead.

Did you say your father had brothers and sisters, or not?

My father had brothers and sisters. One of his brothers came to Indianapolis with him and established his family here. He worked at the old Kingan's—Kingan's

[1] Interviewed by Greg Stone, 18 July 1983, Indianapolis.

Kingan's meatpacking plant, early twentieth century
Indiana Historical Society,
Bass Photo Company Collection, 69862

meatpacking plant. And that brother and him sent all of their children through college, and they became people who had pretty prominent positions in Indianapolis also. Let's see, did he have another brother? That was the one we knew most about was the brother that came here. The others I know very little about them.

When your father went to school did he go straight into law?

He went on to law school—went to Columbia Law School. Well, he was interested and always what he tells me—he had always been interested in the law and felt that it would be a good profession for him—he was always interested in debating and so forth, and he just felt that would be the way for him. So he went on into law school and came back to Indianapolis and started practicing here. I suppose must have been around '09—'10—'11, I suppose . . . somewhere in there.

He must have been one of the first blacks at Columbia—in law school.

He just talked about how hard it was because he had to work his way through. Yes, it must have been awfully hard . . . because when I went to law school at Harvard—when I went—'course that's back in—my daughter calls it the Civil War days—I went, and I was there from '36 to '39, and I was the only black in my class and of course, work—you cannot work your way through here. "You can't do it, because we're going to work you too hard." They didn't want anybody to try to work because they felt it was just impossible . . . and they were about right, about right, because there was no way you could keep up because you had to go, you know, you had to go home and study every night.

Did they give loans for that purpose or were you supposed to pay for it yourself?

Well, back in those days, they didn't have much of a loan program in my day. Now when my son went they had a very, very comprehensive loan program. But, in my day, they didn't have much of that, but then the tuition wasn't so bad in my day. My dad paid all mine.

We have an interesting thing in our family in that I believe that my son and myself are the only black father and son team that's finished Harvard Law School. I think so. I haven't verified that yet, but the other thing is that—what brought this to my attention was the fact that I saw an article in the National Bar Journalists, the black bar journal—telling about this fellow out in—I believe it was Virginia—and they said this is the first third-generation black lawyer. This was just last year. When I saw it, I said, "Now wait a minute," I said, "That can't be right." I said, "Because my father, myself, and my son, and we're ahead of him because my son finished law school in '73."

When did your father get involved in civil rights?

Well, you see, my father became Madam Walker's attorney. He was Madam Walker's attorney, and he was a man that provided the legal background in the business program for the Walker Company, for Madam Walker, and she was real fond of him. He and attorney Brokenburr—that's Robert Brokenburr, he was associated with my father. They were two young attorneys and they worked with Madam Walker. Well, in working with Madam Walker—of course, her company became very prominent, biggest thing among blacks in Indianapolis and perhaps around the country, for that matter. Of course, Madam Walker was the first woman—we think—to make a million dollars on her own and so that in that period of time they were active—my father was active in everything in terms of working with business groups and political groups. And he started out I think he was Republican, but when the depression and Roosevelt came along—that's when he swung to the Democrats and became quite a power in the Democratic party here in Indianapolis and Indiana.[2]

[2] Ransom's father, Freeman B. Ransom, was an attorney and civic leader in Indianapolis. The Ransom Place neighborhood in that city bears his name. *Indianapolis Star*, 9 November 1995.

Now, I'd heard that the Klan was active in the Republican party in the twenties.

They were—that was another one of the reasons a lot of blacks left the Republican party. You see, blacks originally were Republicans on account of Abraham Lincoln back following the slave act, and they traditionally were Republicans, but after the Klan business started, that, plus the depression of 1930, '29, '30, '31 right in there, turned most blacks away from the Republican party and the majority came with Roosevelt.

The vast majority—I'd say it's about 70–30, maybe 80–20. There's no question. . . . But the Republicans now, of course, are working very hard to get blacks in Indiana, which is basically a Republican state, it's where the blacks are usually . . . we're usually on the outside looking in. But, lots of blacks, prominent blacks, have turned Republican. Now the fellow that just came out of my office, that you saw, that was Bill Ray who is the son-in-law of Robert Brokenburr that I was telling you about. And he came—we were talking in here about Alex Haley, who is, as you probably heard or read, he's going to do the story on Madam Walker. He's going to write a book and there's a possibility of a TV series, a possibility of a Broadway musical. We're doing a revision of the agreement between Alex Haley and the Walker Company and the heirs and so forth. That's what I was doing, and he was in here to sign the agreement.

As far as civil rights is concerned, what was your father's role?

And in the civil rights struggle, of course, he [father], as a political figure and also as a business leader, took a very strong role in the civil rights struggle in working the NAACP here in Indiana and working with what they called the Black Business League. But the NAACP was the spearhead, and my father was active in the NAACP.

Was he linked with Henry Richardson at all?

Yes, he and Richardson were contemporaries, and they worked together in the Democratic party and they worked together in politics.

I worked with Richardson quite a bit for his firm when I first started practicing law, and I became state president of the NAACP, and I served for five terms as state president of the NAACP, and I worked on practically every bit of civil rights legislation that we have in Indiana. Richardson was right there with me—we all worked together on those. I would say that Richardson and myself, I suppose, we probably did more than anybody else in terms of the legislation and in terms of promoting it and pushing it.

You first went to school locally—you went to . . .

I went to Crispus Attucks High School. That's another thing I'm very proud of.[3]

And then, why did you go to Talledega?

My uncle—the man I mentioned earlier—Dr. Cox, who was a dentist here, he went to Talledega, and he was a great athlete down there. We were athletes at Crispus Attucks. I must tell you this, we're the only family in Indianapolis that I know about that had—all five of us got varsity letters at Crispus Attucks. We all played basketball, I played basketball and football. And two of my brothers played basketball and football, and two of them played basketball, but all five of us got basketball letters. You see, so we're very proud of that.

Where did you live when you were growing up in Indianapolis?

We lived on California Street, which is about where our house was, it was two blocks from Indiana Avenue, California Street, and very close to Crispus Attucks. So we walked to school always. We walked to Number 4.

[3] Opened in 1927 as the result of the segregationist sentiment prevalent in Indiana in the 1920s, Crispus Attucks High School served the city's African-American population until the gradual reassignment of its staff and students after 1969. Stanley Warren, "Crispus Attucks High School," in *The Encyclopedia of Indianapolis*, David J. Bodenhamer and Robert G. Barrows, eds. (Bloomington and Indianapolis: Indiana University Press, 1994), 481–83.

You asked me about Talledega. The reason I went—my uncle, who was an athlete and a dentist, he was crazy about Talledega, so he persuaded my father to send us there. We took seven guys from Crispus Attucks down to Talledega, and we had had what we called a black national championship high school football team at Attucks. All seven of us from that team, we went down to Talledega, and we won the conference down there. So we had a hell of a team down there.

Were any of the schools in Indianapolis mixed at that time, or were they all . . .

It was all black—School Number 4. There was some schools that had a few, but mostly they were segregated, most of the schools. Now the high schools, strangely enough, when I was coming along in grade school—they were mixed. But then, Crispus Attucks came along—that was the Klan and all the rest of that situation that created that.

Did most of the blacks at this time live around the Indiana Avenue area?

They lived in several [areas]. There was always a group of blacks that lived on the north side, on the west side, which was the Indiana Avenue area, and then on the east side, and that was over at Martindale.

Did very many people try and move out of those areas or did they want to?

They wanted to. There was a long fight here on housing discrimination. We were fighting all the time. Blacks were fighting to get housing accommodations, and there was a great deal of residential segregation. I can remember very well when blacks were jubilant because they got past Thirty-eighth Street. That was a big deal. And I can remember when Railroadmen's Federal Savings and Loan Association—I represented a black family that was the first time they had ever loaned a black as much as $20,000, and that was a big, big event down there. I guess that must have been—I guess about in the fifties.

How do you think Attucks compared to the white high schools, you know, once they became separated?

We got a break going to Attucks. And the reason we got a break was that—not because we were segregated, but because, by the process of segregation, number one—we had the best teachers. The black teachers couldn't go anywhere else, so they had the cream of the crop. I'm talking about in my day, now this changed, of course, later. But in my day back in the thirties and the early—'29, '30 and so forth when Attucks first opened—black teachers that went to Attucks—it's worth a study, somebody could do a study of it—black teachers that went to Attucks were the superior black college graduates who couldn't get a job elsewhere.

So, we had the benefit of getting those superior—one example was Henrietta Harrah. Now, Henrietta Harrah was a graduate of Radcliffe, had a Ph.D. from Radcliffe, in English. She was my English teacher. All of them were potential college professors, but they taught at Attucks because it was the only place they could get a job. Somebody really needs to write the story of those teachers at Attucks.

They didn't realize it, but they had that drive, you know, to keep going. They were the type of people that nothing would stop them. They were going to go anyway, you know. They were just intellectuals who wanted to be damned good teachers. And we were fortunate—we've always talked about that, all of the graduates—how lucky we were because we couldn't have had a better group of teachers. So, we were pretty well grounded, and I've always given them credit—when I went to Talledega I was able to finish summa cum laude down there, and I give the Attucks teachers the most credit.

Did you face any discrimination at Harvard?

As far as Harvard University, once you got in, once you were accepted, they wouldn't tolerate any discrimination within the university. To give you an example—a white fellow was assigned to a room with me, my first year at Harvard, and was very upset about it because they had just assigned us—that was his room, period. Everybody had a roommate. So he went to the registrar and complained, and the registrar told him in no uncertain terms, "Why, I'm sorry, but that's our policy. You'll have to stay with Mr. Ransom or else you'll have to find yourself some other quarters."

Well, he came on back in and after—he decided to stay, but he wouldn't speak. So, that's the only discrimination that I faced as a student at Harvard—he didn't speak to me. So I said to myself, "This guy just has not been exposed to blacks."

He was from Mississippi, and, whereas I had been exposed to whites because in Indianapolis we had some cultural interplay all the time, and we went to Boy Scout camp together and all that sort of thing—the YMCA did stuff together and so on. So, I said, "Well." I said to myself, I said, "I'll just not speak to this guy—let him get over the shock—this cultural shock" [laughs].

So after about three days, he came in the room one evening and he said to me, "Did you understand what the professor was talking about in that contracts class this morning?"

And I said, "Well, I don't think I fully understood it, but let's go over it, let's see what we can do." So we sat down and that was the end of that. We sat down and went over that lesson and then he told me his life story—he was from Mississippi, and he said that he had always been taught that it was just impossible for blacks and whites to live together, and he just couldn't adjust to it for awhile. And it took him awhile to do it. We became fast friends, of course, and that was the end of that.

When you graduated from Harvard did you come straight back here?

I came straight back to Indianapolis and began practicing law, became associated with the Madam Walker Company. My father was still the general manager there. My father died in '47. I came back in '39, was working with him there plus practicing law, and I was associated with Mr. Brokenburr—that was his old associate. Then I got an appointment as deputy attorney general for the state of Indiana. My father's political pull helped get me that. At that time the deputy attorney generals were part time and they didn't pay you any—about $200 a month. But it was interesting work, and I learned a lot. And then after . . . see, after a couple of years, then we were into the beginnings of World War II, and I got drafted in '41.

I went to Edgewood Arsenal, Maryland, then from there down to Tuskegee Army Air Base. I was down there with black pilots with that first group, and I became an officer in the chemical warfare service, something I didn't want to do. I told the general I wanted to get into the legal setup. He said, "Well, I'll tell you. I don't know what I can do about that, but I know I'm going to have to send you to chemical warfare officers' school, because they told me to send somebody."

And so we went. Later, down at Tuskegee—I stayed down there three years, and we fought a civil rights battle down there. Yes, we really fought one down there. The army was segregated—they had—even the officers' club was segregated, and so we broke that up, and we had fights—usually about that. We broke up the segregated eating facilities they had. We just went on strike. We went on this sit-down strike—sit-ins, and the colonel, who was a very smart guy, very shrewd guy, and he persuaded the army to go along with our demands. Everything—'cause you see he sided with us completely, and so they finally just broke it all up on that base. It got broken up in town.

And then the master stroke that we pulled down there: I was president of the officers' club, and I went to the colonel and I said, "Colonel," I said, "We've got a real problem here." I said, "We can't—when the men go into town, they got a segregated city out there, so they can't enjoy the normal social life." So I said, "Why don't you give us an order permitting us to bring the girlfriends here on the base and go into the bachelor officers' quarters with the men?"

And he said, "What! The army has never done that." He said, "And we can't do that. We can't have women come in the officers' quarters."

I said, "Now, colonel, stop and think. We're going to have an incident or several incidents down in that town. Somebody's going to go somewhere . . . some officers are going to go somewhere, and they're going to refuse me, they're going to get somebody killed and all that."

So he said, "Jesus, that is right." We laughed about that thing—he called Washington and they gave him the authority. That was my greatest coup as the officers' club president. The boys all loved me after that. I used to tell them—I said, "You guys all owe me about fifty dollars a week. That's what I saved you from running and trying to get a hotel room somewhere."

So in the late forties, were there a lot of civil rights things going on?

I served over, as I say, in France and Belgium and then was discharged, came back here and that's when we started working on—working with the Walker Company—working on civil rights battles because I became NAACP state president. We reorganized the NAACP and got very active in the civil rights battles around here.

I was just looking at a couple of things, and it said that your wife and sister-in-law lost jobs through this?

That's right. That was not due to—well, it was partly due to the civil rights activities. It was also due to the hysteria of the times—we had McCarthyism coming forward at that time, and they had tremendous fights over that, and I was very persona non grata with the powers-that-be in the town. So they retaliated by knocking my wife out of her job at the planning center, and my sister-in-law lost a job with the Veterans Administration, and I was active in the Progressive party—that was [Henry] Wallace's party, and I was very active and I—in fact, I was the first black to run for Congress in Marion County. I ran on the Progressive party ticket. And that's what they didn't like. And they didn't like the Progressive party period. But what happened to the Progressive party was that we were very successful in what we wanted to do. Of course, we knew we couldn't win. We knew Wallace couldn't win, but what we wanted to do was to get the Democratic party to change its position on civil rights and on the cold war. And we were successful in both of them in that Truman's party changed its whole civil rights program. They adopted the whole Progressive party program, and that's where the Democratic party began to work in the civil rights area.

Now, was there any link between the NAACP and any of these sort of groups, with the CIO in the sense that the CIO was organizing a lot of the black workers, you know, for the first time in unions?

Yes, yes—the CIO was developing at that time, developing a lot of strength, doing a lot to organize black workers, and I think educate, not only black workers, but all workers politically and CIO played a great role. We always got support and assistance from the CIO in all of our civil rights fights, and we could always count on them.

And you ran for Congress?

Yes, I was the first black to run in Marion County for Congress, but as I say, we did it in order to get our platform and so forth before the public.

What did you get in terms of votes?

Oh, we got a few votes. We didn't get many votes because of the fact that they'd made every effort to keep us off the ballot. At one time they even arrested us. We were arrested and charged with false notarizations. You had to have petitions and so forth to get us on the ballot, and they charged us with false notarizations because the signatures have to be notarized. But they dropped the case. Of course, the case was just a harassment to try and keep us off the ballot. As soon as the election was over, why, they dropped the indictments, but they were trying like the devil to keep us off.

For instance, I had a black minister to stop me on the street one time and say that, "Why are you doing this? You're ruining yourself. You're going to ruin everything that your father's built up and your family and so forth. So why don't you just take it easy."

And I told him, I said, "Well, I feel I'm right. We're struggling for principles, you know, and I feel that I'm right." And of course, I think about six or seven years later, the same guy came up and complimented me. He said, "You're doing a good job."

That's because the climate had changed, you see. It had become respectable then. The reason I'm on the Merchants [Bank] board—today I'm on the board of directors of Merchants, but the Merchants, when they wanted to put a black on that board and they had me to lunch, they told me, "Do you want to know why we're asking you to come on [with] us?"

"I don't know, but I have a good idea."

But they said, "Well, it's because we want a black that is not an Uncle Tom, and clearly is not an Uncle Tom, but who has qualifications and so forth."

So, as I said, that paid off for me. That was the first time that my civil rights activities ever paid something. But, it just showed how the climate had changed. People have a tendency to, and this is true with blacks, anybody, any group, if an idea is new and if it's something that isn't accepted, everybody will not stick their neck out to do anything about it.

I remember when there were two blacks lynched in Marion, Indiana, and I can remember my dad's reaction and how much they talked about that.[4] The blacks got to our house, and they talked about that thing and they really became incensed and it really gave them a resolution. They were really tight, you know. I mean any kind of—who was it—some British philosopher—he came to America and they asked him how could America solve the race problem. And he said, "It's very simple." He said, "You should lynch a black every day." What he meant by that was that if you lynched a black every day, the revulsion and the counterrevolution would be so strong that the blacks would solve it. But there's some truth to that. In other words, people react to extremities, and when you force them they will—you'll get a forceful reaction.

But the fifties were when we broke the barriers in terms of restaurants, theaters, all public places—public accommodations—plus we got the law strengthened. You see we made an attack both legislatively and by direct action. Well, in the sixties, I would say we continued progress in terms of legislation. We got stronger fair employment practices laws passed in Indiana, and we got the civil rights commission created—the Indiana Civil Rights Commission created—and we got it established and set up with powers.[5] And we progressively worked to strengthen those powers and so on, and those were the type of things that we were doing, and, of course, the process goes on even today.

I think that the fight [in the 1960s] had shifted to the area of jobs, fighting for better jobs, and also the housing situation was really pretty bad, and people were

[4] In August 1930 two black youths were forcibly removed from the Grant County jail and lynched. The vigilante mob was not prosecuted. James H. Madison, *The Indiana Way: A State History* (Bloomington and Indianapolis: Indiana University Press and Indiana Historical Society, 1986), 241–42.

[5] Created in 1963, the Indiana Civil Rights Commission enforced the antidiscrimination provisions of a 1961 state civil rights law. Ibid., 245.

Front row (left to right): A'Lelia Ransom Nelson, R. L. Brokenburr, Mary McLeod Bethune, unidentified.
Back row (left to right): Violet Reynolds, Mrs. Joyner, Willard B. Ransom, F. E. DeFrantz, Sr.
Indiana Historical Society, C4560

fighting along that line. The jobs we were trying to get blacks—the jobs were probably the major thing that we were doing in the sixties. I remember a supermarket here discriminating against blacks, and they wouldn't hire any blacks and so forth. So we picketed that store and got them to change their policy. That was in the sixties.

There was some frustration, but we didn't have much of an explosion here. I think the reason was that because all this action had come along beforehand and antedated a lot of the things that the riots were about in other cities. Plus we didn't have a large black population as they had in those cities where you got much more of an explosive situation. And the housing situation, while it's been bad here, it's never been anywhere to approach Chicago or Detroit or those places.

But it was very bad. For instance, Eli Lilly, which now has a very liberated policy now, but they used to discriminate against blacks, and they had segregated facilities in their plants—the eating facilities, the toilet facilities, and everything was separate. But they have completely changed; they've got a complete flip-flop, and now they are the leading element in Indianapolis as far as being a progressive employer.

They still are antiunion, but the reason they can get away with that is that they have stayed one jump ahead of the union. There's nothing that a union can propose, that they haven't already done. Now, that's their policy. They have a very conscious policy on that, I think, that kind of paternalism—benevolent paternalism. It has been a good influence on the city of Indianapolis because they've set a standard, and the other employers, whether union or not, they try to reach . . . move towards that.

And now, what do you have, three children?

Yes, a boy and a girl and a stepson. My son is practicing law in Atlanta now, and I got two grandchildren—got a boy and a girl. He didn't come out of school until '73, and then he worked with LSO as an intern—Legal Services Organization—as an intern for about a year, and then he decided to go to Atlanta. What really decided him about Atlanta was his wife got a job down there. He had met her in Boston when he went to law school, and she got a master's in business administration from Boston University and Boston College and she went.

Now, he was involved in the struggles. My daughter and son were involved in the college upheavals, because one time they called me—my daughter went to Spellman College in Atlanta—they called me one time and said that your daughter is locked up with a bunch of striking students in the administration building. I said, "What do you want me to do about it?"

"We just wanted to let you know."

I said, "Well, I suppose you're going to let them out sooner or later." And they did, of course, but . . . and then my son, when he graduated from Howard—that must have been in '70, I suppose, yes, '70—they were still protesting there because many of the men students wore dashikis instead of cap and gown at the graduation. He wore a dashiki. So they were protesting.

Edna Johnson at UAW convention, 1940s
Indiana Historical Society, Indianapolis Recorder *Collection*, *C7794*

A real estate agent for many years in her hometown of Indianapolis, Edna Johnson was also a civil rights activist as well as one of the first African-American women to serve as an elected official of the United Automobile Workers union. She was born in 1918.[6]

Johnson: My mother died when I was twelve years old. And I don't remember too much about what she did. But she did work a little bit—more than likely in private families. Probably domestic work.

My father was a foundry worker. And he also worked for the city of Indianapolis, later on. That's where he was working when he passed away.

I guess I should ask what your maiden name was, you know, your last name.

It was Stephens.

Well, I went to public schools here. I went to 83 in West Indianapolis, and 63 in Haughville, School 56 on the east side and School 37 on the east side. Those

[6] Interviewed by Greg Stone, 10 October 1983, Indianapolis.

were grade schools. And I went to Crispus Attucks. I graduated in '34 and went to IU extension about three years. I took all the usual subjects—psychology and English, prelaw . . . all those courses, appraising, real estate. I'm a real estate broker now, the owner of my own business. That's been thirty-one or thirty-two years. I worked for somebody for one year. Then I went for myself.

I also worked in a plant. I worked at National Malleable and Steel Castings Company, where I was a grinder—you grind steel castings. But I left in '52. When I got my real estate license. And I put on my little glad rags and went out and walked through the plant and said, "Good-bye." And then I went—left that day and went right into real estate office and got to work, so . . . that was what I wanted to do. I quit, see.

When I went to work at National Malleable, everything was segregated. I went there in—let's see, '38. Thirty-eight, yes. We had—even the departments where we worked were segregated. The black women worked in one place and that was one department—in the grinding room where I worked. The white ladies worked in another department, which had to do with nickels. Then there was another department that black women worked in, had to do with nickels. But everything was segregated. No whites or blacks worked together at all.

Everything was segregated. And then the bathroom was segregated. Room for the blacks to go take a bath and go to the toilet. And room for the whites. There was the women and the men. The lunchroom was segregated. We couldn't eat in the same lunchroom, you know. They paid different prices—unequal pay for equal work is what I'm trying to say.

So naturally, when we got all these things together and found how unfair the situation was, of course, we naturally opted for unionism. Which was the salvation of people at that time. It still is, but the biggest barriers have been overcome by now.

Had this drive been going on there before you got there?

Oh, yes, nationally they have organizational drives and the person—when they came to us and we saw the need, so we had our National Labor Relation Board elections. And, of course, I was one of the main organizers. And we had a company union at the time. And Mrs. Lula Hodge was sort of setup of the Mother Superior for the black women out there. And, of course, they had all of the black women so geared to the company union that they were afraid to even express any friendship with me because I was all out for the union. Now, we had the Labor Relations Board elections on that day. And I was so enthused and when I went up and voted I came back with my union button on. Aha! I'll have you know, when I left there that evening I didn't have a job. They fired me for wearing that union button in the plant.

It just so happened that we did win the election. And the National—the UAW-CIO is what it was—made them bring me back to work. Give me my job back. They elected me to the bargaining committee, so I helped negotiate the first contract.

Everybody in the plant voted. By the way, let me tell you this. The makeup of that plant was unique in that we had about a thousand people in that plant. And we had about a hundred women, and the rest were men. The makeup was about fifty-fifty, white and black. So after we won that election and we started to, you know, a bargaining committee to help negotiate the first contract, came around elections. And then I started running for office. I held all the offices in it, in the plant, you know. Secretary, treasurer, and all that. And finally I worked up to president of the local union.

Now, this is what's so unique. Here we have a plant with a thousand people in it and only a hundred of them are women. I was elected president of that union for four or five years. And they said to me, now you know, they said, "Edna, we're for you because you are a fair person." And, in other words, there wasn't any room or even any thought of being—treating anybody differently. Everybody was treated the same. And we had a good union. It was local 761 UAW-CIO.

I was the first black woman ever to be president of a UAW local. Went to the nation[al] convention in Philadelphia, 1943. And got written up—I was written up in a book—it was either *Look* or *Life*. I forget which. One of those magazines.[7]

[7] About 8 percent of the delegates to the October 1943 UAW convention were African-American unionists. John Barnard, *Walter Reuther and the Rise of the Auto Workers* (Boston: Little, Brown, 1983), 86.

Walter Reuther, you've heard of him? He labeled me "that little rebel from Indiana." I was a feisty little fiery thing. When things weren't going right I didn't mind getting up speaking my piece—in a convention or any meetings or anything we might have. I just never have been afraid. You know, I feel like people, you know, ought to be treated right. And I always felt like there's no room to treat me any different than anybody else. And I knew that we were treated unfairly. I have never tolerated discrimination of any kind. I don't . . . I've never done it. I never felt like . . . like it was justified. I've never discriminated. I'm not prejudiced. I've never been prejudiced. Those are my convictions.

The neighborhood that I was born in was a mixed neighborhood, out in west Indianapolis, Haughville . . . immigrants, you know. I can't tell you from where, because I wasn't knowledgeable at that time. But all kinds of a mix—playing in there—native American whites and blacks and . . . whoever, you know. Matter of fact my sister, my older sister and brother went to an open school that was not segregated before they built Attucks High School.[8]

Where did your father work then?

At Link-Belt. And he lost his job during the depression and then he was on the WPA for a while. You know what that is?

Right. Yes.

Getting help and all that sort of stuff. And we used to get baskets of stuff and go to soup kitchens and all that. You name it and we've had it, you know. Name it and I know about it.

Well, my mother died about that time. And we moved from west Indianapolis over to Haughville. That's just a little bit west of here.

When did you start to work?

When I first got out of high school. I worked half days all week, and I made five dollars a week. I did the washing, ironing, cleaning, cooking, and cleaned all the shirts for the husband and son, all the laundry for the two daughters who worked in offices downtown. All of that for five dollars a week. So when I left that job, I said, "Well now look, Edna, you can do better than that." That's the one and only job I had in private families—not that it's a degrading job or anything like that.

So, did you like Attucks High School?

Oh, I loved Attucks. Let me tell you, when you was at Attucks, if you wanted an education, you got it. And I'm one of those who wanted it and got it, see. I would have graduated in three years had I not flunked in geometry. I needed one credit for three-year graduation. The reason I flunked was the . . . this particular lady—and her name is Miss Wickley, if you want to say it—she was one of those teachers who was just so cocksure of herself, and she just rattled off that stuff and, as if you should grasp it. Now geometry's not an easy subject. One day she said something that I missed, and I stayed after class to ask her to explain it to me again. She refused to do so. As a consequence, when you missed something in geometry like that, if you don't get it, you are hopelessly lost. And that's what happened to me.

Was your father born in Indianapolis too?

They were born in Albany, Georgia—my mother and father both. And I was the first born after they got here. My older brother and sister were born there also. And I was the first born after they arrived here.

And why did they come up to the North?

I guess to try to better themselves like most people who leave the South—looking for a place to settle and try to do better for themselves. As a matter of fact, having lost my mother at such a young age, I never heard

[8] Located just west of the White River and north of the Stringtown neighborhood, Haughville's working-class residents over the years included Irish railroad workers and eastern Europeans; many men worked at the National Malleable Castings Company and at the Link-Belt Company. After the Second World War, African Americans and Appalachian whites also settled in Haughville. Cathleen Donnelly, "Haughville," in Bodenhamer and Barrows, eds., *Encyclopedia of Indianapolis*, 663–64.

Crispus Attucks High School
Indiana Historical Society, Bass Photo Company Collection, 242007

them discuss it. And I never even thought to ask, you know, why, because our whole family moved up here—his father, who I remember passing at the age of eighty-two. We all lived in the same neighborhood. My granddaddy owned his own house, and he lived on Pershing.

My brother worked at National Malleable with us. And when the plant closed then he went over there [to Link-Belt] and got a job. Same as my husband did. My husband went to National Starch and got a job after the plant closed. National Starch and Chemical Company.

But, so I guess those other people were still taking people even though that National Malleable closed down for a while. They closed. They went out of business. Well, they closed down for a while, and then they called some people back to work who hadn't gotten other jobs. And doggone if they didn't close completely that time. Messed up a lot of people who had given up good jobs to come back there.

Let me tell you this before we get onto the union: I traveled all over the country with the union—for the union and them. Boy, I learned so fast that, "Hey, this is an oddity." I would go off, and I was so dedicated. I'd come back and make a report to the members, and they would all sit there and look at me. I found myself using all of the language of the labor movement that the people in the plant did not understand.

You have all these things to handle, to take care of. And you meet once a year in your national convention. And very important things are done there. Leon Bates was our representative. He was one of the first black union representatives. He was assigned to our area. And when they started—when they got ready to put a woman on the staff of the UAW I was recommended and was offered the job from the national office. It's a job that's held right now by Lillian Hatcher, who's been in that position for several years. I turned it down. And, I would have been the first black woman on the staff of the national organization. I turned it down. My husband was in the service at the time and you know how you don't have full maturity sometimes on some matters. I said, "I can't leave Indianapolis. I live here. My husband's in the service and I've got to be here when he comes back." I thought of that later and I said, "My God, what a poor answer." Because if I had been thinking and maybe had a little more courage in that area, I might have moved to Detroit at that time.

Even back then I got tired of always having to fight for something. You run out of energy in fighting for your rights and by the time you get them you don't have energy enough to appreciate it, enjoy them, you know. When I left the plant and into real estate I said, "Well, I'm going into something where I don't have to face all this discrimination. I'm just tired of it," you know.

I get in the real estate business, and lo and behold, I found out, I said, "Well now, no matter where you go you find it in everything you touch. Everything you touch." The first obstacle I ran into was trying to get a sponsor to, you know, to get my license. I talked to several offices, all white. And there was nobody who would sponsor me for the exam. You had to have a sponsor even to take the examination at that time. Well, then I had to scrounge around and find out who I could find in the black community—who was in real estate. And I found three people.

You must remember this was in 1950 or '51 or '52. They only started requiring licenses in 1949. And the way those people got in there was because of what they called the grandfather's clause. All you had to do was go down and certify that you are [already] in the real estate business and you could get a license. You didn't have to take an examination or anything. But after that period ran out, then they began to require licensing. And so, of course, then you had to go to school. I passed a state examination. Incidentally, I was told that I passed the exam with one of the highest grades ever made down there.

Was housing discrimination a problem?

The Indianapolis Realtors Association, we had to—fighting for fair housing, if you call it that.[9] Our slogan was, "Democracy in housing," because fair housing is with HUD. If we can't get fair housing, we can't be in business, because we can't—I've had it happen: "Sell our house, but the price is, say $10,000, but if you sell it to a black, we've got to have more." You never heard of that before, have you?

The realtors didn't address the problem of fair housing until they were forced. The government had to get in the act. And then through the civil rights legislation and my organization fighting for fair housing. They didn't want us in their organization, they didn't want us to go into real estate. So they didn't make it easier for us, I feel. They would not deal with us on any listings, we couldn't get the listings. So they refused. So then ultimately they denied a lot of people access to housing, you see. At this time we've gradually gnawing away and getting a little concession there, until now we do have multiple listings. We have an ad hoc committee, an urban league, at which the realtors met with myself and some other members of our organization that represented some of the Indiana Civil Rights Commission. We had to hammer out this agreement.

I was also a member of the Human Rights Commission for awhile. And then on the advisory board of the Indiana Civil Rights Commission for umpteen years. When Hal Hatcher was the executive director, the commission sponsored a bill in the legislature that set up quotas on how many houses blacks could buy. I opposed that vigorously and left the commission for awhile because of that. I opposed it, and I stopped meeting with them awhile, because I opposed it. I told them I opposed it, but they went ahead with it anyway. It wasn't two years, two or three years before they repealed that law. They repealed it. They found out what I told them was right. It's unfair, you know. You're not supposed to be able to tell people how many people can buy a house.

Strangely enough, it was Jim Jones, that had this fiasco in Guyana, was the first director of the Indianapolis Human Rights Commission. He didn't show that personality then. As a matter of fact, I knew him personally and he seemed like a real person who wanted to do something about civil rights. And I think he was a little too strong for them then.

[Mrs. Johnson recalls some other memories of growing up and working.]

You remember when Henry Wallace ran for president? That was at the time. And everybody needed a job, very much like right now. Very much like right now. His slogan was "60 million jobs." I'll never forget it, because I got a book. I got his book, *60 Million Jobs*, I don't know where it is now, but I've got it someplace. I read that book. And I said, "Well, my God, if this is

[9] Johnson served as president of the Indianapolis Realtors Association, an organization formed by African-American realtors.

the man going to supply these jobs, this is the man I need to support." I went all the way to Philadelphia, to Shibe Park for this convention.[10] I was going to school at the time—IU. And I took off and went to Shibe Park for that thing and I was sitting up in there just . . . oh, just applauding, you know, and cheering and supporting.

I got back here and we had to write a paper on something in my English class—one of my English classes. And I decided to write on Shibe Park. I told all about the Progressive party and everything. I wasn't ashamed of it, you know. My English teacher kept my paper and I don't know who she gave that paper to. But, do you know the FBI came to see me about that? They really did.

And I said, "Well, my God," I said, "I'm free. I'm supposed to be able to support anybody I want to. What's all of this about?"

So what happened? What happened? What did they do?

Nothing. They just came to see me. Nothing happened, no. And I wasn't, as far as I know I wasn't labeled a communist or anything like that.

Do you have any other memories like that?

I remember this: it had to do with segregation in housing. And I made this statement something similar to this, and I said, "How would you like it if the good Lord decided overnight to turn all the black people white and all the white people black?" And I said, "And the same thing . . . and then keep on treating each other like, you know." I said, "I wonder if you'd be able to stand it."

And that place got as quiet as a pin. You could hear a pin drop. For several seconds nobody . . . you know, it seemed like nobody was breathing, because that statement really astounded those people. They had to stop for a minute and think about that. And I had so many phone calls and people said, "Edna, who would have dreamed of thinking of something like that?" you know. It was really a stupendous thing that you'd think of something like that. Anyway, made the people think. I think that statement needs to be made more and more, because you couldn't imagine the things that I have faced as a black person, could you? Because you haven't experienced them.

Now the way they control where you go here is by steering, of course. The black person goes to a white real estate office and says, "I want to see your house," you know, a certain house. And they'll tell them, "Oh, well, I can show you so and so." They steer them completely away from where they want to look. And the way they handle us brokers is when we call and want the apartment, it is automatically sold. Or otherwise, they automatically have an offer on it, you know. Now, we get very little white business, you know, for listing. But when they do call, they'll say, "Well, Miss Johnson, I thought you might have somebody who wants to look at it, but I don't want to list it with you," you know. No protection on anything like that. We can't have the privilege of serving the customer, you know, as a customer, you know. But it's all there. I'm not bitter about it. It's just something . . . it's just . . . it's disgusting to me now.

It's just plain disgusting to me, and . . . like in the banks, when we used to go to the banks, we couldn't get a loan anyplace. And we found out it wasn't the bank's policy, it was the employees that got between us and those loans—employees in the bank who were themselves prejudiced. We've taken our paperwork for a transaction to a lending institution—a mortgage company. And they promised us that they're processing the paper. And we go back and they found out they stuck it in the drawer—a file drawer someplace—and forgotten about it. You know, these are the things we've been through. Did you have any idea all this goes on?

Alberta Murphy was born in 1918 in Marion, Arkansas, and lived in Memphis, Tennessee, before moving to Indianapolis in 1948.[11]

How old were you when you started working?

Murphy: Picking cotton? About six years old [in Arkansas]. Picking cotton, and you know, in the spring

[10] Shibe Park in north Philadelphia is now called Connie Mack Stadium.

[11] Interviewed by Richard B. Pierce, 20 July 1995, Indianapolis.

you had to chop that cotton. You know, at that time, we weren't getting but a dollar a day.

What values did you teach your children? If you had to pick one or two values that you really tried to get through to your children what would they be?

Oh, well I always tried to teach them to obey and go by the rules of other people that they're working under. I was just going to tell you, that I was going to teach them to depend on God, and always go to church and obey whatever the teachers tell them to do there. Monday night—you're going to make me bring this up now—they had me speaking on my mission, "Why I am a Baptist."

What did you tell them?

I told them I was Baptist—I'm going to tell you all the truth—I said, "There's no need to be lying, you're in church." I said, "I am a Baptist because Grandma was a Baptist." I said, "But Baptism will not get me to heaven." I said, "I never will forget, when Jesus told Nicodemus, he must be born again." And anytime I start to think about something like that—that really brings it to me—when I was a little girl, when Grandma used to hear me, she used to call me "her girl." She'd come stay with my mother, would stay with my mother and father when I was a baby. And I never will forget her telling me all the time, she used to take me to Sunday school and church. She'd tell me, "Alberta, you go to all of them [churches] you want to, but, now, if you don't get born again," that was their religion, "You're going to hell." I can remember her always telling me that.

And you were telling me about a period when you were working at, actually it wasn't Marion anymore, we were talking about Crispus Attucks.

Yes, that's what we were talking about.

And you started working there in 1979, near as we can figure anyway. Was there any other time during your tenure at Crispus Attucks when, what would you say the racial population was, was it mostly black, was it fifty-fifty black and white students, or . . .

No, when I was working over there, most of them was black.

Did you go to school at Attucks for a period of time?

I was counting myself on graduating with my first son, he graduated from Attucks in '52. And I can remember when he graduated. And I said that I would try, went to high school the same building he went, going to graduate with him. And my nerves got so bad, the doctors stopped me.

The adult school at Attucks must have been a very popular thing for people who moved out of the South.

Oh, it was nice. I enjoyed going. But when I started making them Cs and Ds, I would go crazy over them.

Were there a lot of people from the South, that had moved to Indianapolis in the school there?

Yes, because a lot of people would go in there, I mean, in '52, the adult school was like, you know, the regular school, at night, it would meet at night.

Were there a lot of veterans there, from the war, did you notice that?

That is what it would be, but I didn't pay that much attention, because the classes was really nice, I liked it. They taught you how to sew, ceramics. When they went to teach me that math, that's when I like to have went crazy.

You never worked in Indianapolis?

My husband just never wanted me to—just stay home with the children.

You're talking about John Henry Murphy?

Yes, he'd tell me to stay home with the children. Just like sometime I might see something I want, "I want that refrigerator." In his mind, I wasn't saying nothing. Well I, you know, would come back sometimes, I'd be going to work. I mean one time I worked to pay for one of those little automatic irons, went to work, was working down there on South Washington in a place where they cleaned venetian blinds.

Did you run a machine or something?

No, you just took your hand and washed them blinds.

So your husband probably quit by 1980? Right after you started working at Attucks? Is that about right?

Yes. I think he retired around then, because, that's what caused me to come in here [to the Flanner House].

Because you didn't want to be at home?

When he retired, he started to come up here, I was working at Attucks. He starts coming up here with these men. He's the one who started me. And he would come up here and eat his lunch here with me. [Mrs. Murphy worked in the cafeteria.]

You said he worked—factory work over at Allison?

He worked at Allison.[12] But I worked at this other place two years while he worked for them nineteen years I was telling you about. I worked those last two years. I was living in the east end, I wasn't living in the Flanner House then. I lived east on Twenty-fifth and Baltimore. And he was working at night, and I was working days. And when I stopped working there, when he was working there. We filed our taxes that year, and the money I made wasn't as much as we had to pay taxes. I told him, "I'm not working no more." He said, "I'll be careful you working as much as you want to work, because you get that money every week, and then spend it."

In the job I went on and worked, I liked it, that's how come I went. That was so much convenient for me, to go out and work from four to ten, one of the four hours, cleaning offices. And then they transported me down to this company where I was going, down to Indiana Bell. And I worked there—

Cleaning offices?

I was really cleaning offices. And that was real nice too, but they laid me off then they called me back.

Now, when did you move into a Flanner Home?[13]

Let's see, I would have been here thirty-six years, I believe it is. So that would mean, then, how long it's been.

1959?

Yes, I believe that. The way we got it was [a] miracle, a blessing. We bought a lot out there on Twenty-fifth and Main, and it was already out here when we bought it. But around about thirty-some-odd years ago when these contractors would go through here and build these houses for the people, and catch them in this trap, boy, we got caught in it. We had this lot, we already owned, and we were going to have this house built, and they built this, what they called this shelter. They didn't finish. And we got ourselves a second

[12] Founded by James Allison in 1913 as an engineering parts supplier, the Allison Divisions of General Motors (after 1929) later made aircraft engines and transmissions. It employed as many as twenty-three thousand people during the Second World War. Wanda Lou Willis, "Allison Divisions, General Motors Corporation," in Bodenhamer and Barrows, eds., *Encyclopedia of Indianapolis*, 249–50.

[13] In 1898 the original Flanner House began to offer self-help programs to the city's African-American population. Expanding its mission to include vocational training and health-care services, the agency also sponsored the cooperative building of Flanner House homes in the 1950s and 1960s. Michelle D. Hale, "Flanner House," in ibid., 577.

mortgage, for to finish it. And come time we were so down, we hadn't paid nothing to this contractor, we couldn't get a second mortgage.

So the trap was, they'd build you a shelter, but not a house.

And so, I had a very close friend, she used to teach. And her brother was at Bank One, and he had a lot to do with the Flanner House homes. And she told him about what a trap we had got caught in, and he said, "Well, I'm going to try to help them, John Henry and Alberta, get them a home." And so he talked with us one day and asked if we wanted to sell the house back. And we told him, "Yes." And he said, "Well, I've got something for you." He said, "I've found a house over there on Thirteenth Street." He said the owner was working one day, one night, painting the house. And he had a heart attack and died. And his wife didn't want the house. So he told us to go talk to the real estate lady about that house. So we went to talk to her. She said, about thirty-five people had been past that house, but they chose you all.

Right before you hit the ground.

And so we was only sold a share. And we didn't get enough money out of it for to pay the closing costs. We took the money what we got off the house and paid down on the one where we are now. And John had just bought him a brand new, . . . a Plymouth.

Can you describe the community that was around the Flanner House, did people have a lot of pride in their homes, they all owned them, right?

All of the, . . . from Twelfth Street to almost Sixteenth Street, in the Flanner House homes.

A lot of people talk about how neighborhoods, especially in the central part of Indianapolis, have gone down, you know. People move out, people rent their homes, is that not the case with Flanner House homes?

No. We have had to fight. IU tried to buy the

Men working on Flanner House homes at night, October 1959
Indiana Historical Society, Indianapolis Recorder *Collection*, *C7795*

homes. They tried to buy them from us. I had a lady come to me to buy the house, so I helped her go around, you know, and see the people on the street.

These were not gifts, right? A lot of people thought back in that day that this was charity. But it wasn't charity at all, was it? I mean these men and women had to work and their—

You mean when they was working—and then, there were so many hours you had to put in, on your house.

Can you describe the process to me? How did they, how did they go about building these homes? Did you get to build your neighbor's home, or help build your neighbor's home, or did you just work on the one you lived in?

No, no. You worked on just one at a time. See, that's the reason why John Henry couldn't get it. The hours that he was working on his job would fool with the hours that he had to work. See they worked in the day. We had this son then that, during that time, he was about eighteen years old. And John Henry even talked to him and told him that I'd come and work so many hours and then I'll let my son come. But they still wouldn't accept that.

How has society changed in your lifetime? I know there's a lot of things you could say, but what would you say most specifically has changed?

It really has changed for us, because we're doing a lot of things that we used to couldn't go do. The whole United States has changed. See, you're not as old as I am. Get on that bus, and get on that plane, go somewhere, you'll find out, you'll never be scared now to walk into such a place.

What used to make you afraid when you were coming up? What most made you afraid?

I was just afraid of white people.

Really?

Yes. I was just a normal child, walking three miles to school, and they'd be on the bus, sometimes stick their head out and spit on me. I still had to walk three miles, and everybody at school. Things have changed all over the United States, right here in Indianapolis too.

How do you think Indianapolis has most changed?

Well, I was telling my daughter the other day, I said, "When you go in the store now," I said, "I have been in stores sometimes to try on a hat." And it's, "No, you can't try it on."

I'm sitting here now talking to you—that's important. That's how come I can't see how come those seniors don't want to get on those vans, pick you up for free in the morning, come here and have a good time. This is really something that I've been bragging about. I really enjoy coming here.

Really?

I really enjoy it, and I wanted to come down. What would I do if I wasn't coming here? And I don't come, you know, for me, I come when I want to. I don't come if I don't want to.

William Taylor was born in Indianapolis in 1934 and took a degree in Studio Art from Indiana University in 1956.[14]

Taylor: My father was in the first graduating class of Attucks High School. He strongly requested to go to Attucks High School. My mother also was a graduate of Attucks High School. And out of that union I came about in 1934.

At Attucks High School, and you heard this before, but Attucks High School had a faculty that some junior colleges probably couldn't match. Everybody had a master's. Oh, I won't say everybody. There might have been

[14] Interviewed by Richard B. Pierce, 14 February 1996, Indianapolis.

somebody that was in the process. Had a master's, there were three people who had a Ph.D.

There was one person, Dr. Morton-Finney, who's still alive, I think he's 104 now or something, the only time I talked to him, the only time, we had to put his glasses on to see how many master's he had. I think he had seven master's degrees. He spoke five languages or six languages. He was going to get a Ph.D. until he decided he would like law school, so he went and got a law degree.[15]

[Mr. Taylor explains where he grew up in Indianapolis. After his mother died, he was raised by his grandparents.]

What happened was, when it was time for me to go to school, there was a lady [in the neighborhood] that kept children. Apparently my grandmother was working, because there really wasn't going to be anybody there to let me in the house in the beginning. So I went to stay with a lady named Julia Chun.

I was old enough to be a latchkey kid. And when I hear about latch—I know there are different powers out there now, but, see, the only threat I had as a latchkey person was that if I didn't have my chores done by the time the folks got home, I got my butt burned.

We lived on Capitol Avenue for a while which still got me to [School] 87. Capitol Avenue just south of the Fall Creek was where we lived for a while.

You said your father was working as an elevator man?

My father ended up at the post office. It wasn't exciting, then it started getting more, and then you had more whites that were coming in and getting the jobs because the money had gotten decent to deliver mail and everything. Before it was almost an all-black thing: the truck drivers and that were almost an all-black group. I delivered mail when I was here at the university at Christmas time. That was part of my making some extra money.

[15] In addition to teaching for almost a half century, Dr. John Morton-Finney headed the Foreign Language Department at Crispus Attucks High School for thirty years. Morton-Finney also earned several degrees and practiced law well past his one hundredth birthday. He died in 1998 at the age of 108 in Indianapolis. Morton-Finney was the last survivor of the Buffalo Soldiers, an all-black army unit from the era of World War I. *Indianapolis Star*, 31 January, 1, 11 February 1998.

I never understood that we were poor. I had ample everything. The one thing that I had with my dad working at L. Strauss and Company was I had some upper-decibel clothes and I didn't understand what that little triangle on those corduroys meant. That was big-time good clothes. And he was buying them there and getting a discount.

And what were, what were these clothes called?

I can't think of the name. It had a little name; it would be like a Nieman Marcus label or something like that today.

Right.

We talk about situations in families. When I got married I always put the Christmas tree up on Christmas Eve. And my wife always wanted it to be like a week, two weeks before. And that—it just didn't feel right. Santa Claus brought the tree. Well, what happened was my dad's working at Strauss, he would get the display tree from the store that they had for Christmas—but he couldn't get it until Christmas Eve. And we had magnificent trees, but I never put it together that the reason we had magnificent trees is because these were display trees they let them have. He made friends with everybody. I mean, he was a friendly, jovial person. And with that, there was a Jewish salesman at Strauss, cannot come up with his name now, his father was head of the tailoring down at Strauss at the time. But they became very, very good friends. And the gap between my father being on the elevator or sweeping up and him being the salesman was overcome quickly. And he was still there when I took the job.

So, your first job out of high school in 1952 was as an elevator operator working for L. Strauss and Company. You went to IU, Bloomington in 1953. How was your experience at IU, Bloomington?

Interesting experience. One, it was still a segregated university to a point. Not openly but quietly. You had to send a photograph with your application. I don't know if the white students had to, but coming out of

Attucks, you had to do an English test, to test your comprehension. The halls of residence were open, you know, as long as you had a black roommate, I guess that was cool. I entered into the art education program.

What steered your interest in art? Did you have a strong program at Attucks?

I did art, that was my major area in Attucks High School. That was something I just kind of fell backwards into. I tell people, or the students, that it isn't so much talent that pops out, it comes from encouragement. And so the little things that I drew at home and stuff like Abraham Lincoln, and stuff got stuck up on the wall and got praised and caused me to want to pursue it a little farther.

When I came back [to college] in '53 I was taking studio classes. Most art education says you have to have some studio experiences, but those were very Johnny Casual kind of things, arts and crafts and maybe a watercolor class or something. But I think it's, it used to be, maybe six hours that does it for you.

I was, you know, I was doing this, and folks were figuring I could just knock it off. But what I did was, I ended up with a studio major. It was art education. I had I think sixty, seventy hours of studio. And I didn't realize that. I was told after the fact that I was the first black to graduate with a studio major here at the university. My main area was sculpting. And I ended taking five hours of graduate sculpture. I was the sculptor in the school at the time. And I studied with one of the major metal sculptors, David Smith, when he was here. It was interesting.

I had a good experience, but it was a sheltered experience only because within the art school I lost my black identity, because I was treated as another artist. But on the other hand, I had no history, no study of blackness period. But my upbringing didn't beat blackness into me. But I understood I was black. And I understood that there were those situations. Like in town, at the time, at Nick's, the owners there wouldn't let anybody black in there.[16] And sometimes some of the students would go in, music and art students would go in and occupy the place on a Friday night and fill it up. And then when somebody, they'd have a black student come in about quarter of ten or something and when Nick refused to serve him then everybody would get up en masse and leave—leave the place empty. Those kind of little thing[s], you couldn't, I couldn't get my hair cut down here. I either had to have someone in the dorm do it, or I had to go to Indianapolis. Girls, black girls didn't get their hair done on campus.

So, when did you meet your wife?

Met my wife when I was five years old. And her father was a photographer in that, in that same area. I went up to get my picture taken when I was five years old for Easter, and little Joyce Watts was sitting there watching me, but we actually knew each other through grade school. She went to 87. I went to 87. So, I knew her there. We both went to Attucks. But we didn't really start dating until the fall of 1952, or spring of 1953.

Well, I saw her at a party in Indianapolis. I had known her and didn't know when she was coming down here [to Bloomington]. And what happened was as things would have it, I would come back here to visit here for activities and things, but when I went to school in '53, that fall of '53, her mother was sick so she had to come home. She went back to Indianapolis. And we both were not on campus until the fall of '54. And it's an interesting situation between families. Like I said, mine was a serendipity kind of a family. We would do things spontaneously. And maybe that was because Mother—the structure wasn't that tight.

Where I went to baseball games, my uncle would walk me past the Cotton Club down on Indiana Avenue, when we were walking through going to this house, where I was born. Her mother would have her go down to English Theater to listen to the opera and Marian Anderson. I'm watching the Indianapolis Clowns and the Monarchs coming in here. I saw Satchel Paige pitch and those folks.

Were the Clowns an important part of the culture in Indianapolis?

Oh, yes. Oh, heaven, at Victory Field it was called, that was black folks' day out. And you had . . . I'm try-

[16] Nick's is a Bloomington tavern.

ing to think if it was a Sunday or not. I can't think of a day of the week. But it wouldn't be a workday. It would either had to be a Saturday or Sunday. And, yes, the Kansas City Monarchs, the New York Black Bears . . . I was little when I was going. I mean, we're talking about early forties, late thirties. It would be before the war, before World War II.

You stayed teaching until you got [to] the point where you wanted to build the Flanner House home?

Well, that popped up—we were still living with my in-laws in their apartment, and a new project had just gone on the east side. They'd moved from the west side out on the east side, near Douglass Park.

Can you describe the process by which you had to interview or become a member?

Well, you had to interview, had to be married. Had to interview to get a feeling for your stability, for your income, and you didn't need a bunch of—only needed, they had $250 of good faith money, is what they called it. And actually the $250 was given back to you in some manner to help pay for the cost of the house.

And I believe Boulevard Place and Byrum, I want to say, was the area that opened up to black families on the north side. First time they'd been above Thirty-eighth Street. That was a big, a big deal.

That year was . . . ?

That year had to be 1950? Let's see, I'm trying to think, when they integrated Shortridge High, when they integrated the high schools. That had to be 1950.[17]

Cleo Blackburn was the executive director of Flanner House?

He was, yes. Even though there was probably somebody before him and has been somebody after him, his is the name that everybody knows.

So, you began the Flanner House project on the east side. What street was your home on?

Sangster.

Was the Flanner House Home Building Project a possibility for you to buy a house that you didn't have any other way to do it? For economic reasons? Or was it for availability reasons? Or credit lending?

It was economic. It was economic. Very much so. One, an opportunity to have a brand-new home. And I'm not certain what homes were going for, but I didn't have the down payment before then. And you had to have a down payment of substantial amount, which I didn't have. The opportunity to get into a brand-new home and that my working with that was going to help keep the price of the home down. We worked, we had a time card. And you punched the time card to keep up with the hours. A thousand, a thousand twenty hours was what the total was I believe for our group. I think that came up to a year and two weeks. And they checked the time card when the project was finished. If you had been remiss for some reason and didn't have your thousand twenty hours, your house sat there. And you couldn't move in until you worked with the next project and made enough hours to make up what you were supposed to have.

Actually, I was working at Govco [discount store] when I began.

This was before you became a teacher?

Yes, before I became a teacher which, which in a way was good because I worked at Govco from one to nine at night. So, I would go out and work on the house project, I'd go out at eight in the morning and work to noon. Then I would go over to my cousin's house and shower and change clothes and then go in to Govco. Then on my day off then I would work the whole eight or ten hours.

[17] The Indiana School Desegregation Act became law in 1949. Madison, *Indiana Way*, 244–45.

How long did you live in that home that you built? On Sangster.

As of right now, thirty-five years. I'm still there. I'm still there. I got $4,100 credit for my year's work and I got $4,900 credit because the first mortgage was $10,000.

Who would you go through for your mortgage?

Prudential.

Was it difficult then, was that prearranged?

That was prearranged.

So, everybody in your group went to Prudential, or was there a couple, or three or four different lenders?

Well, I think most of them did because the Prudential person came in and did a presentation. There were options, but it was simple, I mean it was there, and Prudential says, "OK."

Now, prior to that was it difficult for, for blacks to get mortgage loans for home building?

That I don't know. I really don't, although I do know that there was still some redlining going on in the late sixties because I changed companies. I wanted to have a local mortgage firm. Prudential was located in New Jersey. So, I wanted to have a local [one]. So I changed mortgage companies, refinanced, changed mortgage companies. I wanted to get some insurance, and the person at State Farm informed me that my house was too old for them to consider insuring.

What year was this?

This was in the late sixties. And I told the women, I said, "The house isn't but, what, nine years old, something like that." And I said, "I'm looking at new houses around [me]."

And they said, "No, we know that." So that was the redline thing.

So, I went to Allstate, called an Allstate person, and the person said, "Well, I'll come out and talk to you."

And he walked up the steps, and I said, "Well, do you want to, can I take you to see it?"

And he said, "I saw everything I needed to when I drove through the neighborhood." He says, "I don't understand what the other people did, but I'm glad they didn't because . . ."

Because they had a redline around the neighborhood. So, they weren't going to insure anything there.

They weren't going to come, they weren't even going to come out and look.

You grew up in a few neighborhoods, in a way.

Yes. But they were all in the same area.

Can you describe the change that took place in those neighborhoods?

Well, one thing of note here, segregation did something for me that integration is not doing for a number of black youth which is, we knew our restrictions. There's an illusion to inclusion right now. I tell the university students, some of the black students come up and ask me, you know, "What should we do?" And that—you have not arrived. We knew without saying, I knew where I could go and where I couldn't go. And I was loved where I did go, and I was looked after where I did go. And the teachers were teaching me, were preparing me for the situation I was going to be in. I knew that, and I was told that I had to do better than the other people to succeed. And I saw some of this, but with, with the infusion of integration—which is a plus, great opportunities—but you lose something, you gain something. You lose something like, they talk about getting Indiana Avenue back. Indiana Avenue's never going to be back.

My uncle was the one who told me that on Friday, and especially in the summertime, on Friday the men who worked would drive their cars, would come down and park on Indiana Avenue on Friday morning and take the streetcars to work. Then they'd go home from work and change clothes and take the streetcar back for Friday evening in their "shining goods." Because it was known that if you weren't on Indiana Avenue by seven o'clock, you couldn't get a parking space. So, they just left their cars there. They left the cars there.

I can remember the summertime on Sundays after church of going down there, like I said, towards the Walker Building, the ladies under the parasols and walking around . . .

Anne Malott began teaching in the 1950s at School 16, located in a white, working-class section of western Indianapolis called Stringtown.[18]

[18] Interviewed by Richard Phelps, 24 March 1976, at the Salvation Army Shack #2, Indianapolis.

If you can just sort of give the background information and your experience of Stringtown, what it was like when you first came and why you came here [to School 16]?

Malott: Well, one thing'll probably get edited from the tape, why I came here was because that was what I was offered. In those days you took what you were offered, because your starting pay was clear down around two thousand something in the fifties, 1950, and there was one teacher where the rest of my family went to school, School 66. She said, "Mrs. Malott, you're not going to let Anne start teaching over there, are you?" It was a lot larger enrollment, a lot more houses than there are now, less commercial. It's been twenty-five years, it's changed in a lot of ways.

The point we were speaking of a moment ago: we had an enrollment from south of Washington Street, east of White River, we went north of Michigan Street on Cable and a couple other old streets in there to the flour mill, which always put out the fragrance of roasted popcorn, and it's something all afternoon on a balmy

The Madame Walker Building on Indiana Avenue, 1940s
Indiana Historical Society,
Bass Photo Company Collection

spring day that drove everybody up the wall. I think that's one reason why the school itself started popping corn on Friday afternoons.

And at one time we even had movies to go along with it, after-school movies, fifteen-minute cartoons and so forth, motion picture distributors. That went over very well. Boys Club was here at that time, and no one liked to stay after school because then they didn't get over there. I said Boys Club, and that's what it was. The girls had nothing to do, so the girls had no way—just like you had big brothers and so forth to get help from for specific boys, but you never had anyone to get a little help for some of the girls; and they needed it just as much if not more in some cases.

We had gypsy families; we had no Negroes at all at that time. If you want to get into that part of it, the racial part, we had one family move in on the south side of Michigan Street in the old office building. It was sort of a house and coal yard where the Dairy Queen did well, and so forth. It had been a coal yard–lumber yard combination.

The caretaker or the resident guard for that property moved in and sent his little girl to school. It's a shame. Her name wasn't Betty or something, it was a very unusual name, and the kids gave her a pretty rough time until they realized she wasn't going to leave. And she was intelligent too, didn't pay any attention to the rest of us, so it wasn't very long before she was right in with the rest.

And then, as IU expanded and bought properties on the east part of the river, the enrollment of blacks increased. And I think it went probably smoother than any place else. I know it went as smooth or smoother than the busing that has gone on over at [School] 52 the last three years. I'd say smoother than that because we didn't have windows broken out at Halloween or anything else. It was just great. Had a good group come in and the ones who weren't were soon set straight by their own people. And like I said, Friday afternoon popcorn and movies and ball games, there's a general acceptance.

And that was just natural and normal, and that was the way it was supposed to be. There were one or two families—now that was east of the river, they came from east of the river. So as long as they lived there that was fine.

I think one or two families tried to move in, and I say tried moving in. They moved in but they didn't stay, right in what you'd have to call the heart of Stringtown, right there on New York Street. Across the street from the Sycamore Two House, which was built by the Baptist church for retarded children, a family had their windows knocked out and all that sort of thing.

The Baptist kids, that is the children who were in that home supported by the Baptists—they weren't all Baptists renting the house—but they had a pretty rough time for a while, just outside of school in the community was all. Inside of school they were going to classes for special ed at [School] 16. I don't know that they had specific problems other than the fact that children there at the home had more than the ones that were living out of the neighborhood, and they were under all sorts of supervision.

Stringtowners are like a large family. It takes twenty-five years to be accepted as one if you don't live here and haven't for a while. I think I told you the other day that I felt safer around here than I do in the apartment complex I moved into this year. They know you like brothers and sisters. They'll feud among themselves.

This tendency to stick together, is it the same as it was when you first came?

I think so, yes. There are some splits, but generally, any stranger'll walk in and start something, well, the whole gang'll get together and finish it, whether it would be in the school or just in the general area. There are still no Negroes living here. That part's held up. And I rather imagine that if someone moved in that they'd get the same treatment even though they're used to having blacks in school. I don't know if they would accept them now. But that's a real strong point which . . . it'll take a long time to get rid of, and that's probably the one major complaint that I hear the children who are over at 52.

You know, they come to me, "Miss Malott, so and so's bothering me and I'm going to get that so and so and take the whole gang with me." But once they talk it out nowadays, they're okay. They come home, and they don't have any further contact outside of school in most cases, unless they get on a ball team or something like that. There's no further contact. And that goes with other children too; it's still not necessarily an isolated area, but it's still a small—naive, really—community that has not expanded.

I bet there isn't a newspaper boy in the whole Stringtown. They don't communicate on a city or national or any other kind of level unless something that directly applies to them. Now they know more about welfare than I do. They're probably the people that are on welfare rolls, or at least in some families. And they know more about specific interests, like there's one group that's rabid wrestling fans even though they will admit that the whole thing's a big act and faked and so forth and so on. There's this group here that will spend every cent they've got getting down to the wrestling matches.

The boys here at the club, and the girls now too, since the [Salvation Army] Shack has this and they take boys and girls to go to Pacer games and things like that. But they haven't latched on to any one particular person since Buckshot O'Brien and that was back in the forties. But you ask the ball players and they remember Buckshot O'Brien who went to School 16. He got to be quite a well-known basketball player through Butler University and made a trip over to the national invitation tournament or something like that—real little guy that was a sharpshooter. He's an insurance man here in town now.[19]

And it kept a certain standard all the way along the line. There are families who still live here where most of the children have gone away and gotten out, but not all of them. And they don't particularly consider the ones that have gotten out having gotten out of here. They usually are clear out of town. One fellow who went to School 16, graduated in about 1953 or '4 and went on to Washington High School and Indiana Central, got to be the director of Boys Clubs for Indianapolis, and he started out working over here. Now he's in the national end of it some way or other and got another job in Atlanta, Georgia.

[19] Ralph "Buckshot" O'Brien played basketball for Butler University and later for the Fort Wayne Pistons of the onetime National Basketball League. Martin Lauder, "Sports News: Indiana," in Lexis-Nexis database, 17 May 1981, available from web.lexis-nexis.com.

School 16 in Stringtown
Indiana Historical Society,
Bass Photo Company Collection, 32818

How about the change that took place with the Boys Club closing, the School 16 then closing, and the Salvation Army Shack then sort of taking over? In these years of transition, what were the effects?

I think Stringtown shall overcome anything, or mold it to shape its own. They fought the closing of the Boys Club here through two or three years, and two or three years of fighting the closing the school. Actually, they knew all the time that it was going to have to happen. The enrollment had dropped from somewhere between six and eight hundred most of the time down to . . . leveled off around four hundred something, then it leveled off to another hundred lower as different things cut into the school district. They went from eight grades with twenty-some-odd teachers down to eight grades with only five teachers for the eight grades, plus a couple of special teachers.

Parents were saying that they wanted their children to go to school there even if they turned most of the rooms into the disciplinary boys' classes from all over town. "Let them bus somebody else in here, we don't want to go away from here." They still ask, every time you see someone, "When are they going to open School 16? What are they going to do with School 16? When are they going to open it? When do we get to go back to School 16?" And in three years, the children who have been going over to 50 and 30 and 52—were the three schools that took all the ones—everyone asks. They really haven't given up, they're tenacious, they want it to be open.[20]

But they quit on it early, and there again, it was just because there wasn't people that they knew and they find it hard to adjust to changes. Changes have to be gradual. I think the fact that it was under discussion for three or four years and we kept giving them the information, "The school was going to close, maybe not this year but next year, maybe not next year but the year after, it's going to come and there's no way we're going to be able to do anything about it," was what finally got them around to not pulling some of the things that have been pulled in such circumstances, any violence or anything like that.

We had a meeting up in the auditorium one evening in which the parents and some of the school board members were there, and there were parents that came a little fortified and had a few cuss words around and some crying and yelling and screaming and things like that. They can't accept, just don't want to.

In Stringtown . . . now, they protect each other. I think everyone down here now has—if they don't own one, they have access to one, or the one next door's turned up loud enough that they can hear it—police radios.

I thought you were going to say that.

Yes. Everyone has police radios. And another thing comes to mind on that, they use their judgment, each individual family and so forth, if they hear something on a police radio and they want to protect somebody, they'll let them know about it or make sure they heard it themselves. If they don't, they just sort of, you know, sit back and wait and watch.

And they differentiate between a lot of things: the children at a particular age know all the words in the book, three-letter ones and four-letter ones, the whole works. Once in a while, they'd appear on the school and they'd have to be scrubbed off, you know. But you didn't hear within the school or within the club any of that language. You don't hear very much of it around here now ever, although I think there's more of it around here now than—I never heard anyone cuss in the Boys Club.

But you could be on the playground the middle of the afternoon and someone would holler out the front door or be on the porch yelling to one of their kids, and use some of the language that you hear all over Stringtown, to get it in the house right now. The first time that was a shocker. And that was one thing that changed. If you had to complain about a child using bad language in a classroom or something, there were no questions from the parents. The kid got his mouth washed out with soap, or whatever discipline they were going to use they used.

You speak as if there have always been the same people here. Is that true?

[20] As White River State Park and the Indianapolis Zoo expanded in the 1980s, Stringtown's population and area were reduced even further. Cathleen F. Donnelly, "Stringtown," in Bodenhamer and Barrows, eds., *Encyclopedia of Indianapolis*, 1306.

To a very great extent, to a very great extent. In the hard-core Stringtown group, it's three, four generations that I know of. . . . There are families here who have been on welfare or relief or whatever you want to call it since the thirties in the alphabetical groups, WPA, CCC, and so forth. I don't recall those experiences. But I know of at least two families who have never been off the welfare. I think I made mention of the Dirty Dozen; that's one of them. Then the rest of the neighborhood includes them in everything else. If it's for free, they're included.

How did this transition from rentals to one owner take place? It's something I've never heard before.

It's something you've never heard of before? Well, you get someone who's happy here or something like that and they'll buy the property. They aren't stupid. They can anticipate that IU or someone is going to come in here, they [know] perhaps that the metropolitan development downtown is going to move west of the river for housing. And right now I'd say that anybody that does own here is going to hang onto it. But the ones with the fences, the grass cut, or grass period, have had one or more generations of TLC and they're the ones that have been here for several generations in most cases. Even if they own not only the place they're in, but the one next door and two or three others, you wouldn't recognize the rental property from the home-owned.

They trust people too much at times, and maybe I'm beginning to distrust, I don't know. They didn't follow; they do more now. Again, I think it's television. They didn't follow fashion trends or keep up with the usual things. They were completely overwhelmed when they went to high school.

You had an eighth grade graduation that was more of a ceremony probably, or as much of or more of a ceremony as the actual high school commencement, because in a great number of cases it was terminal education for them. They didn't attend more than a year or two of high school, and for economic reasons generally and sometimes physical reasons: they were grown-ups.

Except for the outstanding few, Hoagy Carmichael—they know that he went to school there, but it doesn't mean a darn thing to them. You get to Buckshot O'Brien—who means a little bit more. You get to Kenny Knox, Butch Knox who was the director over here and so forth, and that means a whole lot. You get on to some of the last graduates, there was one or two who've gotten into one of the fast food service deals farther west, and they've made it big and the whole neighborhood knows it. And they go out there and patronize them when they get a chance, hoping they'll get a discount.

Some of the older folks think that, "OK, there's been a great increase in crime and kids are just not handled anymore, there's very little discipline, lot less discipline than there used to be and. . . ."

They blame the Boys Club and the school closing and so forth. I can see where they blame it on those two particular incidents because they think that if they could have kept it together then nothing would have changed. But it would have changed, there's no way that it continues. Otherwise, instead of a lower enrollment at school we'd have a whopping big enrollment and, you know, if they had kept increasing their number right here and not leaving and coming back. The little ones that they're complaining about now, see, the elementary kids and the high school kids now, today, are sassing these older people, which they didn't used to get. They don't remember that their parents were sassed by their children.

Well, how about the type of people that make up Stringtown? I've heard it both ways that, "Oh boy, these are the same old families that have been here forever." I've heard it another way, "Oh well, more outsiders now than there used to be are coming in more often."

The people moving in and out are coming from—oh, what did I hear the phrase used the other night—it was "White Appalachian." You couldn't have said that about Stringtown twenty-five years ago. Twenty years ago or maybe only fifteen some families moved in and a few of them stayed and stayed long, and still live here now, who came from—I'm thinking of one particular family who came from Kentucky someplace and were thought to be foreigners because they said, "snike" instead of "snake," and used phrases like "tote" for "carry" which are more of the southern colloquialisms.

But there are a few families who are sort of isolated in the area. There are others that come and go. In the last—well, I'd say since the Korean War, since the fifties, there have been some and we'd almost count on them. They would come in when schools started in Kentucky, and this would be as high as, oh, thirty-five or forty, maybe fifty children, which would represent ten, fifteen families. Some of them just had one or two and someone else may have eight, all going to the elementary school. They'd come in when school started in Kentucky, which wasn't until mid-October and they would leave early for Christmas vacation and come back late from Christmas vacation and leave early before Memorial Day when school was out in Kentucky. And they came up here to work in the winter, and they went down there for the summers. Not all the family went all the time, and usually they maintained some type of a residence here, as well as down there. They had someplace to go to.

But you had a few transients of the type that had one or two children, and they worked at not transient-type jobs, but changeable-type jobs in bars and restaurants and things like that. And they might move close to their work. They'd come in if they were working at one of the taverns along Washington Street, or working over at the IU Medical Center, and then when they started working in St. Vincent's, they'd move over that way or they worked out at Community for a while.

And how about the community? How has it changed?

The community and the attitudes and things I think are generally mostly the same. I don't think it's basically changed any more so than any other area. All church attendance is off. You'd come around here on Sunday morning and you'd hear—and Wednesday nights—and people went to church. You didn't plan a PTA meeting after one of the churches was having Wednesday night prayer meetings or something like that, if you wanted anybody to attend, because they'd go there first. You had notices you sent out and sometimes church would change their meeting nights. If it were something special like the Christmas program or anything like that, well, they'd change it.

We had things in the daytime instead of evening, but you try to have at least three or four times a year during the evening to get fathers in here. But like every place else, it's hard to get dads to come to anything. They'd get home, they want to take their shoes off, open up a can of beer or whatever and enjoy whatever recreation they're going to have that evening or they'd finish up whatever jobs they've got.

How about the clannishness of the families?

There's a lot of intermarriage, brothers married to sisters, cousins to cousins. There's even one rumor around about one set of grandparents here are brother and sister; that's one of the case studies that's down at IU, which is more than a rumor because it comes from people in the family. . . .

Like I said, they chased one family out. They broke every window in that one house over there when the black family moved in. I don't know how long they lasted, but it wasn't very long. 'Course, at the time we had other blacks in school, and one boy in that family in particular really showed himself off the first day in school, and that could have helped lose his family the house.

What did he do?

New kids always get tested out, and he wasn't about to be tested, and anything anybody else said, he'd top. Anything anybody else did he was going to top that too. And he came up with a few ideas of his own, and he had fight after fight. It didn't take it more than a couple of days to start getting serious and draw blood. . . .

If I remember correctly, he had a couple of sisters in lower grades that were having no problems. But in the school he was the problem, and they caught him at home; they left. That's the one real hard-core fact, and it's no different again from other areas within Indianapolis or all over the country. Certain groups of people won't accept others, until they have to. And at that time it would have been a good chance for someone to make it, except for the one boy in the family who was a junior high show-off.

Anderson

Anderson

Four residents of Anderson reconstruct the world of autoworkers and the struggle to achieve a union in the late 1930s. They offer eyewitness accounts of the Anderson sit-down strike of 1936–37 and of life inside and outside the General Motors plants. The strike was an opportunity to employ communal ties to demand fair treatment. Naomi Wilson describes how women cooked meals for the men as they took over the plant. These people also explicitly compare the past and the present and argue that the generation that has followed them in Anderson and at General Motors does not realize how they struggled and how good the working conditions are now. For a man like Joe Wilson, born in 1911, the movement from the past to the present has been filled with irony. He notes that people had little material advantages in the past, but they were "happy." In our times he feels that individuals have finally acquired more goods but seem less content with their lives.

Naomi J. Wilson worked at the Guide Lamp Division of General Motors in Anderson for almost thirty-five years. She was born in 1917.[1]

When and why did you come to Anderson?

Wilson: I came when I was about sixteen years old. Well, I thought I could make a little more money doing housework and taking care of children here. And I had a cousin that—I worked for her for a while. She had one little boy, and she worked at Delco Remy and he worked at Guide Lamp. He was one of the original sit-downers, too—Paul Holland.

I lived in the YWCA. And I put my sister through high school. She was five years younger than I am, and I was bound and determined that she was going to have an education and put her through high school. And the last year that she was in high school, my father passed away. There, again, there was no insurance or nothing. My oldest brother and I took care of the funeral bill, and my sister graduated. So, she got her education.

My other brother was married and had a family, and financially he was having a rough way himself then. So, my oldest brother wasn't married right at that time. He married later on. So, we took care of everything. And we took care of my mom from then on—both of us did.

When you were growing up and living in Ohio, living with your parents, did both your mother and father work?

Mother never did work. She was just a mother and a housewife. And my dad did odd jobs. I mean, he was a farmer and then during the wintertime, why, he'd clear off along the river to make extra money—trees and things like that, you know—to make a little extra money. It was rough then, but we had a lot of love and plenty to eat. We never did go to bed hungry. It wasn't fancy, but we had plenty to eat all the time. Of course, mother canned everything that she could can. We didn't have a lot of meat, but we had a lot of vegetables and, of course, Mom was a wonderful cook. She could just take two potatoes and make a meal out of it for seven of us. But we had love, and that was something.

How far along in education did you get? To what grade?

Eighth grade. I was raised during the depression, and I quit to go to work. I did housework and took care of children over in Ohio, but I couldn't make the money there that I could from back down here—could make in Anderson, because most of them were just farmers or something like that, you know. So, I decided that I was going to come to Anderson.

Back then, they didn't think anything about it. Education wasn't like it is now. Really, there wasn't anything ever said about it, because I knew I couldn't go on and, of course, my sister was coming on and I wanted to see that she got an education, so I quit. And, like I say, there's a lot of people that's probably got a lot better education than I have, but I'll put my years of hard knocks and knowing how to save and how to get by.

My dream was to be a nurse. And, there again, I was pushing my dream, and I wanted her to take up nursing. At that time it was a wonderful career. And I got her all the way over to Ball Hospital over at Muncie and was ready to enroll her, and she could have went ahead with it. And she, evidently, talked to the head supervisor there, and she called me in and she said, "I want to ask you," she said, "is this your dream, or is it your sister's?"

And I said, "Well, I wanted my sister to have that. *I* wanted it."

"Well," she said, "your sister don't want it."

So, that was—right then I said, "OK," because it wasn't no use to going with it if she wasn't going to be happy in it, which she wouldn't have been.

Did you have children of your own?

No. Joe and I married late in life. I was forty-three when Joe and I married, and it was two years after my mother passed away. And we've had a wonderful life. We've been married, well, a little over twenty years. And, there again, as I said, neither one of us has a real good education, but we come up the hard way. We wanted to have everything paid for before we retired.

[1] Interviewed by Karen L. Gatz, 19 February 1982, Anderson.

We don't own a fancy home, but it's a comfortable home. And everything was paid for, and the only thing we owe is our utilities and the taxes on the property. We did not owe one debt.

When did you first start working at Guide Lamp?

At Guide Lamp, when I first started, I started on the assembly line. And, of course, there wasn't any union then. And they had a point system, and I can remember us girls just working so hard, because if you made points you got a little bit more money. I think—I think my first paycheck was $19.00 for two weeks, and I felt that was something wonderful, because I'd been working for $2.50 a week. And we worked like the dickens, and we got our points. We made points.

But—and if you made over that—whatever they had for points—well, then maybe you got paid a little bit more. Until the foreman come along and took our points away from us and give them to the line next to us because they was way in the red over there, so we didn't get any. Now, those are some of the things. And then, also, you didn't have any choice of working nights or days. Now, I worked nights, but if they decided they would need me in at seven o'clock in the morning, I'd go home at midnight, they'd say, "Well, you be back in here at Monday morning—I mean in the morning at seven o'clock," well, I had to be.

So, now, they've got a choice, see. And there's seniority. Then, there wasn't anything like seniority. And this one foreman that we worked for was quite a ladies' man, and he had favorites on the line. Well, a year after the union got in, he committed suicide. But anyhow, he was a—he was a son of a gun to work for. And you had to work hard, and you—there just wasn't nobody looking up or anything hardly at all because he was just right there all of the time, see?

Guide Lamp, 1936
Anderson Public Library, Frank Baker, photographer

In the days right before the sit-down strike, or the time leading up to it, do you remember there being a lot of concern about having to work too fast, things being speeded up, and this being a real problem for workers? Was that one of the reasons that people might have supported having a union?

One thing, and then another thing was getting seniority, where you didn't get laid off. You know, they'd come along and lay off whoever they wanted to. They'd keep—if he got favoritism, he'd keep her, lay her off. Maybe she'd been here quite a while longer than she had. See, the union stopped that. And then shift preferences. That was another thing. They could put you on, like I said, on nights or on days, whichever one you wanted to do. Well, when the union came along, the youngest one was the one that was on nights, unless somebody older wanted to go on nights. There's a lot of older people didn't want to work days. They preferred nights. I worked nights for a long time. In fact, when I came on days—to stay on days—was Pearl Harbor. Before that we worked nights.

Did you have a vacation?

No vacations. Didn't know what that was. And no paid holidays. Didn't know what that was. If you got off Christmas, you just was off, period. And we—I think when I first started there we had an hour lunch, and then shortly after that it was cut down to a half hour, and that's all I ever did get was a half hour.

Even after the union came in you still had a half hour?

Yes, even after that. Yes. And on your relief, well, you just got so many minutes. You'd have to go to the rest room and back. Before the union. And then the union didn't exactly say fifteen minutes, it said personal need, but we got fifteen minutes. So, that helped.

Did your conception of work change, or the reason that you were there change over any period of time?

Guide Lamp, ca. 1970
Anderson Public Library, Norm Cook, photographer

I, myself, got personal satisfaction out of it, because there were things I could do that I couldn't do before like, as I said, put my sister through school, and I took care of my mother, and I can remember back when we were growing up we didn't have a lot of clothes. You had what you went to school in, and when you come home you took that off and put on something that wasn't so good. But it just isn't like clothes we have now. And I wanted my mother to have a nice wardrobe, and I saw that she did have. So, I did a lot of things for my mom, and I got a lot of satisfaction out of that. And, of course, for years, because they didn't have money for a car, I'd ride the bus from here to Portland, Indiana, and then my brother would pick me up in Portland, which is about fourteen miles, and that's the way I got on home. Then he'd take me back on Sunday night, then I'd catch a bus back Sunday evening to go back to work Monday morning. Didn't have a car. So, I can say that I got a lot of satisfaction out of my job. And, as I said, today we've got a nice life, Joe and I have. We can do things that we always wanted to do but we couldn't do before, because he took care of his mother.

Do you remember when the strike was called and when the shop was closed down?

Well, I was working—of course, it's not there now, but it was an upstairs at Guide, where—we called it "the balcony," and they had an assembly line up there, and I was on this assembly line. And I had heard that there was going—they were going to or they were thinking about it, you know, but it wasn't anything for sure. And we was all working on the assembly line.

And, again, Ed Hutchley, who is dead and gone—of course, I was young, inexperienced young girl back then, and I looked up and saw him coming upstairs to shut the power off, and I thought that was the biggest man I ever saw in my life. And he was. Ed was a big man. A good guy, though. Ed—he made foreman out at Guide—who, as I say, is dead now. But he was a good one, a good guy. Now, he shut the power off.

And this foreman that we was working for—I told you that committed suicide two years after the union—he turned it back on. And he had a—Joe [Wilson] can tell you what it was—anyhow, some kind of an iron rod, and he told him, he said, "You turn that back on one more time, and you won't be able to turn it on again." And he didn't. And, of course, at that time I didn't know Ed like I—of course, Ed's gone now—like I knew Ed now. And I thought that—it was frightening in a way, in another way. They said, "Get up and leave your job and leave," which we did.[2]

Had you wanted to stay in the plant and be a sit-downer?

Back then there wasn't anything like women lib at all then, see. Women—they just didn't do that. Let's put it that way. Not like now. It was a man's job, and men took over. And the women were on the outside. Well, somebody had to take care of the kitchens and make coffee. Of course, we had so much food donated to us, you know, at that time.

Was it a big step for you to support the sit-downers?

I knew that it was going to be better for us in the long run, and we had more to gain than we ever had to lose by it. And, it's just like I said, it gave you a little bit of a choice, too. And, of course, now they've got it a lot better than we had it when we first started. You could work nights if you wanted to, or you could work days, according to your seniority. And, instead of coming along and saying, "Well, I want her job," and just up and give it to you. Well, that didn't happen anymore. So, the union was, to me, it was just wonderful and all.

Back in '36 and '37, you supported the sit-downers, you went to work making food for them. Where was the food prepared?

We had a kitchen, and this—it was on Twenty-fifth Street—and this man owned a restaurant at the time, and he just turned the restaurant over to us. And, of course, as I said, about all we had then was coffee and

[2] For a short history of the sit-down strike at GM's Guide Lamp Division, which lasted from 31 December 1936 to 16 January 1937, see Claude E. Hoffman, *Sit-Down in Anderson: UAW Local 663, Anderson, Indiana* (Detroit: Wayne State University Press, 1968).

soup. Just couldn't afford anything else. People would maybe bring a soup bone or something like that, you know, and we'd make great big pots of soup or chili. . . .

Did most of the workers themselves support the sit-down strike?

Of course, there's a lot of them that didn't want to join the union. I know that. A lot of them didn't want to put out the money for it. And they didn't realize, though, just like before, see, we never had vacation, and they come along—first, we had one week, then we got two, and I think it's three weeks now that they get. And, see, we never had anything like that. And then we come along with paid holidays, and then they got where—like you was off on Christmas or Thanksgiving, well then they made you work the day before or—and the day after, if it was working day.

When you left, the union and GM were still very prosperous and didn't really have a lot of problems of unemployment. How did people in general, younger workers, feel about the union in say the late sixties or early seventies when you were getting ready to retire? Were they very supportive and did they—were they willing to partake in, say, union meetings and activities?

UAW Local 663 sign, 1998
Tim Borden

Some of them, not all of them. Of course, it's—there again, this is a whole new generation. You take most of them that's working out there, they've never known what a depression was. They grew up with plenty, because nine times out of ten one of them works at Delco and the other one at Guide—father and mother, see—so, they've always had plenty. And they've never known, really known, what a depression is—recession, whatever you want to call this now—and it is a big adjustment for them.

Did you ever take grievances to the union about discrimination? A woman wanting to go into a job and not being hired?

No, because there was a lot of jobs that I knew that I couldn't do. And if I was going to be classified with the men, you would have to do those jobs. Just like one time two or three of the girls that I knew real well decided they wanted to come in and they're—they was going to knock three men out of work on Saturday, and their job was to clean these tanks—big, very big acid tanks. Well, they come in, and they made them put coveralls [on] and they made them go do it. Well, that was the last—that was the end of that. There wasn't any more women wanting to hold that job, see. So, I never wanted to because I just felt that I wasn't—I didn't want to be classified as a man. I was—I had my job there, and that was it.

So, there seemed to be a real cohesion among you?

Most of us. Yes. Now, we got where—when I worked on assembly line, we'd celebrate everybody's birthday just one day out of the month. We didn't celebrate each one's birthday. And we'd bake cakes and bring them in, you know, bologna and cheese and crackers, things like that, just that one day out of the month, and that was everybody's birthday. We'd take a big cardboard and put everybody's name on it that had a birthday that month. So, we—you know, we—it broke the monotony of things. And if anybody had trouble, you know, like maybe a wreck or something like that, or an operation, we'd all send get-well cards to him, and it—we had a nice friendship down there.

When I went—when this mirror line went down and I went over to glass units, that was the worst place

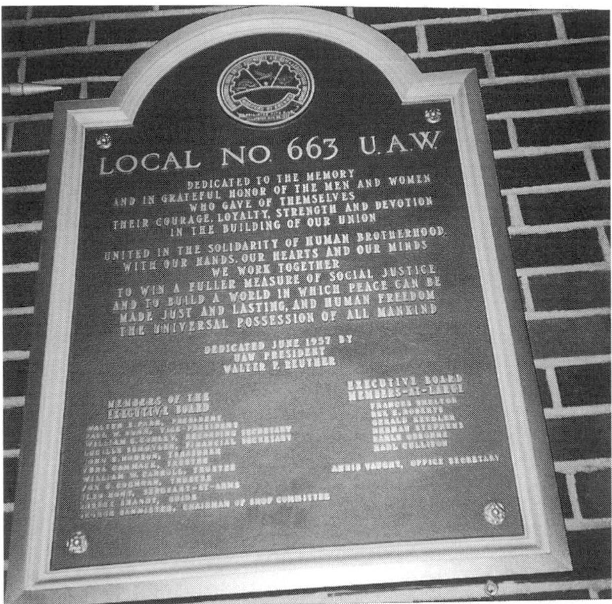

UAW Local 663 dedication plaque
Tim Borden

I ever worked at. It was cutthroat, cutthroat over there. They—some of those girls had never worked anyplace else but back there. See, I'd been all over Guide at that time. Not now, but at one time I had—see, as I said, when we got ready to be laid off, we would start from the press department and you just kept on going back, and I would end up back in service shipping and then be laid off then for about three months. So, I had at one time worked in just about every department there was out there. You would, as the work began to slack up here, maybe on down it was working, then you'd go there and work, and just keep on going, and then you'd finally get laid off. So, when I went back to service shipping, I mean, where I retired from, most of those girls back there had never worked anyplace but there. And they just resented anybody coming in with seniority more than they had.

Born in 1911, Joseph R. Wilson started working at the Guide Lamp plant in September 1935 and retired in 1971.[3]

Why did your family come up here to Anderson from Kentucky?

[3] Interviewed by Greer Warren, 19 February and 19 March 1982, Anderson.

Wilson: There wasn't no work down there, and strawberries and tobacco is your main crops down there. And they wasn't bringing anything. You'd starve to death on a farm down there—about a few miles out of Bowling Green, where I was born—Warren County, Kentucky. Oakland is the county seat of it.

My dad came up here first, see. Him and about four or five others. He had an old Model T touring car. And they heard that Indiana—Anderson, Indiana, was hiring people, which we had a bunch of little factories here and they were. And he came up here and then got a job and then when he got enough money ahead that he could have us to come up on the train, we came on the train up here, see. My sister, me, and my brother, and a baby brother, in arms, see. We rode the train up here. My mother did by herself. And she'd never been in anything like that. My mother was a person that didn't like to go.

And we come up here and moved on Cedar Street, which is colored now . . . lived there for quite a few years, and he finally sold the house. Then we moved right across from Anderson High School on Lincoln Street. Lived there for awhile. And the guy that owned that decided to make apartments out of it. And he wanted us to move in one section of it while he made apartments, then move up.

And Dad went, said he didn't want no part of that. And so we moved down on Ninth Street, there in that old shack down there that you could see out the walls anyway you looked. And about froze to death, and the water would freeze up every winter. Then we finally moved to Central Avenue, then moved back to Sheridan Street after we left Central Avenue—the water froze up on it, and you didn't have no bathroom in the wintertime.

Then we moved down on 1100 Sheridan Street. My mother lived [there], and we lived there for forty-four years when I take my mother out of there. And that killed her. Of course she was ninety-some-odd years old. But she couldn't leave that old house, see. My dad died while we was there.

Lost my sister on Central Avenue. She worked at Delco Remy. And she worked on a little switch that they dipped in oil, but they didn't have nothing to pull the fumes away and she breathed that and they said it was TB that she had and she was just poisoned from that. And she died.

Shift change at Delco Remy, Anderson, ca. 1948
Anderson Public Library, Norm Cook, photographer

Now I've just got one brother left. My youngest brother died of a massive head stroke. He had had headaches all of his life, and nobody then knowed what it was. And a blood vein busted in his head. It was balloon—what they call ballooning up, and then he'd have headaches and he didn't know what he was doing when he had those. I mean, they had them headaches. There was nothing . . . no pain killer would do it, see. He was working in the job shop over in Muncie. And I think they took him to the hospital and x-rayed it and seen what it was.

But then I talked to him—another doctor, well, a friend of mine talked to him and he said, "Yes, from the neck up when we operate like that it's not too positive. If you got one that's in the body we can do it without any problem. But when you go up in that head, you can either [become] an idiot or a violent person, see. So it's one that we will do if the people will agree to it." But he said, "We just don't like to do it," because it's too much. . . . So eventually you're going to die anyway so you don't make too much difference.

Where did your father work when you came up here?

Well, he worked at a box factory, Midwest. He worked for American Steel and Wire. Worked at Hayes Wheel, made wheels. But all them factories folded up, see. Then we worked for . . . about five summers with the Central Indiana Gas Company working on main lines, putting in main lines. We serviced all these little towns around here and put in lines in this town, see, main lines. Then we had a big gas plant out here, which we don't have now. But all them little places, all except Container, has folded up. They ain't here anymore, see.

How old were you when you started working?

I worked all my life. I worked while I was out of school. I went to work at the gas company. I was only sixteen, but I went up and got the working permit and took ink remover—they didn't type stuff out like that.

Tract housing, probably southeast side of Anderson, 1920s
Anderson Public Library, Norm Cook, photographer

Meridian Street, Anderson, 1930s
Anderson Public Library, Norm Cook, photographer

I went and took the ink remover and had somebody else to put in my age as eighteen. I carried water the first year for them. That was two dollars a day for ten hours a day, six days a week. And I could get four dollars a day for working as a man, see. I was big enough to work for a man. One of the foremans told my dad, said, "Why don't you put that boy on as a man down there? They make four dollars a day." That's four dollars a day. Four dollars that we was going to be carrying home a day, see. It got us out of debt real quick.

Did you graduate from high school then?

I was going to junior high school, was in the eighth grade. My dad, trying to get a job, walked and walked and sit and cried at night because he couldn't feed us. So I told him, I said, "Well, in the morning, I ain't going to school. I'm going to see if I can get a job too." Because if *one of everyone* could get a job, could feed the family, see.

So I went . . . we went down to Container. They weren't hiring anybody. We had the tile shop, went out there. On the way out there we stopped at this Leval Foundry down where the high school was. I got a job working for the yard gang down there.

I'd been working before that at odd jobs, any kind of jobs I could get. I worked at Wellington Mill. I dug basements with a team of horses, a pick, and [a] shovel.

What was your parents' attitude about education? Did they want you to continue to go to school?

They did, but how can you do it when times is tough? It would just be like you, if you didn't have some way of getting money, how could you go to college? You've got to have some money there someplace or another that you can go with and be able to not have to work. If you have to work in that college and try to keep up your subjects, hey, you're going to get in trouble. You can do a small job here and there, but after I got out, why there was no sense in me going back, see. Because it was still the same tough time, see. Times are as good now. You're looking at good times. I looked at it when it was bad, real bad.

Did you ever feel like your parents wanted something for you, something better than what they had?

No, because we wasn't brought up that way. We were brought up that we had to work for a living. And I've done it all my life.

When did you start working at Guide Lamp?

September in '35.

What did you do with your wages when you were still a single person?

Blowed them. I've been around. I had nobody to worry about. When my dad died then I give my mother money to keep the place going. Sometimes I was there, and sometimes I wasn't there. I just done anything that I wanted to do. Which wasn't good, but then that's the way I seen it then, and I had a lot [of] fun then. All the things I've ever done in my life I had a lot of fun at. I don't regret them, some of them I shouldn't have done. But I done them. And you can't recall the past.

I used to drink, heavens. Drank a quart of whiskey every day for about fifteen years, seven days a week. And plus what I drank in the tavern with other people, see. My dad didn't say anything. My mom raised hell about it. My dad said, "Well, I ain't going to tell him. He'll know when it's time to quit."

I was already up in my forties. I got started drinking when I was in my late twenties. But I got a lot of fun out of it. It costs a lot of money. I spent a fortune on it. I made big money for a while in gambling.

When you started working at Guide Lamp, what did you expect from there? Did you expect personal satisfaction or was it just a way to make money to support the family?

It was a way to make money. Didn't really want to go. In fact, I didn't like factories. I worked for the *Anderson Post* in advertisement. And when I had to go in the shop and build that lattice work that goes between them billboards it'd bug the hell out of me. I didn't like it. When I was out there digging holes and putting up them billboards, which was a lot of them at that time—a Jew from Chicago come down and bought it—I enjoyed that kind of work. I enjoyed working for the gas company with a pick and a shovel. I worked a lot, a lot of little jobs like that, but they didn't last long, see. I worked for Bell Telephone one summer. They was putting the tile underground, and I was in ditch grating. I could sit and look down a ditch and tell you where every hump was in it, see. And I was traveling along behind that old boy, was in the southern part of the state, working with a little old short guy. But gruffer than the devil.

When you started at Guide, what job did you do?

Buffer. That was your main thing at Guide Lamp, at that time, was buffer. There was the majority of the people there were buffers. Because the die-cast parts was shipped in. We had no die-cast department. It was small place. Oh, my God Almighty, it wasn't nothing out there. Hell, you could walk all to one end in five minutes. And I got back there in that bumper guards, and boy, that's the worst job I've ever gotten into.

The fumes, oh my God. I eat enough grit for ten people. Your blowers didn't work, see, they had blowers but they weren't powerful enough to suck the stuff up the pipes and take them out to the silos where they was supposed to go. They just wasn't powerful enough blowers. It was too small to do the job that they were put in there for. This is what we argued, and that's what we finally eliminated.

It's not too bad out there now. There's a lot [of] fumes, yes. But when I went there, oh my God. Come down the damn aisle with a bucket of water with oatmeal in it that—you couldn't drink the water. If you did, got sick at your stomach. I didn't drink no water. I just quit. Absolutely that made me sick, so I said, "Well, if I'm going to get sick drinking water I'll go to the drinking fountain." And it was as hot as it was running out of a tap that you take a bath out of. And I'd get my mouth full of water and rinse my mouth out and that's all I'd drink until I got home. Well, when I got home I sure give the water the devil and I'd drink seven, eight glasses of water.

My mother'd say, "Why do you drink so much water?"

I'd say, "I'm thirsty."

"Don't they have water out there?"

I'd say, "Yep, but you can't drink it. It ain't fit to drink, see."

How did you get into the union? Did someone come and approach you?

Yes. Somebody figured that you was honest and wouldn't turn them in as talking to you about joining the union. They come and asked you how you felt about the union. I don't know nothing about the union so I asked one guy, "What do you mean, union?" I said, "I don't know what the hell you're talking about," see.

So he told me, "We're going to group together and we're going to try to form a union here so that we will have some say-so over what's happening to us."

We didn't have no say-so over it at all. Because they tell you you've got to run so many parts an hour and tomorrow you'd come in, they'd add fifty or sixty more parts on it. You thought you was going as hard as you could go here, see. And if you didn't make it, you went out the door, see. You had no security of a job at all.

And I had just went in there in '35, see. So, it was—you had no security of your job. If you was twenty years, and they decide they wanted to hire me off the street and give me your job, that was it. You had no way of keeping them from doing it, see. This is what they explained to me. That the union would establish something for you.

Was the money good for the times?

Any money was good then considering the times. See, the things at that time, you didn't have the huge production of automobiles and like that. Man, they make more cars in one day than they made in a year, see. One time they come out in the paper about it, General Motors wanted Ford to do something about his cars—Model Ts now. And he told them. He said, "Hey, I can make that car and sell it for a hundred dollars and I'll make a dollar on each one of them and I can sell a million of them and I'll make a million dollars."

Why they wouldn't think—a million dollars is nothing to them now, see. So they shut up on them, see, Ford went to paying them big wages long time before the union ever dug in there. He raised the wages, said, "The people produce that stuff, they're making me money, let's give them a little more."

General Motors wouldn't give you nothing. We had to fight for *everything* we got. All the way down the line.

Today it's a good place to make a living, I'll tell you that. It pays. And now, under this way the contract is, if we don't lose it, it is a good place. You can go in there and make good money. You can go in there and work overtime and get seven days a week out of it. You can come up there with 250, 300, 400 dollars a week. Plus you get your insurance paid and if you have to wear safety glasses, you can't wear regular glasses—they'll give to you prescription grounding safety glasses, see. These are safety glasses I got out there. Think these cost me eleven dollars and something.

I was never what you say "happy" at Guide Lamp because I didn't like to be pinned in. I don't like to be pinned in now. I was in the hospital and liked to went nuts. I've been in the hospital three times in my life. One time to have my nose worked over because I couldn't breathe out of it. And that was from fighting. And I got it broke about four or five times and two or three times playing football when I was a kid. And it got to the place where I couldn't breathe out my nose, see. So, I went out there for surgery on my nose, carved on me. But that room like scared me to death before I got out of there.

I can't stand close quarters and knowing I have to stay there, if I don't know it, see. But I had some good jobs at Guide Lamp. I had a job doing oiling. I oiled all that equipment out there. And I finally worked into the toolroom, which is all the skilled trades equipment and equipment in there costs a lot of money, see. And me and the foreman didn't agree upon the way things was going, and I told him to go to hell. I didn't have to work there, and I could ask for another job or transfer, which I did. And he stalled me for three weeks because the general foreman chewed him out for losing me. Because he said, "Hey, that man is in the toolroom, he knows all the oiling in that toolroom, what has to be done in there. He does a good job in there. There's no complaints from the toolroom since he's went in there." But he just wouldn't give me a break, see.

Was there any discrimination against women in the plant? I mean discrimination in that . . . did foremen give them a hard time?

Women had a certain bunch of jobs that they could work on, see. And then finally they kept raising Cain with the people in the union that they wanted equal seniority, see. And equal pay for performing jobs like I performed, see. Well, a great deal of them didn't want it. But then the majority of them voted on it were younger people, see. And they found out that these jobs were not women's jobs, that women could not perform them, see. You'd go in there and to lift up something weighed 150 pounds, you ain't going to do it. It's going to ruin you if you do, see. And you clean out tanks, see. You go in on overtime, you go in them tanks and you have to shovel out that muck that builds up in the bottom of your tank, you've got to shovel that out. You have to put on a pair of coveralls, boots, rubber gloves, and they didn't like that too well. But then they got to where they were working in about all kinds of jobs that there was in there, see. In other words, we got more women under that agreement than we had originally carried. Because it was mostly men's jobs.

What's the general attitude of people working in the plant now with this unemployment problem? I mean, how do the people who are working feel about it?

Well, I think they figured that they got the top seniority, and there's no way they's going to get laid off and they don't care what happens to the other people. Now that's my opinion of it. And I've talked to a lot of these young boys out here and some of the officers that's in there and that is the way that plant is. It's got to be greed in there. It was before I left. Anyway to chop you and get the overtime, they would do it, see.

It's greed—"Greedy, greedy, want more money," see. The people are not grouped together like they was when we formed this union. We was all for one and one for all, see. Now they're not. They're individually for each other. And that don't get you no place in the world.

They come into good times. Most of the people that's in there now has come into good wages and good times. Come in under a contract that didn't let them shove them and push them, see. When I went in there, they'd tell you what you done and if you didn't do it, you didn't have no job, see. You either done it the way they told you to if it was right or wrong. It's still that bad in there now. Man, they run junk in there something pitiful. If the foreman gets his feather in his hat, by that counter on the last press in there, if you've got a line running stuff, he don't give a damn whether they *fit* that automobile or not. Makes no difference to him, see.

Oh, I had it with the foremans out there awful. Hell, they fired me one time, lost four hours so I got drunk and went in. I told him. I was sitting right out in the middle aisle, had a soap tank and I have sinus trouble. And you dipped them auto parts, see. Had a girl that put them on a rack, there was a rack that you set up and just dipped it in this hot soap. It would just come up in your face every time you took them out and put one in, see. And I kept telling the man, "Goddamn it, can you get me off this son of a bitch, I can't take this. I can't breath at night. I can't lay down and sleep, I've got to sit up to sleep all the sleeping I do because this would run down my throat and choke me to death."

So about half the time I'd get drunk and that's the only way I'd know to survive, see. But I went in there that morning about half drunk, got me a chair and set right down in the middle aisle. And he come over, got a big shot with him.

"You get up there and run that soap tank."

I said, "You go to hell. I ain't about to run that soap tank."

"I'll fire you."

I said, "No you ain't firing me because I ain't took my sweater off yet. I haven't went to work yet so how in the hell you going to fire me. I have quit as of this morning."

"You can't quit."

I said, "I can do anything I want to. I feel I'm big enough to do it, I can do this." I said, "I know where there's a job that will pay me two dollars more on the hour. And I go to it in the morning. I'd leave here right now, and in the morning I'll be up there and walk right into that job and go to work." Well, they didn't believe me, see.

When was this?

That was during the war. So I went to the front end, see. Tried to give them a badge. Well, I badgered him, and that little old fellow wasn't going to take it. And I throwed the door in and cussing up a storm because I'm mad, and when I'm mad, I'm crazy. And he wasn't going to do it, so he was going to take me in to talk to the personnel man who was taking another guy's place when he was in Detroit, see.

And he said, "I can't do nothing about it, Joe."

I said, "You don't have to do nothing about it."

"Well," he said, "you can't quit."

I said, "Whoa, one minute, I can quit."

Said, "You better read what the government said on that. I can change jobs in three states: Kentucky, Indiana, and Ohio, if I'm not working at my highest skill."

I said, "If they need me in my skill in some other job in them three states, I can go it."

So what finally happened, you stayed there?

Yes. I lost four hours and went back to work.

Was there fear during that sit-down strike? Were people afraid they were going to lose their homes?

Most of them didn't own homes, see, at that point. They rented off the real estate people.

Would bad things start happening to them if they had participated in the strike? I mean, were they sort of persecuted for it after the strike was over?

No, most of them *got* homes after we finally got some wages and some kind of a setup that was going to let the older man stay, if he went out and tried to buy himself a home. Homes wasn't like they are now. You could buy them for about six or seven hundred dollars for a nice house, see. Now, when I worked for the gas company, an old boy bought a little old house down on the river there, on the east side, give six hundred dollars for the house and three lots, and lost it. Couldn't pay for it. Because when he couldn't find anything to do during the wintertime, see, you don't put lines down in the wintertime, 'cause the ground's froze. So he couldn't find anything to keep the payments up, and they slid him out of it.

Were you all prepared to fight, then, when you were inside there? How did you prepare yourselves?

Well, we made some awful beautiful knives and sharpened up them, and made some awfully good billy clubs.

What we had mainly in there during sit-down was a lot of people out of the mines. The mines was down, the coal mines was dead, see. Small operations where they would have been, they just shut the things down because the business outfits would dig coal, sell it cheaper than they could. Well, say a dozen of us run a mine, see. We couldn't dig it as cheap as that because hey—we had a dozen families to take care of, where the big operators, see, we'd work for them.

But see, they went down there, at Guide Lamp, we had a hardball team out there. They went down to the southern part of the state, and Illinois to the mines, and brought them back, see. Gave them a steady job the year round to play hardball. And we won the championship between Delco Remy and us, see. Some of them are still out there. Well, one of them still comes here, Jack Jourdan, was captain.

Them old mines was union—that was beat in their heads right—two hours after they was born. Hey—when you went down there in the coal mines, and tried to scab, you didn't get out. They would set up on top of them hills up there with a .30-30 rifle, and them guys would knock a squirrel's eye out at a hundred yards, and never touch another hair on its body. And they'd kill you.

That's something.

Well, it was a different life than it is now. We're living in a different ball game. Now whether it's going to . . . people then were happy. They had nothing—nobody had nothing. Now they're not happy with whatever they got, they're not happy. They want more, and more. Well, there's got to be a stopping point someplace. And I blame the federal government for allowing that. They should have set up a system for where management made so much profit and labor stopped at a certain place. We'd still be booming if they'd set up like that. But see, they just kept raising the prices. I've got a '78 Fairmount setting out there—the little wagon I just drove in. It's in my wife's name— I bought it for her. And

Sit-down strikers leave the Guide Lamp plant, 16 January 1937
Archives of Labor and Urban Affairs, Wayne State University, Detroit

I bought it late in the year—before the first of the year. We didn't get no raises. We had no raises. We got one in July and that was the end of it, see, until the next year when our next raise would be.

What did the workers hope to gain from the sit-down strike?

A contract. That was what we was after. That one little piece of paper that you got there. Be recognized as a union. That's what we wanted.

We wanted to be recognized as the bargaining unit for the people in there that punched a clock. And that's what we got in that there—that's all that's in there. Ain't nothing in there says we get any more money or anything, see, then we had to negotiate that, see.

It was to get ourselves recognized as a union in General Motors. Then we could go from there. Then we started building on to it, adding on to it, and won all this stuff that these people's got now, through all these years, see.

Who ordered that strike in the beginning?

I never will know and nobody else will, it was too secretive. I'll be honest with you. It was some of them boys from the mines, see. And a great deal of us was told about it through being uptown in taverns, see. One guy said, "Joe, tomorrow we shut her down, we pull the main switches."

There's some in there that didn't know about anything, know nothing. They just sat there with their eyes open, see. 'Course they got up and left. Some of the supervision didn't want to leave, but when you got an iron rod about bigger than my finger and about that long that could split somebody's head with it, you're moving. And one guy didn't quit running, once the guy said. He pushed the switch back up twice on this one guy. He's dead and gone now. He said, "You push it the next time, and they'll call the ambulance to get you, and try to, see if they can put your head back together 'cause I'll split your head with this."

We wasn't trying to beat anybody. We was just trying to get enough money to live off of. We weren't getting it. And we wanted a little say-so of how we was treated out there. You done exactly what they told you to do. And you had no say-so. You couldn't talk back. If you said something back to the foreman, he took ahold of you, took you over to the office, and they'd hand you your money, took you on out, reached out there, and got another gal and brought her in and put her on your job. You had no say-so.

I was running a little bitty old bracket about that long—die casted—that fit in the headlight—that was headlights that fit on the top of the front of the fender. And I was running so many cardboards a day on this wire brush that was taking off the roughness that, that was taking it off before it went to the guys that polished it, see. It was chrome. Or painted it, whichever one it was designated to do. And you just barely had enough to get your fingers on. Whereas on that wire brush, I looked like a porcupine the first day I run that thing. Them wires coming out, sticking all over me.

Do you think that union members today appreciate the work you did to create the union? The struggling that you had to do?

Some does. Some does, and some don't.

How about the young people?

Well, there's a great deal of them young ones that don't see why they should have to pay that hour and a half dues a month, see. That's quite a bit of money, see.

But there's some young people who are listening to you all?

Yes, there's some people who, now well, they're soft. They never thought they was going to get this. Hey, most of them people's never been laid off. Did you realize that? Up until this [recession] hit?[4] Never had a layoff. Done mostly seven days a week, ten and twelve hours a day. They had a silver spoon all this time. Now

[4] In the recession of 1979–82, durable goods manufacturing employment in the state dropped by one fourth, and unemployment in Anderson reached almost 20 percent, the highest in the nation. Madison, *Indiana Way*, 276–77; *New York Times*, 2 March 1982.

Reunion of the sit-downers of 1936 at Local 663 in 1953
Archives of Labor and Urban Affairs, Wayne State University, Detroit

then, they're going to go back to where I started. The reason I helped make this union and kept helping and helping and trying to do everything I could to bring it up to where we could hound a deal, see. This is what they don't understand, see. Because hey, they go out on a strike, they get some money, cash, every week.

Do people come to union meetings anymore?

No. They don't even come to our retiree meetings. They're just spread out all over the country.

Victor G. Reuther held several posts in the United Automobile Workers union. He was born in 1912 in Wheeling, West Virginia.[5]

[5] Interviewed by R. T. King, 26 September 1980, South Bend, Indiana.

It's my impression that Indiana in general was a difficult nut to crack for the UAW, and that certainly Anderson was.

Reuther: Well, first of all, one must keep in mind that the UAW was an infant movement at the time, taking on one of the most gargantuan corporations in the world. Hence, it was not in a position to challenge that corporate strength in each of its bastions. I don't think that the officers of the UAW at that time gave any great priority to unionization in Anderson. I think the workers there were caught up with the euphoria and the excitement of the organizing campaign that was beginning to sweep the auto industry.

I don't believe there was a calculated move to strike the plants. This was a voluntary action by the workers in Guide Lamp, and undoubtedly influenced by the success of the Bendix strike of November 1936 in South Bend, Indiana. The Kelsey Wheel and Bohn Aluminum strikes of December 1936 in Detroit contributed to this euphoria, this spirit of excitement and hopefulness that the time had come when worker action could be successful. Flint—the Chevrolet and Fisher Body strikes of December 31, 1936—was obviously striking at the very heart of the corporate power. Atlanta, Georgia—Fisher Body, November 1936—was not so crucial; Cleveland—Fisher Body, December 1936—was very important. And it wasn't until the Cleveland strike, which tied up, of course, a very crucial Chevrolet operation, that the union was forced into action in Flint. Forced into action much before we were prepared for it.

We certainly weren't prepared for it in Anderson, Indiana. The state politically was a very conservative state and to this day it remains quite conservative in its political outlook. There were no strong unions in the area that could provide assistance. You had some scattered building trades groups. I suppose the closest allies we had was in the little town of Alexandria, where we went to rally our forces after that sad night when the union headquarters was broken into on Main Street [in Anderson]. So actually what happened in Guide Lamp was not the result of an order from headquarters to go on strike and tie up the plant. To the best of my knowledge this was an action on the part of the workers, in solidarity, of course, with what was transpiring nationally.

Can you cast any further light on that?

Well, as you know, I was in Flint at the time, deeply involved in the efforts there. It was only after the Battle of Bull's Run—when it was suggested I get out of town because the General Motors–controlled judge was trying desperately to throw us in jail—that I was named director of organization. So I came into Anderson after the strike had already occurred and after they had evacuated the plant.

There had been this attack on the union headquarters. I arrived on the overnight train the very night of that attack. So that I was not on the scene at the time the strike occurred in Anderson, was not privy as to who gave what orders.

But let me say this, it's quite understandable to me that there were conflicting stories about this because there was division at the highest level in the UAW about whether to take strike action against General Motors and when. [Homer] Martin, who was then the president of the union, was notorious for making inflammatory speeches. We had just gone through the sad experience with him in Bendix [South Bend] where he came in to pep people up and to arouse them and then ran out on them when it came to negotiations. National CIO really had to bail out the fledgling UAW by negotiating a settlement in Bendix while Martin was off somewhere else. And you know that Martin sent out telegrams to General Motors locals across the country telling them to get ready for strike action without having discussed that with his fellow officers of the UAW—and certainly not with those who were most responsible for determining strategy in General Motors. So my suspicion is that local people at Guide Lamp took the telegram from Homer Martin as an order to go on strike, which it was not. And hence, long before they were prepared for strike action, they went on strike. And this accounts for, I think, a lot of the confusion about it, and the fact that the stalwart union members were so outnumbered at that point in Anderson.

Mind you, I think once events in Flint developed the way they did, it would have been very difficult to hold back General Motors workers elsewhere even if their plant was not a strategic plant. To this very day, with a highly organized union that's powerful and very centralized, to strike only portions of a major corporation and to permit other segments to continue functioning requires an enormous amount of self-discipline and highly centralized decision making. Well, an infant union, a fledgling union that hadn't even learned to crawl yet, let alone to walk or run, was hardly capable of that kind of discipline. So the situation was very confused, and I am not at all surprised that you'd get conflicting stories from participants in Anderson.

One of the really remarkable things about the strike was that it began with so few people actually signed up as members and yet the quality of leadership that existed among that small group was remarkable, because they were taking on the richest and most powerful corporation in the world. And John L. Lewis couldn't be sitting at their elbow every minute telling them what to do. They had to make hard decisions, and they did. And the leadership of the local strike people was really incredible.

When I realized how tense the situation was in Anderson . . . the open violence against active unionists with almost a Klan-like or Black Legion type of vigilante movement against the strike with open terror being used against strike leaders where their homes would be circled by cars at night and they'd be warned,

Victor Reuther
Archives of Labor and Urban Affairs, Wayne State University, Detroit

and people beaten up individually as they were waylaid. With this kind of terror in the city I knew that they would be undergoing an enormous risk personally to their lives to try to reestablish the picket line the morning after that attack on the union headquarters. And that accounts for the decision that we made, and we made it jointly with the strike leadership. I didn't presume to tell them what was in their best interest, but I asked them where it would be safest for us to begin to hold meetings again. The strange suggestion was made that we begin to meet in Alexandria, which was twenty-five miles away. We drove there in our ramshackle cars and talked strategy about resuming the picketing.

Now, psychologically the resumption of the picketing at Guide Lamp was terribly important symbolically to indicate the strike was still on, that we didn't throw in the sponge. But no one was under any illusions that Anderson and the strike there was exerting any significant pressure on General Motors for a settlement of the strike nationally. But it became a matter of symbolism, not only to the strikers in Flint but to the potential membership in Anderson, that the strike was still on.

I remember when we moved in a caravan of cars with the American flag in the lead car and pulled up at the Guide Lamp plant and resumed picketing. I especially recall the harassment by the local police and some of the deputy sheriffs who deliberately tried to pick a fight. And one of them slugged me, and I called upon the people in the picket line not to respond in kind, because I knew what they wanted was to start a melee, a fight of some kind, and use that as a pretext for a brutal attack on us. We were subjected to the worst kind of harassment and physical abuse.

But the pickets and the strike leaders understood full well what they were up against and responded. It was their decision—it wasn't mine; it wasn't the international's decision. We talked through, you know, "We've got a very desperate situation here. How do we handle it? What can we do?" And it was their decision that we would meet in Alexandria and then come back. Finally we resumed the picketing. But the outlook at that time was very grim, very grim indeed.

What was it that made Alexandria a safer environment for meeting than Anderson?

Well, it was known as a union town. You had old building trades unions there, barbers union, and so on, and it was just considered a little haven close by. There was no other community that we could have turned, and quite frankly the Anderson city officials, Chief [Joseph] Carney and the police, the mayor were so openly on the side of the corporation.

Do you realize we couldn't rent a union hall? Even when the strike was settled in Flint. And I thought, "My God, at last peace has come to Anderson. We can have a meeting without fear from vigilantes." We couldn't get a church, we couldn't get a school, we couldn't get the armory. All the doors were closed to us. That's why we had to rent this old ramshackle Crystal Theater, in the middle of February, bitter cold, to have a meeting to explain the terms of the strike settlement. People came there, many of whom weren't members of the union. They wanted to go back to work, they wanted to hear what the terms of the settlement were. They jammed the rafters of that place, you know. You couldn't get them all in.

And then what happened? The vigilantes gathered outside, fired through the windows. We almost had a riot on our hands there. I aged ten years in that one night. And Chief Carney came in and says to me, "Reuther, if you will submit to protective arrest the crowd will disperse."

"Protective arrest?" I said, "You mean you can get me through that motley crowd without a hanging, without a lynching, but you can't disperse that crowd? You're the chief officer of law and order? They're breaking the law. They're trying to deny us the right of peaceful assembly." Fire station across the street . . . mid-February . . . did it ever occur to them to use the hose on a motley crowd that was armed? Oh, no! Even Governor [Maurice Clifford] Townsend said, "The local authorities can handle everything." It was not until the workers of Anderson decided to defend their own rights and called for help from Flint and Toledo and Detroit and that caravan of cars started down the highway toward Indiana, then we got martial law. But I'd gone to the governor and asked for martial law.

I went as soon as we got the last group of people out of that theater safely, and it wasn't until five o'clock in the morning, mind you—five o'clock in the morning—before we got the last ones out. We had to escort them out in small groups. And I went with the delegation to see the governor and I said, "Governor, local authorities are not in charge of the situation. Vigilante groups are running wild in Anderson." I begged him to declare martial law. And you will read in many history books of American labor and not find another incident, to my knowledge, where a trade union official asked for martial law. Because in most instances we knew the troops would be used against the strikers. We wanted physical protection for our people to have a meeting.

When the caravan of jubilant workers who were victorious from Flint, Detroit, and Toledo started converging on Indiana, then the governor declared martial law. And let me tell you, with troops stationed at the door we had the biggest union meeting because people lost their fear of coming out. And the union began growing then, and we began winning community understanding and support.

I think also we had a chance then because national attention focused on Anderson. The violence used against us brought prominent people in. Reporters and distinguished people like Roger Baldwin and Norman Thomas came in, and from their visits here, articles began appearing and there was pressure then exerted on the local authorities. And I think community leaders then became a little more shamefaced about their silence and church leaders began speaking out, and we began assuming a proper role in the community.

You mentioned that it took until five o'clock in the morning to get everybody out of the Crystal Theater.

No, it began to dwindle as the hours of morning wore on and when the mob became small enough that I felt that some of the organizers and stalwarts from the strike committee could conduct women and children out of the place and get them to their homes, we got them out first—the women and children. But it was five o'clock in the morning before the key leadership evacuated the theater and we went straight from the theater.

I would say that it was certainly three o'clock in the morning before we got all the women and children out. And that's a long time to keep . . . in a building that's cold and tense and kids were crying and, you know, women were menstruating, and it was horrible.

One of the things that shocked me about the community situation in Anderson at that time was the degree to which the corporation dominated every aspect of community life even to a far greater extent than Flint, which was certainly a General Motors town. But even in Flint there were educators, there were ministers, there were social workers, there were people who felt concerned about the crisis through which the community was going and expressed some interest—offered their services to mediate, to try to avoid open clashes and so on. In Anderson, there was a stone wall of silence. No ministers spoke out, no educator, the whole town was silenced by the enormous power and pressure and dominating presence of General Motors. There was no community base to which the union could appeal, for instance, in a moment of crisis and say, "Look, the strike is over. Is there no church in which we can meet to explain the terms of the settlement?"

Everyone was fearful of having contact with us. It was a terrible thing to go through of being so isolated and so alone when your very roots were the same as those in the community. You couldn't possibly succeed in Anderson without the support of large numbers of citizens of Anderson—the workers. And yet the community had permitted itself to be so divided into two warring camps. There was no middle ground. There was no one stepping forward and saying, "You know, there must be a better way of doing this." And that was shocking.

Rex E. Roberts was born in 1913 and worked at the Guide Lamp plant, starting in 1936, for thirty-eight years.[6]

Roberts: I was born in Hancock County in a small town by the name of Maxwell, July 21, 1913. And I just was the average kid growing up. Went through grade schools. We settled in Anderson in 1928, and that was my freshman year in high school. And I graduated from Anderson High School in 1932.

My stepfather had obtained employment at Guide Lamp Division of General Motors, and so that's what brought us to Anderson. He had previously worked in auto factories. One that I recall most was the Pierce-Arrow Company in Buffalo, New York, and he was a metal polisher. Since they had metal polishing here at Guide back in those days, why, he was able to get a job here. I have been here ever since.

Did your father ever tell you anything about what it was like to work in Guide Lamp before you became employed there?

Oh, yes. And, of course, ever since I can remember, he always was a great union guy. Or at least, you know, he talked union and organization and getting the people to band together in order to benefit themselves. Right after I got out of high school I had got a job at

[6] Interviewed by R. T. King, 13 August 1979, Anderson.

Delco Remy, and I worked over there two different times.

In fact, the last time that I worked over there I finally got fired. I always say it was because I was more militant than other people, and I didn't take a lot of stuff that the foreman put out. One night I asked the superintendent for a hospital pass, and I went over to the hospital—which was located in Plant 1 at the time, over at Delco Remy—and the doctor told me that I had a slight hernia. He said, "I will order you a truss."

And I said, "OK." I finished out the night, but the next evening when I went in I was having more discomfort than usual, and I decided that I was going home. I couldn't find the superintendent; I couldn't find my foreman; so I just rang out and went home.

The next night when I went in to work I was feeling a lot better, and lo and behold, when I got to the time rack my card wasn't there. So I just waited around until I could get ahold of the superintendent, and I asked him where my card was. He said, "Well, it don't make any difference where your card is," he said, "You haven't got a job here anymore." So I was fired. That ended my employment at Delco. That was in—possibly 1935.

After I was fired I got a job with the State Highway Department mowing weeds along the highway, on the right-of-way, by hand with a scythe. In the meantime I had put my application in at Guide Lamp. And then in the fall of 1936—in October, to be exact—I was called to Guide Lamp, and I stayed there for thirty-eight years. Then I retired because of a heart condition. So that ended my job at Guide, but I'm still very active within the local union, UAW Local 663, and with the retired workers.

When you were at Delco Remy did you belong to the union, or was the union even . . . ?

When I was at Delco Remy, there was no union. They had a company organization—I believe the name of it was the DREA—the Delco Remy Employees Association—which was just strictly company dominated.

Rex E. Roberts (middle), along with the first Guide Lamp retiree, Ray Seward (left), and Howard McClintock, 1950
Archives of Labor and Urban Affairs, Wayne State University, Detroit

One incident . . . after I got fired, I had become pretty good buddies with two or three of the machine operators. We went out and drank beer and, you know, socialized a little bit. And he came to me and he said, "Rex, I'm awful sorry but there's not a thing I can do." And he was the departmental representation of the DREA at that time. So, you see, they didn't have a union. In fact, they didn't have a union until the UAW was recognized after the sit-down strike in Guide Lamp.

Do you recall what your wages were in 1935 at Delco Remy?

I think they were thirty-four cents an hour. I would say that possibly that was one of the best jobs that a guy could have at that time. You know, wages in 1934 and 1935 and 1936 were all right in that same category. Of course, it's possible that there were some people making more money than that, but they were few and far between regardless of what kind of a job you had.

I hired in at Guide in October of 1936, and I can remember what we called the "candy room"—it was just a little room up in front where there was a guy who sold candy and chewing gum and milk and things like this. When you came in to work, if there wasn't a job or if there wasn't any stock or you couldn't run your job, they'd say, "Well, you go up to the candy room and stick around, and if we can get some stock in I'll come up and get you."

Your foreman tells you this, see. And there has been time—I can't personally say this had ever happened to me, but I *know* it happened to other people—that you'd set there for all day and never get a job. You'd never earn a dime, but was afraid to go home, because if you went home and then that foreman come around fifteen minutes later and wanted to know where Roberts was, or somebody, and you wasn't there, well, nine times out of ten the next morning when you come in you didn't have a job, *period*. Because there was so many guys who was always willing to take your job. All that was changed because of the January 1937 sit-down strike, but back in 1935 and most of 1936 this was an everyday practice of the Guide management.

If you had to go to the rest room, you had to get somebody to relieve you. You were supposed to get in there and get back out on the job just as quick as you could do it. Of course, a lot of the guys, they'd stay too long. Maybe it was necessary, but maybe just to goof off for a few minutes. If the foreman thought you was in there too long, he'd probably come in after you—you know, come in to see what you was doing.

Of course, a lot of the guys, they'd take a smoke when they was in there, which was against the rules. You couldn't smoke anyplace in the factory when I went to work there. Later on in a contract we finally got so that we could smoke in the rest room only—not out in the plant, no place—at anytime. Consequently, the rest rooms became quite crowded and really smoke filled, because the guys would all . . . if you wanted a smoke, you had to go to the rest room. Even before working time or at noontime, you had to go to the rest room. Later on, then, we got the privilege of smoking out in the plant in restricted areas.

Can you describe the pace of work in the fall of 1936?

It was pretty hectic, and I know that . . . well, the parts were coming down a line—a belt—and there was a part there to be buffed every time you got one done. There was no lapse in the parts coming down the belt, and you was expected to just work all the time. There was always, most generally, plenty of material to work on because of their coming down on this endless belt. You were supposed to get one and run it on your machine and put it back on the belt and pick up another one and put it back on the belt and you know, just continuously.

There were several reports of men losing fingers and thumbs and so on on punch presses at Guide Lamp. Are you familiar with that?

I think the greatest safety thing on this particular buffing line was the blower system wasn't adequate enough to keep dust—primarily dust—away from you. That's the only thing right now that I can think of. But the operation on headlamps, before I got them as a buffer, come directly out of the punch press department, or a draw press, we called them. At that point they didn't have any guards on them, and I know of guys that have lost their fingers and their hands. I later on had worked on punch presses. I worked on draw presses, but I was fortunate enough not to have an accident.

But there *were* accidents. A lot of times these punch presses or draw presses would double trip. By that, I mean when you tripped them once and it run the operation that it was supposed to, a guy would reach in to get it out of the die . . . bang! It would trip again, and that's how a lot of people would lose fingers and hands.

Was there any sort of protest against that sort of thing?

I'm sure there was protests, especially after we got our union. Prior to that most of the protesting was done among the men theirselves. You could protest to high heaven, to management, and it wouldn't do much good. They'd always tell you that "if you didn't like your job, why, you could quit. Because, we've got guys out in front that's looking for a job." Well, a guy was married and he had a family, he just couldn't quit every time something like that happened. He put up with it because he had to.

Were there seasonal variations at Guide Lamp?

At one time—I think it was in the year 1938—I got laid off. Back in them days if you was off a year you lost all the seniority you had. I was off almost a full year, and I was thinking that I was never going to get called back and I'd lose my seniority and then I probably wouldn't have the chance to get back. But just a few days before the end of my time of losing seniority, I got called back to Guide. As I recall, that was in the year 1938. I was never laid off anymore for any length of time after that one time when I thought I'd really lost my seniority. Of course, in other contracts we took care of that, you know.

What did you do during that period you were laid off?

You done odd jobs. You drew unemployment compensation. Unemployment compensation became effective—as I can recall—in 1937. I was laid off at the very time that unemployment compensation become effective, and it was fifteen dollars a week. I applied for it, and I drew it for just a short time, and then I got called back. That was in 1937. Nineteen thirty-eight, though, is when I mentioned that I was off almost a year. Well, I drew my compensation then, but it didn't amount to too much, and it didn't last too long. But you done odd jobs. I finally had to move in with my folks. So you just done whatever you could do to earn a little money.

Can you remember whether Guide Lamp provided any athletic facilities for its employees, such as baseball fields or anything of that nature?

Yes, that was one of the popular ways of some of our people getting their job, because they were pretty good athletes and most of them played baseball. If you went to the employment office and told them you was a baseball player, you had a very good chance of getting a job. And, of course, they provided a baseball field and uniforms and equipment. But that's the way a lot of our people did get a job.

Was there already some organizing activity going on in the fall of 1936?

At Guide Lamp we had another organization known as Local 52 of the Metal Polishers, Platers, and Buffers Union. That's the AF of L. Some of our first leaders was involved in that, but they knew the fallacy of having craft unions in Guide Lamp. They wanted an industrial union that would include in their membership production, skilled trades, janitors—the whole outfit, you know. So there was a move on. And I'm sure that we had a charter and it was federal; they called it federal unions. I wasn't involved in that. That was just prior to my time.

Shortly, then, they actually organized and was given a charter in the UAW which was known as Local 146, which was an amalgamated local, and employees of Delco Remy were also in this amalgamated union. This is the first industrial union that ever hit Guide. My stepdad was very active in that. Well, I knew when I went to work in October of 1936 that I was going to be a member of the union. Of course, I didn't let anyone know that I knew anything about the union.

When you went there, approximately what percentage of the workforce were members of the UAW?

It was a very small percent. I couldn't tell you exactly, because back in them days you just didn't brag about being a member of the union. If you did, you'd *had* it, because they would find some way to get rid of you. So consequently they had meetings in secret, and they signed up people very secretly, and once you did get signed up, why, you didn't talk about it to anybody.

Prior to the strike, I know that guys would have meetings in their home or they would have a very informal meeting downtown at a beer place, and they would get guys to sign applications. If you talked to anybody in the plant, you'd do it secretly as you could, because if you thought anything of your job at all, or if you wanted to keep your job at all, you just didn't talk union out in the open.

Were there any local bars or taverns that were known to be union bars? Any places where union men gathered?

Oh, yes. There was one here in Anderson called The Club House that every Friday night—and I was working nights—I remember the guys—not everybody, but several guys—would always go up there and have a beer or two and cash their checks. That's where I joined the union—in a bar. And there was another one over at our neighboring city up north, Alexandria. The guy that owned it was favorable to the unions, and the guys got to knowing about it, so they'd go up there.

Right after you got in the union, you know, you didn't tell people. We did have a pretty nice hall, and, of course, we had people from Delco Remy and Guide. That was in the amalgamated local, see; that was Local 146. And then we'd have dances and card parties and pitch-in dinners and things like this even prior to the sit-down. And I became very interested.

I got on what we called at that time the Flying Squadron. Say we would have a meeting someplace or anything that happened that we needed a bunch of guys there, why, we had this Flying Squadron. They'd either call you or come by and say, "Hey, come on, let's go." The only thing I ever carried was a blackjack. I never carried a gun, but I had a blackjack that I carried frequently. I never actually used it. But it just seemed like it was a weapon I knew I had, and if I got in a situation that I couldn't handle and it got to be physical, I thought, "Well, this is just a little protection." It might not have done any good at all, but at least that was my thinking.

Did you ever meet Mr. Ed Hall?

Paramount block, 1956
Anderson Public Library, Norm Cook, photographer

In fact, Ed Hall give me my obligation into the UAW. And that occurred up in the circuit courtroom of the county courthouse. I always admired Ed real good. He was quite a guy. Of course, he was one of my early heroes, so to speak. I always looked up to him.

Well, he had a pretty deep booming voice, and whenever he spoke he spoke with authority. You know, sometimes people can make a very eloquent speech, but they don't have too much forcefulness or ability to really get the person involved in their thinking. But Ed always put me in mind of John L. Lewis, another guy that I always had deep admiration for. Never did meet John, but I read quite a few books concerning him.

Ed wasn't much bigger than I am. I doubt if he was six foot tall. He was pretty chunky built and just the kind of guy that didn't seem like he was afraid of anything. But he was knowledgeable, and he could impress upon you anytime he made a speech. I'll never forget the obligation that he read to me and two or three other guys the night that I was formally made a member of the UAW.

Is it a swearing-in ceremony?

Yes. It took place in the circuit courtroom in the courthouse. You know, people today don't have to come before the local union and take an obligation, because it is on their application card. When they first sign up in the union they also sign their obligation, and they are held to that. But back in the old days you had to come to a meeting. Now, once in awhile if we should happen to have some new members, we ask them to come up in front and the president reads the obligation to them. But that very seldom happens anymore, because they've already signed an application card and agreed to abide by the constitution and the obligation of our union.

Was there any tension between the UAW and the AF of L?

We still had guys in the plant that were strictly AF of L craft union people, and they didn't want guys like me, which is a production worker. They thought that we shouldn't be allowed to join their union. They wanted to hold it strictly to craft people. Just like they didn't want, we'll say, an electrician or a pipe fitter, which is a pretty good craft in itself. They wanted them people to be craft people. Not only because of the crafts, but they thought the UAW was communistic. Well, in my opinion, just the very fact that we wanted to include all the workers in one union. And, of course, there was a lot of publicity in the papers against the CIO, the Congress of Industrial Organization, sometimes known as the Committee for Industrial Organization. In other places I have read it in the paper that they was communist dominated. You know, "They were agitators." So this was another thing that they didn't want any part of the CIO.

At that time, John L. Lewis was pretty active in forming the CIO. A lot of those craft union, they didn't like John L., because he had already got out of the AF of L, and he was for the organization of industrial workers. Well, they just talked against it, as near as I know, in the plant. But when it come time later on for our NLRB election—and I was honored at that time to be a member of that election committee when we won the right to be represented by a union. Of course, the company union was on the ballot. So I was just a guy that had primarily grew up with the AF of L, so to speak, and they thought that was the only union. Maybe they had that right to think that. Just like I thought—and I think now—that there is no union like the UAW.

Did you become a shop steward before the sit-down strike?

No. As I said before, I joined the union in November, went to meetings, but I sat there and listened. I didn't say much, but I was listening and I was trying to do what my stepfather wanted me to do—learn something about the union. The morning of December 31—by then my wife and I had moved away from home—my stepdad met me at the gate, and he walked in the plant with me. Going in, he got up pretty close to me and he said, "Now, at nine o'clock we're going to shut this plant down." And he said, "I just want you to be careful and not get hurt."

This was entirely a surprise, because although I was a member of the union—they had decided this sometime prior, and I never knew one thing about it until that morning going in the plant. And you can imagine how I felt. Well, I was scared, because I didn't know what was going to happen. But we went in the plant. A guy who, incidently, had got a job at Guide Lamp because he could play baseball, but who had been a miner prior—a big, burly young fellow who wasn't afraid of the devil himself—came over to me and said, "Rex, we're going to shut this plant down at nine o'clock."

I said, "Yeah, I understand."

"Well!" he said, "You see that switch up here on the wall?"

And I said, "Yeah."

"Well," he said, "I've got a job for you." And he was acting in a steward's capacity. Of course, the company didn't recognize stewards or committeemen or anything at that point. He said, "I want you to pick up your wheel wrench and go over there and pull the switch, and then stand there by that switch and if anybody tries to turn it back on," he said, "knock their damn head off."

Well, a wheel wrench is a big iron bar about so long with a curve on the end that you use to tighten and loosen nuts on your buffing wheel—on your lathe. "Why," I said, "you don't want *me* doing this. *I* don't know what's going on."

He said, "Yes, I've watched you." And he said, "You're the guy that can do it."

"Well," I said, "OK. If you think I can do it, by God, I'll do it."

Well, when nine o'clock come, you could just hear that plant getting quieter and quieter all the time because the machines were going down. And I went over there, and I pulled that switch and there wasn't anybody come and tried to turn it on. And I was damned glad of it, because I was determined that if this guy thought I could do this job, that I was going to try to do it.

Well, things went off pretty good. Of course, we was in a buffing department. But back on the assembly lines where we had a lot of women working, and where they were assembling headlights and all, they was a little more hectic back there. Some of the guys—I didn't go back there—some of the guys went right on back to these assembly lines. We had one foreman who thought he was pretty hot stuff, so when somebody turned that assembly belt off, he just went back and turned it on, and he told the girls, "You go back to work." He said, "There ain't going to be no strike here." Well, he done that a couple, three times. Every time, he'd turn her back on, you know.

And finally a buddy that worked in my department was back there, and he was another big, burly young guy, he went up to this foreman and he said, "Now look, I'm going to turn that off. Don't you even *attempt* to turn it on or we'll knock your head off." And, of course, there was several other union guys around. This guy, he didn't turn it on anymore, and it wasn't too long until there wasn't a machine running in Guide Lamp.

Were there any women members of the UAW?

We had women members. We told them that they could stay in the plant until four o'clock that afternoon, and then they all had to leave the plant. We didn't want any women in there overnight for obvious reasons. You know, they was married women, single women; and married men, single men. We didn't want to get involved in anything that might not look good. So by four o'clock that afternoon all the women was out of that plant, and there wasn't any in there for the following seventeen days. But they worked in the kitchen and done things like that.

That was an education to me. During the seventeen days, well, it was during that time that all the guys made blackjacks.

What did you do to pass the time?

Oh, we sang, and we got up a band, and we had one guy that could really make an accordion talk. One fellow had played drums, and he had got his wife—they brought their instruments in, you know, a little later on. Guitar and banjos and we made music—all the guys can remember that you could hardly wake up any time and not hear that accordion playing.

Some of the guys, they'd play euchre; some of them would play poker; and the women brought us in food—or brought it to the gate. We would take a little four-wheeled cart and go out and they'd bring in soup beans or other kinds of soup by the big washtub full. You know, like ladies used to wash in—a big washtub is what they called them. We had tin plates, and we converted one of the washrooms into a place that we washed the dishes. I was on the dishwashing crew at one time. Of course, we kept constant patrol.

I'd say one guy was our leader. A great big burly guy by the name of Riley Etchison, who later became our Madison County sheriff. He could influence our people; they'd listen to him. We had regular patrols all down along the dock which was right by a railroad track just in case something happened. I remember one time we got word that the police were coming out to throw us out of the plant. Of course, we had fire hoses in Guide Lamp, and we designated people to man various hoses. We was just getting ready to make a stand if they did come, but they never did come. But had they of come, it would have been a fight, that's all.

Of course, we'd have meetings periodically—all the sit-downers. We all come to realize that if we was going to ever better ourselves we had to have a union to speak for us. Our main objective, as I said before, was to get recognition of our union to bargain for our people on anything that we wanted to bargain on. That was the main objective. Back in them days the word pension, nobody ever used it in their vocabulary. That was something that was never dreamed of. We never talked about vacation. We didn't talk about call-in pay. Subpay was the furthest thing from anybody's mind. The fact is, time-and-a-half for overtime, we wasn't thinking about that. We were just thinking about getting General Motors to recognize our union so we could talk for our people.

We also, in Guide Lamp, had an organization called the Loyal Two Thousand. This was nonunion people. Company union. The company had made up the oblong badges, had them chrome plated, and said, "Two Thousand Loyal Employees." So, you know, it was always in our minds what a back-to-work movement would be, what we'd do. We knew that there would be a fight, because we wasn't just going to stand by and let people go back to work. Up on Main Street, at that particular point, we had an office. The Loyal Two Thousand and some of the DREA people from Delco Remy rotten-egged that place. Some of the guys even got up there and throwed our files and typewriters out the window. It finally got quieted down, you know. Oh, another time out at the Gold Band Tavern out here in the west end of town they had a shooting.

Now, on 16 January the UAW decided to give up the sit-down strike. What led to that decision?

If I can recall, they had reached some kind of a tentative agreement, probably in Detroit or Flint, that all the sit-downers would evacuate all the plants. Word got down here to us that on this particular day we were supposed to relinquish our hold on the plant. And we did. We marched from Guide Lamp uptown to the armory, and we had a big mass meeting and rally up there and had a big time. All of us was glad to get out of the plant, of course, but we also thought we was on our way to getting an agreement. But things got kind of fouled up in Flint, as I recall, and they didn't go out—they didn't evacuate the plant right on that particular day. They stayed in for a few days because of something happening; I don't know what. Anyway, we left the plant at the designated time. Of course, we set up picket lines and so after that. Really, it was after that time that the trouble started. Tearing up our hall and the Gold Band thing. And we had a picket tent right outside the gate, and it was burned.

We had a rally shortly after that, and we were going to have it down at Athletic Park. Homer Martin, who was the president of our international union at that time, was going to be here to speak. We all met at the union hall and marched down to the Athletic Park in a body. But some of the guys—I didn't personally; when I say "we" I mean the union—had got word that when we was going out of the hall our Loyal Two Thousand was going to tear it up. And there was a couple of guys stayed back at the hall. They didn't go down to the Athletic Park. And they came to tear our hall up, but they were met with buckshot. A couple of guys got shot—didn't kill them—but anyway, they didn't tear the hall up.

Can you recall the arrival of Victor Reuther; what effect that may have had on the morale of the strikers?

I became very, very close with Vic and Sophie Reuther. I am today. Every time I go to Washington or go to Florida, I always visit. Since we have named this hall here after them, why, they have been here more frequently than in the past years. But anyway, the first real encounter that we had with Vic was . . . we was on the picket line and the sheriff or the chief of police, I don't know, came out and he walked up and smacked Vic. We've always thought that he done it to try to incite a riot. But Victor, the first thing he done was he started hollering and telling everybody not to do a thing. You know, we had enough guys there we could have beat the guy's head off. But Victor wouldn't let us. He said, "No. Absolutely not!" And nobody touched him.

Athletic Park
Anderson Public Library, Norm Cook, photographer

At that time Sophie was in town, too, but nobody knew that she was Vic's wife. And he didn't want us to know it, so she went by her maiden name of Good. As far as we knew, she was just a member of the organizing staff.

Do you look back on those seventeen days as having been an enjoyable experience?

Oh, my, yes! That was an education to me because that was the first time I'd ever been in anything like that. That's what started me, really, in being active in the labor movement. Of course, I haven't stopped.

You asked about various offices that I might have held over the past forty-two years. The very first job that I ever had in this local was as steward. This same guy that asked me to turn that switch off on the morning of the strike, after the strike was over came up to me one day and said, "Rex, we need a steward." And he said, "Here," and he handed me a little badge that said "Steward" on it—"UAW-CIO."

My greatest satisfaction came in 1950 when we first had the pension program with General Motors. It became effective in October 1950, and Walter Reuther was director of the GM department at that time. He appointed me as a pension committeeman for this local, and I held that job for twenty-one years until in February of 1971 I had a real bad heart attack. I was at that point, also, the recording secretary. But my doctor recommended that I retire if I could. There's no problem about that, so I retired. And in October of 1971—and I've got a picture around here someplace where it shows me pinning the pension committeeman's badge onto my alternate, and he is still in office today. He's getting ready to retire, probably at the end of this year.

I've had more personal satisfaction working with retired people and being instrumental in retiring people those twenty-one years than I did having any other office in this union. In 1966 the national convention OK'd the retired workers' structure as it is today, whereby we have a local union chapter of retired workers.

It's just been a lot of satisfaction over the last forty-two years of working with people. You know, to be retired and to pick up and take off and leave the country to live—I couldn't do it at all. As long as I can still be of service to people, well, I'm going to do that.

Meridian Street, ca. 1948
Anderson Public Library, Norm Cook, photographer

South Bend

South Bend

The eleven people who tell their stories in this chapter relate how central a large employer like the Studebaker Corporation was to a community and to the people who lived in it. In many ways it was the foundation upon which the ideal of mutualism rested because it provided economic support for families and reinforced the idea that the investment of work and devotion in a key institution would ultimately be recognized and rewarded. This type of investment stood at the heart of many American communities in the twentieth century, before the era of massive plant shutdowns after 1960, and helped sustain feelings of communal ties. Stories in this chapter also provide perspectives from various social levels in the plant. A midlevel supervisor such as Otto Klausmeyer, consequently, is able to offer an extensive look into "popular knowledge" about why the plant eventually closed. When Klausmeyer looked down, he criticized the local union for fighting to keep too many men on the payroll. When he looked upward, Klausmeyer found fault with management decisions, especially those that rejected his designs for smaller and more fuel-efficient cars in the 1950s.

Christine Drabecki, Mary Schoonaert, Louise Dzierla, Theresa Grayzck, Mary Nowicki, and Mary Van Daele, 1985
Robin L. Zeff

Christine Drabecki, Louise Dzierla, Theresa Grayzck, Mary Nowicki, Mary Schoonaert, and Mary Van Daele all worked in the Studebaker plant in South Bend.[1]

Schoonaert: My name is Mary Jane Schoonaert. And I was born in South Bend August 28, 1907, figure that out. And I hired in to Studebaker's at May 22, 1943.
Grayzck: And I'm Theresa Grayzck. I was born in South Bend and started working at Studebaker's in 1947.
Drabecki: I'm Christine Drabecki. I was born in Chicago November 21st [1913]. And I live in South Bend now.
Nowicki: My name is Mary Nowicki. And I was born in Stuebenville, Ohio. I was born in 1914 in Ohio.
Dzierla: Louise Dzierla, born August 16, 1914, in Michigan City. And I started to work at Studebaker's in 1942.
Schoonaert: When I hired in at Studebaker's, I hired in to sew for the Weasel. At that time during the war they were making the Weasels, and we had to sew the curtains that fit the top of the Weasels. And that was my job during the war. Then after that we were laid off until they got ready for the regular work. You know, on cars 'cause they quit, the war was over then. They quit making Weasels.

How did you get that first job?

Schoonaert: Well, the forelady was looking for experienced sewers and I had worked before at Wilson Brothers sewing so I had ten years of experience when they hired me in at Studebaker's. We needed the money for our livelihood at that time. I mean things were rough. My husband wasn't feeling too well. He was off of work a lot, and it was just necessary for me to go to work.
Nowicki: I worked at Studebaker. I started 1940. And I started working on the carpets, binding the carpets for the cars for the floors. Then I worked there for about nine weeks then we got laid off. And then they gave us ninety days to come back, didn't they, to lose your seniority?

[1] Interviewed by Robin Lee Zeff, 25 July 1985, South Bend.

The sewing room at Studebaker, 1940s
Studebaker National Museum, South Bend

Well anyway, they gave us eight months or whatever before you lose your time, your seniority. So they called me back just about half a day before I lost my seniority. Then I started on sewing those for the cars, for the cushions. I started on that for Alice Nash. Then after that, then they put me on the door line, making those doors. Remember, the doors, with the conveyor line? So I worked over there. We was making the doors.

And then the war broke down. Then they laid us off for awhile. Then I worked at South Bend Awning. For about six months I worked there. Then after that they called us back. Then I went to work at the aviation on inspection. Then I went on piston line, working for the piston line. And then I got pregnant with my Carol. So I took off for about six months, then came back. The war was over, so I worked on the inspection across the street from, packing all those pistons, packing in oil. Packing and shipping out. Then they called us back working on the sewing for Alice Nash. That's when I worked with you girls. And then after that I went to the core room. I started making cores in the foundry.

Who was Alice Nash?

Nowicki: The sewing room. She was our forelady in the sewing room. We all had her. She only had her own friends. Certain friends that she was good to, wasn't she?
Van Daele: God, I'll never forget. There was a bunch of us, I don't know if you ever heard it, but we used to call her "the devil on wheels."
Schoonaert: I have to say, Alice Nash was good. She watched her . . . I mean, she was particular about the work. She was always nice to me. I have to say that because it's true. To me, she was always nice.
Dzierla: 'Cause you were Belgian, and she was Belgian.
Schoonaert: Well, not really, because I think she went with the Polish group the most. She hung around the Polish group the most. But she was always nice to me.
Van Daele: She was nice to me too. We never had an argument. But I did everything she told me to.
Nowicki: Yes, I did everything she told me to.
Schoonaert: She knew that I was very particular as to how I did my work. And she would give me some hard jobs. And that was on leather, binding leather. And

that was very hard. I said, "Why do you give me that job?"

And she said, "Because you do a good job, and I don't have to worry about it if I give it to you."

So I was sewing on, and that was hard work, sewing leather seats and tops.

Did you find that there were cliques?

Nowicki: Yes.
Van Daele: Sure.

What were some of the cliques that they had?

Nowicki: Oh, they would bring some coffee cakes or something or food or do her special favors.
Dzierla: Well, she had an awful lot of Hungarian friends too.
Drabecki: I think that she was more of a company's man, company's woman. She stuck for the company a lot. She thought, you know, she tried to more or less help them out, you know.
Nowicki: She picked on her own mother. We used to all sit there, and we had a fifteen-minute rest period. And her mother sat with us girls in that room there, and she happened to take a needle and start doing something. She grabbed her mother by the back and she said, "Leave that alone and go back where you belong." She gave her hell, her own mother. She would make sure that everybody, that they were supposed to do on their own.

How did you all feel about being laid off at the end of the war?

Nowicki: We felt bad. We felt hurt. Because they sold us out, our union sold us out. Didn't they?

Then they had a big union meeting, and then we came back. We all got a cut, didn't we? Didn't we get a cut and then found out about a year later our new president from Studebaker came in and then that's when we lost all our jobs after the new president came in.

So when the war ended, did you expect to be laid off because the military work had ended?

Van Daele: Sure.
Nowicki: Yeah, we expected, but not for too long. We thought we'd be all called back to work on our cars.
Dzierla: I got hired in 1942, December 21st. And I went into aviation. I now was the first woman that went into making the motors for the airplanes. And like she said on the breaks, I put the piston into the motor. And everything had to be micro. And you had to write everything you done, and how many milligrams and everything it was. And I didn't want the job because I was the first woman that they said they would try and see if they could teach a woman to do that job. So Mr. Smith was the boss and his son was under him and I wanted to get where I could get off it, 'cause it was too nerve-racking. And he said, "No Louise, I'm going to help you, and we're going to make you the first doing this job." So I stayed there until the end of the war. And then my best friend, Helen Shumaker, came and bumped me out of my job and the war was almost over.

So after that, I don't know why, but I did not get laid off. I had a right to bump so I went and bumped in in different parts of the Studebaker place. I went to the cafeteria where they cooked. And I worked there for about a year and a half. And after that was done, I was bumped out of that. I went into cleaning offices at night. I worked from about eleven o'clock at night until five o'clock in the morning cleaning offices at Studebaker's and that was a tough job.
Van Daele: I started at aviation in 1943. And I inspected screws, and we worked on a machine that had a diamond point. And you would turn the lever, and it would have to be a certain texture. And if the metal wasn't quite right you discarded it. Then after the war, I can't remember my first job there. It was on sewing. But I never had enough seniority to stay there. So I worked in the foundry. I worked at Plant Eight. And I worked on taping doors. And there were so many jobs. They would only last maybe a few weeks, a few months, until I got bumped again.

How did you feel about getting bumped?

Van Daele: I didn't like it. Terrible.
Dzierla: If somebody got eliminated, well, they had the right to bump with less seniority. It was seniority rights. So if you had even a day more than the one that was on the job you had the right to bump them.

How did you hear about that you were bumped?

Drabecki: They'd come and tell you. The union official and the boss would come and say that you're being bumped. They'd bring the person right along and you'd have to teach them the job. In fact, if they could, do it in a day or two.
Nowicki: I think they gave us three days. They gave us three days to learn.
Drabecki: If you bumped a job and couldn't make it in three days, carry on the line, you were gone. You were out. You were eliminated again.
Van Daele: You always looked for something you'd think you might like, right? Or that you could do. But sometimes you didn't have much of a choice. If you wanted to work you took whatever was there.
Nowicki: And you had to work fast, working on that line.
Van Daele: Oh, my.
Nowicki: When the line was going with the cars moving, you had to be fast to keep up.
Van Daele: I had one job, I didn't even have time to blow my nose.
Dzierla: Washing car windows was one of them.
Nowicki: That's me. Getting in, going out, going in. The time you washed one window there's another one ahead of you waiting.
Van Daele: And there's these times they would come around with the piece of paper and pencil and they'd wanted you to work like a robot. Remember? You never did enough.
Dzierla: They say that people at Studebaker's didn't work hard. Maybe there were a few that had good jobs. But most, majority of the people really had to earn their money. There's a few freeloaders everywhere, you know that, but you had to have a good connection with the boss and the union to get away with that.

What was it like working there during the war?

Drabecki: Very strict. Now, when you come in the morning to get in the gate, you were searched all over.
Nowicki: Not every time. Once in awhile. They'll count to about every tenth person, they'll pull you in. Especially when you get out at night.

What were they looking for?

Dzierla: To see what you're bringing in. If you're bringing in any alcohol and if you were carrying anything out.
Nowicki: Or taking pictures or anything like this, spies or anything like that. They kind of watched you. Then they search you a certain number.

I'd like to talk a little bit about the unions.

Drabecki: Oh, the union was active for both parts. There was no separate union for the ladies or the men. And of course the women would never have a chance to go out on a strike and be able to lead their way. So the only time we went on strike was when the men voted for it and we'd have to follow. There was never a strike on account of the ladies. When we had grievance or anything. They'd talk about it but there was never, nothing special done for the ladies.
Dzierla: You had to belong to the union to work at Studebaker's.
Nowicki: Yes, they took our dues through the paychecks. So we had to belong to it.
Van Daele: I'm for the unions.
Dzierla: Me too.
Van Daele: They have a lot of faults. They've done a lot of things wrong. But where would people like us be without them?
Schoonaert: I think we needed the unions at that time. But the unions have caused a lot of these layoffs today. Today they have hurt the people.
Van Daele: I know.
Schoonaert: Instead of helping the people. And it was all for their own pockets.

How did they help the people? When, you know, different times?

Nowicki: Well, instead, like the boss will fire you. You go to the union and ask for help. And they did fight for you.
Dzierla: And get your job back.
Van Daele: Well, before the union, there was no seniority. And if the boss liked you, you had a job, and if he didn't you got fired. Or if, I remember one lady, what was her name, before the union she used to tell us she worked for a boss that insisted on taking her out, and she wouldn't go with him, so he fired her.

Did that happen much?

Nowicki: No.
Van Daele: No, that's the only one incident that I know of. And I know my father worked in the core room before the union. And if they told you you had to work twelve hours, you worked those twelve hours or else you didn't have a job. He used to work a lot of overtime.
Dzierla: It wasn't overtime, it was straight time.
Van Daele: Well, I mean, straight pay, but he worked fourteen, fifteen hours a day sometimes.

Right after World War II, the union kept seniority and you started bumping rights, women immediately started bumping men?

Drabecki: Men started bumping women. The only place they didn't bump was on the sewing. Yes, that's the only place.
Nowicki: I thought somebody tried it one time, and they didn't make it out.
Schoonaert: They didn't allow it.
Dzierla: She disqualified him before a day was even . . .
Nowicki: I say one man did try once, and he couldn't make it. He couldn't do it.
Schoonaert: I think what was sad about this is when they did close in 1963, why these people that had thirty-six years' seniority and . . . I mean, they were not sixty years old. They were maybe just a little few years away from sixty and lost all their pensions. Never got a dime pension. I mean, they were paid so much for the years they worked in one lump sum, but that was it. But not for the rest of the days now. Now I don't get anything, and I worked there twenty years. I wasn't sixty years old, so I don't get a dime.
Nowicki: Yes, but at least we got something out of that. Like I got close to $750 when they closed.
Schoonaert: I say one lump sum you got, but these people who have it. I mean, there's people who have retired that had less seniority than I that are getting maybe $25 a month for the rest of their lives, you know. Where I don't get anything, and I had more seniority than they did. Look, a lump sum, what's a lump sum of money? I mean, that isn't anything.
Nowicki: Well, we had a fella here. He was about fifty-five when they shut off. He took his life away.
Van Daele: I know.
Nowicki: He just shot himself.
Van Daele: Oh, sure.
Nowicki: Lots of people shot themselves, or they took poison because they couldn't take it.
Grayzck: Committed suicide.
Van Daele: Actually family men.

How did you hear Studebaker's was going to close?

Drabecki: Rumors.
Van Daele: They told us. We heard rumors, but the official time came one morning and we walked out that same day.
Drabecki: It came in the morning.
Nowicki: In the morning, about eleven o'clock, everything was shut off. And they was out taking pictures.
Nowicki: That was shocking news to us. Very shocking news to us. We heard rumors, but that morning we all came in without knowing anything. And about 9:30, ten o'clock, they're shutting it off.
Drabecki: The *Tribune* knew it because everybody was out there, all the newspapers and everything.
Nowicki: Except the Studebaker people didn't know nothing about it. Just happened just like what, a surprise to us, didn't it?
Van Daele: Some ladies cried.
Nowicki: Some ladies cried.
Van Daele: And the bad part was at Christmas time. You know, right before Christmas [10 December 1963].

What did you feel the role of Studebaker was in the community? You all lived in South Bend. You worked for Studebaker. How did you feel that the Studebaker Company helped the community or in different ways?

Nowicki: Well, they did help a lot after they lost out. A lot of people didn't think that they'd ever come back to themselves again after they lost their jobs. They felt bad about it, didn't they? It was a big loss.
Drabecki: It was a source of income, a source of living, was Studebaker's.
Schoonaert: The businessmen did not drive a Studebaker. We did all of our shopping at their grocery store. And bought all our groceries from the store. And yet the proprietor of the store had other cars and didn't even drive Studebaker cars and then made us feel real bad. And then even the people that worked at Studebaker's, they were driving all other cars. Now I never drove anything but a Studebaker. As long as I worked at Studebaker's that's all I ever drove.
Drabecki: But when the first car was made in, what was it, 1947? If you bought a Studebaker and sold it and bought another one, then you lost your job.
Schoonaert: But in the end they asked everyone to buy Studebakers. That would help the Studebaker Corporation. But they didn't. They didn't. When they parked their car, they were all cars from everyone else's but Studebaker's.

Clifford MacMillan retired as vice president of Industrial Relations for the Studebaker Corporation.[2]

MacMillan: I was born in Hebron, Indiana, in 1908. It's about twenty miles southeast of Gary. And I lived on the farm until 1926, when I went into the U.S. Army.

What did you think you would do about making a living or doing with your life?

I had no career aspirations. I had a general feeling that I wanted to accomplish something in my life, but didn't really know how to go about it. I was attracted to the adventurous kinds of things and that's why I ended up in the army.

I was rather frustrated as a kid. I got very little guidance from my father. He was an immigrant from Scotland with a third-grade education, and his own ambitions were to work with horses. He used to go to Scotland and bring Clydesdale horses back. But I never remember him making any recommendation to me about a career or anything like that.

When did you first start working?

Oh, I worked in the fields at the age of nine. I could drive a team, I plowed corn—everything was horse then, you know. I plowed corn, and I helped in the haying and other things like that. Just whatever there was to do—milk cows—which I hated. I liked the horses. I took care of the animals.

I used to help the neighbors. There wasn't enough work on the farm for my dad and two boys, though. It was more labor intensive then. You know, everything was done with horses or by hand, and eighty acres, now, would be a very small farm. It was a modest, a fairly decent farm, in those days. But I started working with the neighbors, and then one summer I became very unhappy. Another guy and I started down the railroad, and I went to work on a railroad crew in Economy, Indiana, and I worked there most of the summer, living in boxcars. Strictly a colored group, too.

What were you unhappy about?

I don't really know, except that I wasn't satisfied with my life. And my father and I didn't get along very well; he was a man who believed in direct action when he was opposed. And I had problems with my father. For awhile I didn't run toward anything, I ran away from things. And that's when I went to the army. I was really running away from a situation that I didn't like. I'd had trouble at school. It was probably because I mouthed off. I was rebellious, and I had a teacher who was kind of rough in the way he handled things. The incident that really triggered it is that he said something about pulling my arm off and hitting me over the head with it. And I stood up and said, "Come on and try it, goddamn it, if you think you can." Well, I got throwed out of school. I was in my junior year at that time, and I was a fairly husky kid. I did some work around, and finally I decided I wanted to get away from the whole thing. And I went into Chicago and enlisted in the Army Air Corps. I was seventeen.

Well, I was sent to the Air Corps Technical School in Chanute, Illinois, and I took a course as a parachute

[2] Interviewed by John Bodnar, 11 May 1984, Hudson Lake.

rigger. But I had learned to type in school and there was an opportunity, over the short period of time, to go in an office there. So I went in and got my typing straightened up. When I graduated from school you could bid . . . you could apply for wherever you wanted to go. And I figured, well, I'm going, I might as well go as far as I can, so I asked for an assignment to the Philippines. And I was sent to the Third Pursuit Squadron at Clark Field, in Pampanga, north of Manila. I spent a year there. Nothing like it is today. It was a base that had 135 enlisted men and 12 officers. I commenced to decide that I needed to do something to improve myself so I applied for a transfer to Manila, so that I could go to Artereo de Manila, the college down there. And the transfer was granted, and I went to Company A, the Thirty-first Infantry. And I had the honor of being the youngest sergeant in the regiment; at nineteen I was line sergeant, which made me feel pretty good. There was an accomplishment.

I waited out the depression in the army. I came out in '29 and went back in because of the opportunities outside. And I was relatively well off because I had ration and quarters and allowance, I wore civilian clothes. I was a staff sergeant with shooting pay of an expert rifleman and that gave me an extra five dollars, so my income was in excess of one hundred dollars per month. And this was when people were working on WPA for thirty-five dollars.

But the children started coming, and so my wife and I decided that maybe I could make it on the outside. And I got my discharge—I bowed out—which you could do at that period of time and came back to Hebron. I contacted some people that I knew, was introduced to a National Guard colonel up there, who was an engineer in the steel mills. And he introduced me, in turn, to the employment office, and they put me to work. And my first job was the hooker—not the kind you may think about. It was hot, dirty, difficult—physically difficult—kind of work.

It was Carnegie–Illinois Steel in those days, it's now US Steel. About that time—this was in '36, '37—the Steelworkers Organizing Committee, which is now the Steelworkers of America, organized steel across the country. I stayed aloof from it for awhile but one day, because the management suspected that union meetings were going on in the washrooms, they turned off the heat in cold weather. And that did more to recruit union members than any union recruiter ever did. Then I went over, and I became involved in union management, or union affairs.

You mentioned that at the Gary plant that Arthur Goldberg, who later became Secretary of Labor of the United States, was a young attorney helping the Steelworkers Organizing Committee in Gary, and you had a chance to work with him.

That is right. I guess I was what today you might call a goon squad. I remember helping tip over a streetcar coming into the Broadway entrance of the Gary plant. I was just an enthusiastic volunteer and organizing men was, you know, nothing like it is now. It was a catch-as-catch-can thing. There was violence there in situations and so forth. But I had worked with Arthur a couple of times because of picket line incidents and things like that, where I'd come in contact with him. And I think he remembered me because I was a fair witness; when he needed testimony or needed to find out what was going on or what had happened, I probably was a little more accurate than most of the men. I imagine that's why.

How long did you stay in this Gary plant?

I was there five years. But about the time that the union was pretty firmly organized, I had an opportunity to go in the mill office. This was in the axle mill. And the mill superintendent was a guy by the name of Bob Lucas. I think if I had to give anybody credit for a leg up in my career, it was Bob Lucas. He was understanding. He gave me books to study. He gave me assignments—I was mill clerk—well, I got assignments that were well above that. I worked for the safety program, I worked with the industrial engineers when they came in to do some job evaluations and things like that.

And I had had enough experience in the steel mills, working with safety and so on, that I got a job [during World War II] as a safety and explosive engineer. I went to school at Illinois Tech. And my first assignment was to go to any one of 125 ordnance plants in the United States to make an investigation of industrial and explosive safety, control of confidential documents, and so forth. It was decided to set up a training, a safety training program, and I was selected with about twenty-five others to go to Newark, New Jersey, and work with some consultants out there to develop a ten-hour training program, a conference-type training program, for managerial and hourly people in the explosive plants. And the last day we were out there, much to my surprise, I was called over to one side and told that I'd be chief of the unit. I thought I was good, but I didn't think I was that good. I was very, very surprised. So I then handled the recruiting of the traveling group.

And part of my job was to go out and sell the management in an ordnance plant to accept the program, and schedule people, and then have a staff member put it on. When [World War II] started winding down, I was told that if I wanted to get the jump on things that I could get my certificate of availability. You had to have that to move in those days, under the Manpower regulations. I got a certificate of availability, and I went with the Ranger Aircraft Engines in Farmingdale, New York, as employment director. In about a year, an opportunity opened up in Chicago, near home, with the Container Corporation of America. And I got that job and became involved, or reinvolved, in union affairs, but on the other side of the table. We were being organized there, and I worked with the people from corporate who came in, and they liked what I did. And finally I had a chance to go with them in some other plants, more as an experience sort of thing, than anything else. I then was offered a job as director of industrial relations for the Lufkin Rule Company in Saginaw, Michigan, and I had the privilege of presiding over the longest strike in Michigan, at least at that time. We had some problems in that plant.

My ego commenced to grow, and I decided that I shouldn't just have one company profit by all this vast wisdom of mine, and I set up my own consulting firm. So, in between things, I had taught for the University of Michigan, and I had become acquainted with John Riegle, who was the director of the Bureau of Industrial Relations. In fact, we became friends and were friends

1952 Studebaker publicity photo showing brothers Charles and Arthur Smith, their uncle Deloise Smith, father Orville Smith, and grandfather John R. Smith. According to the photo's caption, "Studebaker fame has been built around hundreds of father-son teams in the plant."
Studebaker National Museum, South Bend

for several years after that. The University of Michigan's Survey Research group was about to go into Detroit-Edison with a study, and Riegle suggested to them that to supplement the academics would be a good idea to have someone who had actual business experience and so forth. This was interesting, and when that one was finished, one opened up at Studebaker.

A survey was going to be conducted at Studebaker?

At Studebaker, '47–'48. I liked the idea of coming back into the area. It was close to my home, and the children were growing, and so the wife and kids went back to their farm. My wife came from a farm about two miles from where ours were. We were childhood sweethearts. When I came back from the Orient we got married.

We had a staff of twenty-four or twenty-five people at Studebaker, and I carried the title of associate director for the studies. The purpose of the study, slimmed down, was to determine why Studebaker, after the war, with the same militant union that represented employees of the other automobile companies, had never had a strike.

And we must have been in for four or five months, but we talked with every management person, from the assistant foreman to the president of the corporation. We interviewed a cross section of six hundred employees. We talked to all of the union officers. So it was a study of some magnitude.

Well, by the end of the second day, I could have written the report that we were in there to make. The reason that Studebaker had no strikes—and now you have to do some definitions. And the definition that we were going in on was authorized strikes. That is, where the union had taken votes and had formal action and got international approval. And it was true that Studebaker hadn't had any of those, but it had wave after wave after wave of walkouts—wildcats. And the management did not succeed in stopping it. The reason they didn't is because they always compromised. People would go out on the street and there'd be a meeting called, and everybody'd sit down, and some sort of an accommodation was invariably made. So all that did was foster more of them.

So you think management was excessively accommodating?

You want to go into the reasons?

Well, sure. I mean, why, for example, should the management at Studebaker be any more accommodating than the management at General Motors?

Studebaker was in receivership in the thirties, and two men, Paul Hoffman and Harold Vance, bought it. It's the only automobile company that ever recovered from receivership. They did this by enlisting the assistance of the people. I've been told that the first Champion that came out were made for nothing, that the employees made these for nothing. And my own theory is that there was a gratitude there. We went through this thing together and we, you know, we've shared this sad experience and you've been loyal people. And the president, Harold Vance, at the time that I was there, would not permit the kind of strong reaction that was necessary to break this thing up. I can remember sitting in his office one day with the vice president of manufacturing—at that time it was P. O. Peterson. He's dead now, but P. O. Peterson—he went up there and became president of Mack Trucks. And Peterson had come up with a program to move in and restudy the jobs of certain workers in the plant. And the meeting went on until about noon. I was assistant director of standards and planning at that time, and I was there with my boss, who was the director of standards and planning. And when—I can see him yet—Vance reaching for his coat and turning to Peterson and saying, "Now Pete, I don't want any trouble. Don't do anything to get those people upset."

So he's saying to Peterson, "You can go and institute time studies but don't cause any problems?"

Well, if the stewards objected, quit, is really what it meant. And that's exactly what happened. They went out with a whole bunch of time study men and started the time study. The employees threatened to walk off, and they pulled the time study men out.

What else was going on at the time in '47 and '48 with Studebaker that gave you the impression that management was lax?

Well, the most startling example I can give you is the stamping division, which was scheduled to operate from 7:00 to noon, and from 12:30 to 3:30. They were on a piecework system, and by noon every man had made his quota and not a wheel turned three hours in the afternoon—not one thing turned in that division. The people sat around and told stories, played cards, and read newspapers. Some of them would sneak over the fence, and go home and their buddies would punch them out. And there were literally whole laundry lists of practices like that. They were overmanned. They had too many people for the work that they did. The man-hours that went into a Studebaker were probably 25 percent more than the man-hours that went into Ford, General Motors, and Chrysler. They had idle time allowances that were the envy of the industry. It was a mess.

In '58 or '59, there was the first formal strike?

Fifty-eight was the first union-authorized strike. There was another one in 1960. It was over work standards. That was in 1960. And Nagy, Joe Nagy, was the president. Nagy was president of the union. And he had run on a platform of sweatshop, that Studebaker was making people work too hard, and everything else. There may have been a few operations where people were loaded heavier than they should be, but here again, they didn't want to file the grievance procedure. Work standards were not subject to arbitration in the agreement we had. They wouldn't go to arbitration with work standards. So they went out on that basis, and it really didn't hurt us because we were overproduced. We had cars running out of our ears, and it really didn't hurt us that much. That one was the silliest thing that ever happened, and it went on for probably three weeks or four weeks. And we finally resolved it by agreeing upon a special grievance procedure for production standards.

Sixty-three was the most vicious strike that we ever had, because we needed a production increase time but we had to break this thing. And finally we decided that we'd declare an impasse and that we would notify the union that if we didn't have a settlement by January 1, that our proposed terms would be in effect. And that did it. That started the strike. But this was, we knew it would, we were sure that it would. But we had to end this horsing around. Something had to break and that was the only way we could think to break it.

We had picket line incidents for the first time. And this was when president [Sherwood] Egbert got arrested. He broke an agreement that I had with the union about driving into the plant.

I had agreed to that we wouldn't drive cars into the plant, that we'd leave the cars outside, because they were accusing us of smuggling stuff out, you know. Well, you couldn't smuggle enough out to make any difference, but a matter of principle. And I also agreed that we would show our company passes when we went through the picket line. And I got back for that even more than I give out, but Egbert was furious over it. And he and I got into an argument—and I won't go into that one—but anyway, I come out of it feeling I stood up for myself, anyhow. But anyway, we were developing a vehicle called a Turtle, and it had a Nonan engine in it. And it was like a motorized wheelbarrow. It was to be used for the military in taking stuff up the hill instead of the mules, you know. We had it in the engineering building. And there was some lieutenant general came from Washington to see this thing. I was taking care of another picket incident down at the parts plant. . . .

I came back, and Egbert's secretaries were crying. "Oh, Mr. MacMillan, can you do anything? They've got Mr. Egbert and a client over on Sample Street, and they won't let him out." He had taken this Mercedes Benz, which made them all mad, anyhow—why can't he drive a Studebaker, you know? He had taken this Mercedes Benz, and he loaded up the attorney and a couple other guys and this general, and he drove right through the picket line. And they were surprised and let him go, see. When he started back, they wouldn't let him out. And there must have been three hundred of them just milling around the front of the Sample Street gate.

And I finally got over there, you know, and I went in and talked to Egbert, and he was leaning on his car looking at them disgusted, you know, "the sons-of-bitches." And he said, "Well, we called the cops," he says, "they're going to come down."

So I said, "Well, let me see what I can do." And I jumped into this melee out here, and I got ahold of the collar on the leaders and said, "Look, goddamn it, we're trying to get a settlement on a labor dispute and this isn't helping any. Why don't you let him out?"

And I wish we had that film. They had about forty cops there, and all of a sudden they formed a V and they went right into the circle and locked arms. He shot out with the Mercedes.

I hope that I haven't indicated that I'm critical of the union. The responsibility for making decisions is management's responsibility. The union cannot be asked to help you do your job, and that was the situation. When Vance was there, Vance thought that if you went out and talked to the stewards that they'd put their shoulder to the wheel, like they did in the good old days, you know.

You said you took some aggressive moves in the fifties in terms of civil rights?

Yes. We had decided that we had potential in the plant that we weren't using. And there wasn't any morality attached to this. I think that the fact that I worked with a black crew on the railroad when I was sixteen years old and got along with them—I have no bias on color. And that's not just conversation, I really don't have any bias on it. But we decided that, looking ahead, that there's going to be trouble. And so we thought, well, let's break the color line. And we selected three blacks.

Forest Hanna was president of the union then. And very quietly, I asked Forest for his recommendation. I wanted blacks who, I wanted a superb black for what my purpose was. We put one into foreman training. His name is Odell Newburn.

We picked a girl by the name of Martha LaSane, and she was black, and put her in the administration building. There wasn't a black over there. And then we picked another guy by the name of Felix Curtis and brought him into our office and made him a trainee first. And here's the things that make you feel good: he's just retired as an industrial relations executive from Chrysler a year ago.

You moved up into another echelon in the company in the early sixties?

I was made vice president in early 1960, and before the year was out I was made the vice president of the corporation. And in November 1963, I spent a helluva lot of time in New York, with the board and without the board. The chairman of the board was a man by the name of [Randolph] Guthrie. And let me take you to Friday night, which would have been the seventh of December. I'm in New York, Saturday night, and I'm down doing some paperwork. Well, let me go back a little further than that. Let me go back three or four days before that, and we're out there and we figured that we've got to tighten the belt. And I am told, "Mac, I want you to go back to South Bend and you get the executives together, and you tell them that we are in a desperate situation and for them to go over their budgets and see how much they can take out."

So I go back to South Bend, and I called them together and I said, "Fellows, we're probably in the worst predicament we've ever been in, and each of you should go back to your operation and come back with your revision of a budget." I said, "Take out everything you don't have to have tomorrow morning." So I went back the next day with this revised budget.

But now I'll move ahead to probably Saturday night. We're sitting down there and Guthrie comes down, the chairman of the board. And Guthrie was talking about flying to Germany that night to Daimler-Benz and seeing if he could sell them the Mercedes Benz inventory for eight million bucks. Now this was the kind of thing that was going on back then. Then Saturday afternoon the decision was that "We'll make the decision tomorrow, and we'll release it." Or on Monday. They were going to make it Monday and release it Tuesday. And my assignment was to go back and get the union together on Sunday and warn them that the decision hadn't been made, but that in my best judgment it was going to be "Shut her down."

Now you stayed with the corporation after the automobile plant closed, for awhile.

Oh, yes, I was there about seven years. Everything was done to provide other employment for the people that was in our power. There were a lot of people whose parents and grandparents had worked for Studebaker and who worked for them, and they would look on

Studebaker employment, with all its ups and downs, as they're going to be there the rest of their lives. The reactions of some of these people were tragic. They went into their homes and wouldn't come out. There were some reported suicides. I don't know if there was any of those. And it was a tragic thing.

But most people did get some other employment?

Well, one of those things that was helpful to them was the fact that a lot of Studebaker employees were laid off periodically. And some of them owned farms and filling stations and moonlighted and so forth. So they were accustomed to surviving for short periods of time without Studebaker.

What were some of the programs that the community undertook to help these people?

Well, I've mentioned the ABLE program, and that was a group of people, both union and management people, who were under Les Fox. And one part of the group cultivated jobs. They looked all over; they went and talked to people within a fifty- to sixty-mile radius, anyplace with the possibility of hiring people, and were persuasive in getting them to consider the older Studebaker employees. The other part were out in the homes, getting guys out and getting them to try again. It was a very big problem with some of them. The world was over as far as they were concerned. "There's not a chance of me getting a job. I'm forty-nine, I'm fifty-three, now where could I get a job?"

There was, as I remember, about $28 million in the pension plan. Now this was a formal plan; it was a legal agreement between the company and the union. It had provisions within the plan, in the event it was ever liquidated, as to the priority the money would be allocated for. Well, the priorities established were the first currently retired people, so part of that was set aside to buy annuities for them. The next priority was people sixty years or older, and another chunk came out for them. And then there were the disability pensions, which was the third order of preference—the money was taken out and put over there. There was something like $2 million left—in that order.

I was called into Washington to a committee that was investigating pensions, and along with me was the actuary from the UAW. We'd worked together for years. And they probed into the thing. But there was a congresswoman from New York—I don't remember her name—but she said, "Mr. MacMillan, how much money did Studebaker take from the pension plan?"

And I said, "Not one goddamn cent, Madame."

Well, that's the picture. Now, never mentioned, is the fact that substantial sums of money were coming into this area and other areas where Studebaker retired people still live. The last I knew it was something over one million a year, it was being paid through the annuities, being paid into the community. Let me add one other thing and then I'll quit being so defensive about this. If that termination had been under current law, we would have had no liability either.

Otto Klausmeyer retired as a plant engineer for the Studebaker Corporation, where he worked since 1923. He was born in 1899.[3]

Mr. Klausmeyer, why don't you tell me where you were born and when?

Cairo, Illinois. Both my parents were born in America. My father was educated in Purdue. My father was born in Huntingburg, Indiana, a seat of early German culture, and my mother was born in Lafayette. Of my four grandparents, both grandmothers were born in America and one from a family that came here in 1775—settled in Philadelphia. Both grandfathers came from Germany to escape military conscription there and settled in Indiana.

My father was an idealist. He was an author, a good writer. He could do almost any kind of physical work, any kind of mechanical or electrical work. He was probably one of the greatest naturalists I've ever run across. He could walk into a woods and name all the trees and bushes in the woods. And he was a very, very excellent operator of farm animals, stock. He had a rather nomadic existence, and he left after he married.

[3] Interviewed by John Bodnar, 11 May 1984, South Bend.

He left Huntingburg and went to Dayton, Ohio, to work for the National Cash Register company, which was where I was born, in 1899. And one of my first recollections is when we lived in a three-room house on West Washington Street in Dayton, which is now a black ghetto. I remember one cold night my father came home, opened the door rapidly and knocked the snow off his derby, and shook off the snow off his overcoat, and announced, "McKinley has been shot." This was 1901.

Then we moved from Huntingburg to Oklahoma City, in the time when everybody was in the business of "Go West, young man," was at a fever pitch. And the principle reason for him going to Oklahoma was that the doctor, my mother had acquired a very, very severe throat, raspy throat condition, and in those days, when a doctor couldn't cure or help anybody, he very rapidly sent the patient out into another location. So he recommended that they go west in a dry climate, so we moved to Oklahoma City. And my dad was employed by the city in a street department, and we started school there. And at that time Oklahoma was not a state.

How long did you live in Oklahoma?

We moved there in 1905, and we left there two years later. And the reason why we left was because Oklahoma City had a serious water problem at that time. They had no municipal water, and everyone had their own wells. And all the wells were contaminated, and the whole family got typhoid fever. And so my father decided to move to some healthful place that at least had healthful water. So he moved to a little town in northern Arkansas called Mountain Home. And it was an old, old, old town. We lived there from 1907 to 1911, and then we moved from there to Little Rock, where my dad operated a hotel for railroad men. And we moved from Little Rock, then, to a little town north of Little Rock, called Cabot, where I met my wife. And we were later married, in 1920, and we lived together for sixty-three years.

And in early 1918 my dad decided to move north, back where there was a little more opportunity, since there was no industrial work at all in Arkansas at that time. So we moved to Detroit and principally to give my younger brother a good education and to give me a chance for a job.

That's the main reason you moved?

I had gone to the University of Arkansas—I went through high school at Cabot—went to the University of Arkansas, and one year, the World War broke out. And while I was at the University of Arkansas I discovered something about myself that I didn't know prior to that, and that was that I was a natural, very, very rapid draftsman.

While you were a young boy, down in Arkansas, did you have any ambitions or aspirations at this time?

I certainly did. I certainly did. I was an automobile man from the time I was five years old. I had nothing in my mind . . . as my uncle said. My uncle brought me back, disgustedly, one Sunday, and brought me into the kitchen and dumped me unceremoniously into a chair and said to my mother, "Dena, this kid is never going to be anything. He's never going to be good at anything. He's got nothing in his head but wheels."

Well, in Arkansas, when I was in high school, I traded for a motorcycle and three or four more motorcycles, and I traded for three different kinds of automobiles and rebuilt them before I ever went to the university.

When we moved to Detroit in '18 I went over to the Highland Park Plant of Ford Motor Company. I had always wanted to design engines, automobile engines. "Well," they said, "we don't have any opportunity for car parts draftsmen. We do have an opportunity for tool designers."

So I said, "OK."

So I went up there to the fourth floor to the drafting room, where they had 125 draftsmen, and they were designing tools, and jigs, and fixtures, conveyors, and furnaces, and special machinery. And they built their own machinery in the Ford–Highland Park Plant. Well, this was really something, and I really went for that. And my first job there was an armload of changes the foreman brought to me, to make changes brought in, sent in from the shop. Change orders came in from the shop to change certain dimensions of something else, see. So the foreman and the checker were a little bit upset when about the end of the first day, I brought them all back to the checker, all finished.

Well, to make a long story short, I was there about three years and at the end of three years, I was designing special machinery. At the age of eighteen, I was designing special machinery for Ford Motor Company.

Did you ever meet Henry Ford?

I never met him. I'd say in my tenure of three years at Ford Company, in those days, I saw him probably three or four times. And my drafting board was right on the Woodward Avenue front, on the fourth floor, and I could see right down into his office on top of his desk.

He had a large office at the back of the administration building, on the first floor, between the administration building and the manufacturing building. I'd seen him drive in many times, but close up, he was rarely ever there. I could see in his office, and it was a rare occasion, indeed, when he came into the office.

He had an uncanny ability to know exactly what was going on in every corner of that giant plant. At that time, Highland Park was producing fifty-five hundred Model Ts a day and had sixty-five thousand employees.[4] When they came streaming out to change, out of that plant, to change the shifts, this was something to behold. You couldn't believe it. The street would be black with humanity.

Why did you leave Ford?

My dad had an old, old home his parents had accumulated, or found and bought this thing, and many years had gone by. It was in Bloomington, Indiana. And it was a big old house that sat on First Street, back of a grocery store, right opposite the city hospital on South Rogers Street. And so he wanted to do something with this thing because it was in such horrible shape. And so my brother had then just graduated out of high school and had enrolled in Indiana University, Bloomington. So my dad said, "Well, we'll just sell this place and go down to rebuild that house, and live there while Leonard goes to school." So we moved down there, and Leonard and I rebuilt this house in about six months and made a two family out of it.

When I left Ford I got a leave of absence for a couple months to go down and help my dad rebuild this old house. And when we had it rebuilt it was late winter, December. So there was nothing to do in Bloomington, so I decided to go back to Ford. So my brother and I got in this little Model T he had, a roadster, and started out Saturday, Saturday morning. And we came, we drove to Detroit by way of South Bend. Why we did, I don't know. We left Bloomington early in the morning, and it was beginning to be dark when we got into South Bend. So we hunted up a lodging place, and I bought a *South Bend Tribune*, and there was a big ad in the *Tribune* stating that the Studebaker Corporation needed plant engineering draftsmen. And I said to my brother, "You know, I think I will just take another two, three weeks and case this job. I'll take this job and get on it and see what it looks like."

So, Leonard went on to Detroit in the Model T, and on Monday morning I went in and applied for work. I had my tools with me. And I went in to see the general employment manager who was a man by the name of Nelson H. Kaiser, who had started to work as a sixteen-year-old boy as a letter carrier for J. M. Studebaker. Well, he interviewed me about five minutes. I didn't need to get a physical examination. And he said, "OK, you're hired. Go on up and go to work." So I wasn't in the employment office over fifteen minutes until I was assigned a drafting board in the plant engineering department. And things were moving so rapidly I could hardly catch my breath. So I started to work in the planning and engineering department.

You know, a very good old-timer at the plant over there was R. A. Vail, apparently one of the best executives they ever had at the plant, vice president in charge of production and engineering [around 1926].

He said to me, after I was gigging him a little bit on a trip to Philadelphia, about some of the errors some of the upper-class, upper guys had made in the manage-

[4] According to Stephen Meyer III, *The Five Dollar Day: Labor Management and Social Control in the Ford Motor Company, 1908–1921* (Albany: State University of New York Press, 1981), Ford's Highland Park factory employed 12,880 workers in 1914 and 32,679 in 1921. Production figures for those years were 248,307 and 933,720 automobiles, respectively.

ment, and he said to me, "Remember one thing: the mistakes that make or break corporations are always made by the organ-grinder, they're never made by the monkey." And this was Studebaker's problem from start to finish.

The first half, or production of horse-drawn vehicles, and the second, automotive, and it's almost equally divided. In other words, from 1852 to about 1910, and then from 1904 or '05 on to the shutdown in 1963, the early first half was managed by the Studebaker brothers. And the second half, the automobile half, never did achieve superior location in competition that the first half did. The most prestigious operation in the world of the two halves was during the horse-drawn era. They started from sixty-eight dollars, and they wound up multimillionaires.

The horse-drawn vehicle outfit was preeminent in their sphere. They were the largest manufacturing company of horse-drawn vehicles in the world. There was nobody like them. But the reason why they were preeminent was because they were not only good managers, good financiers, honest people, but they were also engineers. They had the biggest toolroom in the Midwest. They made their own machinery. They had special machinery for making almost every part of the wagon and buggy. They had automatic machinery for assembling wheels, believe it or not. And they built hundreds of wagons and bodies, buggies a day when these other people operating by hand couldn't.

What was going on in the late twenties though?

They were in fairly sound financial shape and were making money until late 1928 or early 1929. And they started losing their shirt in '29 and '30 and '31. Then, of course, in 1933 [Albert Russell] Erskine stops his part of the business quickly.[5]

Why is that?

Erskine's wealth was in Studebaker stock, and he was interested in staying afloat financially, and he was dishing out dividends to take care of himself. And not only himself but some other people who were in a like condition.

Were you plant manager at this time?

Yes.

Are you aware that, or aren't you aware that more was being paid out in dividends?

Sure, I was aware of it, why not? I thought it was none of my damn business because I thought that this guy's been running this thing now for twenty years, he's been doing nothing but handling money all his life. He sure ought to know something about it. Probably at least more than I do. So I had no idea why he was doing this at that time. But the money dispensed in dividends was during the thirties, just before he died.

Yes, he committed suicide, didn't he?

Yes. The reason for it is not known. I can tell you the reason for it. In 1931, Studebaker's . . . let me back up just a minute and tell you something. Studebaker products were designed generally in the engineering department or by outside designers. And the decision on what products they made was made, according to the bylaws of the corporation, by three men: the chairman of the board, the president, and the chairman of the finance committee, who was always appointed by the banks. So we had three men appointed by the banks that made the decision on what kind of a car to make, and they were perpetually making the wrong decisions.

As long as I have been there, there was never a time when the production couldn't easily more than take care of what the sales could sell because of this stupid business of designing their own kind of car.

We didn't recognize such a thing as labor and management. People just did a job they were supposed to do, and everybody talked to everybody else. I mean, of course, Erskine never got out of the ad building. He

[5] Albert R. Erskine came to Studebaker in 1911 as a treasurer and served as president of the corporation from 1915 until he was removed from office during Studebaker's receivership in 1933. He committed suicide on 1 July 1933. Donald Critchlow, *Studebaker: The Life and Death of an American Corporation* (Bloomington: Indiana University Press, 1996), 66–67, 103.

never went in the shop in his life—never. And one of his characteristics was, too, that he was a great gambler. He would gamble on anything. Every time he got on the golf course he wanted to gamble, with anybody. He was just a gambling—he had a fetish with it.

Now, let's skip to the fateful day of the twenty-first of October 1929, and after. There's another very, very strange and extraneous group comes on the scene about this time, and that is the gang that designed the Rockne, built the Rockne. And this goes back to 1928, to the Dodge brothers' plant, when the bankers sold the Dodge brothers' plant to Walter Chrysler. When Chrysler moved into the plant at the front door, the old Dodge management went out the back. They wouldn't have any part of Walter Chrysler. And I can tell you some reasons why, but I won't right now. At any rate, out of that group was R. A. Vail, who was vice president in charge of production, and had been with the Dodge brothers since they started making Model T engines in 1905. He was a vice president, and he was one of the most marvelous tool designers you ever saw. And Roy Cool, who came from Chalmers and Hudson, he was the chief engineer, and there was about six or seven other people.

So Willys hired this group to design a six-cylinder automobile for them. And they took these two cars—Vail and Cole took these two cars—down to the management, the board of directors at Willys-Overland in Toledo, and submitted them. And Willys-Overland said, "That's fine." They took them out and drove the cars and they said, "They meet, or fulfill our needs completely. But we're broke. We don't have any money. We can't build them. But we've already paid you, our commitment with you is over with. Now we will give you these cars and you can do anything you want to with them."

So the old man drove—I call Vail "the old man" because he was really the old man—drove to South Bend. And at noon he got to South Bend, and he happened to think, "Well, South Bend—Studebaker. Guess I'll go see if Erskine's there." So he drove over in front of the ad building, and old man Erskine was there, alone. Nobody else in the ad building, Saturday morning. Vail went up to see Erskine, laid the whole thing out in front of him. Erskine came down, drove the car around, and bought it [snaps fingers]. Just like that.

He bought the car, the design, and all the people. They come to work for Studebaker. So this whole gang came to work for Studebaker then in 1931, but they didn't have any money to pursue this thing. Then Mr. Erskine discovers that the White Motor Corporation had $4 million cash.

And old Erskine was a salesman. He sells White Motors on the idea that there should be a merger, a stock exchange, merger deal, see? So they worked out this stock exchange and merger deal and as soon as the merger was complete the parent company, which was Studebaker, declared a $4 million dividend in favor of Studebaker, and took their money to build the Rockne.

Then this dissident bunch of stockholders—3 percent of the stockholders—Erskine discovered that he was being subpoenaed into superior court in Cleveland to answer some questions from the judge. So he didn't think much about it.

And then the trial came off, and these lawyers had discovered an old Ohio law which said that a merger of two corporations cannot be complete unless 100 percent of the stockholders on both sides approve it. And only 97 percent had approved it. So they were in complete—it was completely illegal. And the judge said to Erskine, "You don't have any problems, Mr. Erskine, all you have to do is go back to South Bend and get the $4 million and bring it back."

He couldn't bring the money back. He had spent it. He had 20,000 bucks, his home was mortgaged, everything he had was in his wife's name. And he came back, stayed about two days in the ad building, and went out there and shot himself.

You were plant engineer at this time. How long did you remain plant engineer?

I was plant engineer from 1926 until 1947. Then I was made foundry superintendent. I stayed here, but I built the South Bend Aviation Plant, I built the Chicago Aviation Plant, and I built the Fort Wayne Aviation Plant during World War II.

What did Studebaker do during World War II? They couldn't produce cars, what exactly did they do?

Employees gather around the last car produced before Studebaker turns over to war production, 1942
Studebaker National Museum, South Bend

Well, we made 57,875 nine-cylinder Curtiss-Wright 1820 rotary radial engines that powered the Flying Fortress. Then we made some 80,000 trucks, military trucks, in the old plant. And then when the Korean War came along we made General Electric jets.

In the late thirties, the workforces of most of the auto plants, now, are starting to organize—the unions. They hadn't been extensively organized before. . . .

Well now, let me tell you one secret. It establishes the date when the union started getting a toehold. Roosevelt was president.

Studebaker was reorganized in 1935. Well, first of all, they went bankrupt. And one of the conditions under which they went bankrupt was set by the government, and that was that the union be permitted to come in and organize Studebaker. That was set by Roosevelt. So this place was organized right after 1935. During—the minute we came back out of the receivership, we were organized. And about the same time Bendix was struggling with their bunch over there and they had a sit-down strike for about two to three months and, of course, that's when you had all the other labor difficulties, a little later, in Detroit.

But now, I've seen both sides of this labor deal. I have been in a Ford plant and a Dodge plant, and I want to tell you right now, that whatever is said about Ford being good for labor, and the Dodge brothers being good for labor, is so much baloney. Of all the slave drivers you have ever seen in your life, they always had them hired.

How about at Studebaker? Was that true at Studebaker?

No, they went the other way. The unions were in control! Let me give you the reason why they were in control. Again, management. First of all, the bankers in New York City weren't interested too much in what the labor cost was as long as they just added to the price. As long as we could sell cars. And that still goes today,

OK? The union served a notice on Studebaker when we came back to work in automobile plants in 1945 that they would produce no more than 80 percent of what they had previously produced.

If only they had produced 80 percent it wouldn't have been bad. But I'll give you a good example, see. I'll give you a good example. One day I got a call from old Ed Vance. And boy, I'll tell you, I could have killed that guy a dozen times. He was a very, very soft-spoken guy, who could get up and filibuster for two and a half hours until everybody went to sleep and never say a word. He was a typical politician, see. Well, he was chairman of the board. Hoffman had gone. He had had Hoffman fired.

Well, you could see why, because the bylaw says that the corporation shall be run by three men: the president, chairman of the board, and chairman of the finance committee. Now if the president and the chairman of the board is the same man, he runs it, don't he? OK. If he got into that position—he talked the stupid board into that position—and he hired Hoffman, had Hoffman fired in 1947. And the bankers went to Truman and had Truman give him the job of operating this giveaway program in Europe.[6]

Now, so Vance was running the show, personally. One day he called me on the phone. . . .

"I'm getting a lot of static from our boys in the union who say that they can't get out of 84 Building quick enough. We only have three stairways, main stairways. I want you to immediately get prices on three additional stairwells on the north side of the building so we can give them rapid egress."

So I said, "Mr. Vance, that property is not ours. It belongs to the railroad. Moreover, the railroad is on the second floor, so there is a chasm in between there that you will dump people into. Furthermore, I can tell you, that you are talking about three times $1,750,000 for three new elevator towers anywhere on any building in South Bend."

He said, "Well, don't give me so many objections, just do it."

And I said, "Now, may I make one suggestion?" I said, "I know where this objection is coming from. It's coming from the fire marshal office in Indianapolis. And he is a charter member of the AFL-CIO."

"And I know these guys here are pushing him and he's pushing you." I said, "Why don't we send Courtney Johnson, who is the corporate's best diplomat, down to talk to the governor."

"Well," he said, "that's a good idea."

The next day he sent Courtney Johnson down to talk to the governor, and that's the last I ever heard of it. Then in the meanwhile, just to satisfy myself, I called up the industrial engineering department—Jay Curry. I said, "Jay, how many men do you really need on the sixth floor of 84 at this production level?"

He said, "I don't have to study that, I can tell you. You need 222."

I said, "How many are up there now?"

And he said, "890."

What were they doing up there in that shop?

Nothing. Throwing parts at each other, hanging out of the windows. They'd go away for a month's vacation and come back, and somebody would punch their clock in the meanwhile.

And so it finally got to where Vance, the corporation head, would tell the foremen and the lower echelon people, "Stand your ground. Don't give anything in to the union." Then the union would go up to him, and he'd give them everything they wanted. He was double-crossing his own people. And in one instance, at a meeting out at the aviation plant one Sunday morning, and he made a decision in favor of the union, and he told the union president to go locate the plant superintendent and tell him what the decision had been.

Were you surprised when they finally shut down auto production in South Bend?

Not at all. I'll tell you why. After I had been here three weeks and observed some of the top decisions, I remember talking to my brother and telling him that I might as well quit because this outfit isn't going to last another month, they are awful. They don't know what they are doing. The first three weeks I was here, they decided, all of a sudden, to dump all the present transmissions. So they get ready and start scrapping all the

[6] Paul Hoffman led the European Recovery Administration under President Truman from 1948 to 1953. Critchlow, *Studebaker*, 126.

Sherwood Egbert with the Avanti
Studebaker National Museum, South Bend

tooling to make this transmission, and we're moving half the machinery out, and all of a sudden they decide, all bets are off, we're going to go back to the old transmission, we don't want that transmission. So we had to go back and grab all this tooling and put it back, and this kind of monkey business went on all the time. You just, you can't imagine. I used to get so disgusted that I'd just come home and just almost cry. It was just hopeless.

In 1940 I made a chart based on Studebaker's position, competitive-wise, in the sales market, which is the real criteria on whether a company is successful or a failure, right? They started out in number three in the market. And I plotted that whole curve from figures I got from R. L. Polk on the production and sales. And in 1940 I plotted this curve on a chart and extrapolated that curve until it came off the chart in 1962.

It was obvious in 1940—that early—during a period of fairly good prosperity—that unless the top management changed their policies, or unless the top management was changed, Studebaker would be out of business by 1962.

I made a very careful study in 1955 on the growth of the Japanese car and imports, and the size, and the reasons for their sale. And made a chart showing the terrific upward spiral of the Japanese vehicles in America, and examined their engineering very, very closely, as well as that of the Volkswagen and others. And I was one of the ones that was instrumental in having [Harold E.] Churchill cut down the size of the Lark like he did.

And I've always said that the automobile is a vehicle, a device to transport people, individuals, from here to there. It's a quick way to get from here to there, seated. OK. But it's not designed for a bus. And this is the reason for the oncoming trend of small cars. And I saw that, and I tried to convince Churchill of that, and I finally convinced him and he cut the size of the Lark down, that's why we sold them. And then come '60 and I said, "Church, we've got to get a little four-cylinder out."

Church was so sold on it that he actually had the styling department style and build it in the foundry. I built twelve engines, castings, and machined three of them, and in the engineering department we built two little prototypes of that little four-cylinder car. And it would have gone over like nothing. We would have been in business yet.

And then along comes this leggy high school dropout, Egbert, who has got nothing on his mind but super performance and super style. Then he goes to the board and wants money to build a super-stylish car. And what does the board do? They supply him with a designer, their own designer. His name was Raymond Loewy. Raymond Loewy worked for the banks. And he was a German Jew who lived in Paris—he got run out of Germany—and he talked with a thick German accent. And he was the biggest con artist you ever saw in your life. Well, he's the guy that [is] supposed to have designed the Avanti. And Egbert knew absolutely nothing about automobiles. He was nothing. He knew nothing. He had one thing in mind when he came here. And he brought a man along with him to foster this idea, his own personal PR man. He said, "The thing that is most important to me is my image."

Harold E. Churchill began working for Studebaker in 1926. He was the president of Studebaker upon its closing in 1963.[7]

Churchill: I was born on July 4, 1903, in Penn, Michigan, a little Quaker settlement in Cass County. I think I was a very fortunate young man in that from the earliest, I can remember what I was interested in. I look back now after many years and I can discern things that indicated an aptitude and an unflinching desire on my part to be in things mechanical.

Unlike a lot of people, my life's work was pretty well oriented from the time I was about ten years old. I can remember well that a neighbor and I decided to build an automotive piece of machinery consisting of the running gear of an International Harvester mower, a four-wheel buggy, a stationary mower gasoline engine, and a driving belt off the dynamo on Pullman cars that we found along the railroad track. We put this thing together clandestinely. We got everything all together. This was when I was about eleven or twelve years old. We decided on a date we were going to inaugurate it, launch it, and we both professed to have stomachaches the morning that my father and mother hitched up the surrey and went to church. So we didn't go. We had this thing in components that we could bolt together quite readily, and we did. We lived on a 288-acre farm, and shortly after we were left home from church, we started this thing up and drove it down a large hill. We couldn't get it back up the hill because the belt slipped. We thought my father would really chastise us no end.

Pretty soon, they came home from church in the surrey, brothers and sisters, the family. And I'll never forget my father's grin from ear to ear when he saw us at the bottom of this hill in really a peck of trouble. And he finally, rather than castigating us, said, "Well, come on boys. Get in. Let's go home and eat. I'll come back and help you get this thing back home, 'cause we got to pump water." That was one of my first experiences in automotive transportation. And, as I said, I was about eleven years old.

But this desire and mechanical aptitude was nurtured by the local blacksmith who let me come into his shop. Any other kid up there would have been chased out posthaste, but he'd let me use all his tools because I always put them back. And I got in the bee business, built hives and foundation frames and that stuff, all as a means to an end.

The blacksmith shop burned down one day, and I negotiated with the blacksmith about a power drill there, a hand-fed drill that burned up in the fire. It was frozen fast, and I asked him how much he wanted for it. He said, "Fifty cents." My father gave me fifty cents to buy this thing, and I fastened it up. My shop was going to be on top of the granary in the back barn that we had. I finally got this thing freed up, and this drill was the beginning of my shop.

In 1925 I worked the summertime at Dodge Brothers Manufacturing Company in Detroit on drawing-board layout work in the engineering department. That was just about the time Dillon Reed bought the Dodge Brothers and formed the Chrysler Corporation. Walter Chrysler came in.

A friend of mine [in 1926] and I were invited to a house party up north of Pontiac. I don't remember the name of the lake now. But the chaperon of this group was a group engineer, a group leader, in the engineering

[7] Interviewed by R. T. King, 28 and 29 February 1980, South Bend.

department at Studebaker. And he then told me, "Harold, we need some help down in the lab at Studebaker. Why don't you come on out and . . . ?" I went out Monday morning, and they hired me at a hundred dollars a month. I was supposed to go back to school, and at the end of the month, they said, "Well, we need you."

Of course, you were there during the time when Albert Erskine was the president of the corporation. Can you give me any evaluation of Erskine's character and of the impact that he had on the fortunes of Studebaker in the late 1920s, early 1930s?

Well, he lived in an ivory tower to me. I was a little laboratory technician. Albert Erskine was a good financial man. He, I think, inspired the building of smaller, more compact automobiles, challenged the product-design department to build a small, well, experimentally it was known as Job 100, which was later named commercially the Erskine. And it was a small size, I think the forerunner of the compact automobiles that we know today.

Of course, the car did not prove to be a sales success.

You have to look at it from this standpoint too: there was an economic collapse in 1929. And who's to say what the impact of that was? It certainly had an effect on the whole economy of the country, of the world. And maybe it was not the propitious time to launch something of that kind. I'm sure that industrial expansion was really slowed down during that period.

This brings us up to 1933, then, and the receivership, the first collapse of Studebaker.

We were aware that they were losing money. I don't think there was any of us in the lower echelons of the engineering department that realized to what depth it had gone. I'm sure the chief engineer and vice president of engineering was aware of this.

Can you recall any efforts on the part of Studebaker management to do anything within the organization of the company to rectify the problem?

Well, the day we were placed under Chapter Eleven receivership, there were no employees in the engineering department. The vice president of engineering was the only employee of the corporation left. We were all terminated.

Tell me what happened the day you went into receivership, then. Describe that day for me.

My wife and I were up to my folks' home. And my mother rapped on the bedroom door Sunday morning with the Sunday paper. Studebaker had hit the headlines. That's the first I knew of it. We didn't know what was going on, and we were all terminated.

Well, we were in shock. And I don't particularly remember. But we were told to go home, that we were no longer employees. I and seven other people were rehired in the engineering department. There were eight of us. The receiver realized that product planning had to go along, and they gave us some money—modest, meager budgets. And we went on with a zeal that we were going to whip it. I don't know why now, because we weren't going to be there forever under those conditions.

What can you tell me about Paul Hoffman?

He was a highly successful dealer in Studebaker cars in Los Angeles and later came in 1925 into the corporation as vice president in charge of sales or general sales manager, I'm not sure which. But he later became an officer of the corporation, vice president in charge of sales. He was a tremendously forceful stimulator of people, saleswise. His success in the Los Angeles area was due to his personality, his gregariousness, and his ability of motivating other people. He had a tremendous facility for that.

Do you know why Hoffman was appointed as a receiver?

I don't know why Hoffman was appointed receiver. But I can speculate that he and Harold Vance were the key people after Erskine had bowed out by putting a gun in his ear. They were the principal in-house motivating force of the corporation—Vance in manufacturing and Hoffman in sales. And I think it was logical for the trustee to appoint someone that could handle the assets of the corporation under his direction probably as good as anyone else.

Did the character of the company undergo any remarkable changes after Paul Hoffman and Vance took over?

No, I don't think so. There was a strong underlying father-son heritage in the corporation. You were a Studebaker man, your son became one. His children became Studebaker people. This is the small-town influence of a dominant industrial complex in that period of our history. There was no place else to go—which is not quite true. Oliver was here and Birdsell's and the O'Briens, and those were family industries. I think that's a part of America that this kind of relationship existed. And I think the proprietors of the business really had a fatherly feeling of responsibility for the employees.

I think as much as anything the emotional aspect of the thing was sold quite forcefully to the public and to the employees themselves. This "More than you promise," and father-son relationship and the quality of the Studebaker name and that sort of thing. Emotions were really sold by Madison Avenue. This institutional advertising did a great deal for it. And the budget was small. He didn't have money for four-color center page foldouts in the *Saturday Evening Post*, but nevertheless, a good job of selling that aspect of the business was done.

I think that's the thing—that the character of the corporation certainly had a great deal to do with carrying it through not only from the standpoint of employee-management relationships, but employee-public and management-consumer relationships. I think that a tremendous job was done in that respect. After all, historically there are damn few institutions or corporations of this size that Studebaker was at that time that ever got their head above water after receivership.

It was done because the employees had faith in the company. There was no competition for their services here close by, and they had roots here. The community esprit de corps was great. You not only got it from the pulpits but from the gin mills as well.

We were coming out of the destitution of the 1932–33 depression, and people were looking for an opportunity to show themselves. This is a bootstrap operation. The national economy had something to do with it. There's the "I'll show you" atmosphere. It probably couldn't be done today.

Were there any immediate engineering changes that took place after the reorganization of the company?

The Champion in 1938–39 was a product that came out of it. I think it began after 1934 and 1935. This was a lightweight, small automobile, energy efficient, that weighed, I think it weighed 2,340 pounds or something like that, shipping weight, which nobody had done before in that size.

That brings me to World War II, then, which is of course a very important period in the history of Studebaker as well. I understand that Studebaker took advantage of the National Defense Plant Act to enlarge its business here in South Bend at that time.

We tooled the Wright Cyclone engine and were a prime supplier of engines for the B-17 with plants in Chicago and South Bend and Fort Wayne. There was about two million square feet of manufacturing space and about 400,000 square feet of testing space for the Wright Cyclone engine.

How much of that was located here at South Bend?

Probably 40 percent of it. I think about 1.1 million in manufacturing space, and there was 400,000 [square feet] of space devoted to engine testing. Power plant testing was all done here in South Bend. The vehicle manufacturing plant, the downtown plant here, about five million square feet was put into the manufacture of two-and-a-half-ton, six-by-six trucks, of which we built 293,000. And we built 67,000 Wright Cyclone engines.

Was it necessary to recruit outside of the immediate area or outside the state of Indiana?

Well, the only reason we had plants in Chicago and Fort Wayne was because of the labor scarcity here. See, Bendix had a war effort going on here too, and they were employing some of the workforce. So the aircraft engine parts [plants] in Chicago and Fort Wayne were put there primarily because of the unavailability of labor here.

Then we also built the Weasel, which was a full-track-laying snow vehicle intended primarily for snow work, but it ran from Saint-Lo to Paris on the Red Ball Highway hard surface road. We did the job on the Weasel under sponsorship of the Office of Scientific Research and Development on a high priority. We did the job of designing and producing 765 of these vehicles in about 210 days. That was design, building the prototypes, proof testing, and tooling and manufacturing in, I think it was seven months. March through September, that's seven months. And that included some work up on the Columbia Glacier in 1943. This vehicle was a snow vehicle that OSRD wanted ostensibly for attacking the heavy water plants that the Germans had set up in Norway. It was a classified project that we produced. Now, cost was no consideration. You had to get the job done.

I'd rather hesitate to think that cost-plusing was any great advantage to organized labor. I can't think of a circumstance wherein it would, except that it produced a state of mind that the well would never run dry. And I don't think it produced any continuing bad habits in the minds of management, because we understood the necessity for getting these things done. Particularly in the automobile industry, you work on a very short fuse anyway. When you used to take twenty-two months from the time you decided what a prototype was going to look like till the day it started down the production line up here, it required a lot of planning and watching nickels and dimes and pennies and tenths of mils. So it was a condition of the moment that had complete justification so far as I'm concerned. And after you look back at it in retrospect, you can always find something wrong with it.

Weasel production
Studebaker National Museum, South Bend

The charge has been leveled—an accusation made—that the major abuse of cost-plus contracting was that entirely too many people were often hired to do a given job.

I'm sure we had too many. But we didn't have time—you had to get the job done, and you had no increment of time in there to do something over. Sure, you can look back upon it and say, "Well, you had too damn many people." And I can justify it, because you didn't dare come up too short.

What was the immediate consequence of the end of the Second World War?

See, we had a pent-up demand for consumer goods that in the automobile industry lasted until 1953. You had a seller's market. You could sell *anything* that you had. People would come and take it away from you. And it abruptly ended in the summer of 1953. Then we went in to stimulate the effect of this pent-up demand, to reincarnate it. We got into two-year styling circles in the automobile industry to create and perpetuate this demand. I think this is what happened. Because we did go into two-year major body cycles. Or the Big Three did. And that was an effort to create sales.

And what sort of policies did you initiate when you came in as president in 1956? What sort of changes did you make immediately?

Well, cost reductions. We had high overhead. And we, in collaboration with Curtiss-Wright, immediately went to work on manufacturing costs. There were capital improvements in the plant that could be done to eliminate costs. I can cite many examples.

One of the first things that I did was to ask all our management to go through the plant and inventory capital investments upon which we could get returns in three months, six months, nine months, twelve months, and longer periods of time after that.

I think that my comments on the investment of capital may have been a little vague as to what the return embraced. It embraced savings in labor and material handling that are one of the sins of multistory building manufacturing facilities. As an example, we vacated one floor of a six-story body manufacturing building and eliminated the indirect and direct labor of handling bodies between floors.

About what period were these things done?

This was probably in the period 1957, '58, '59, along in there. And it was a very significant improvement in our competitive position with respect to labor costs. Previously our labor costs were running considerably higher than the national averages of Detroit. About thirty-two cents an hour indirect labor. And we whittled that out so that we were competitive with the industry in both labor performance and cost performance, cost being a factor in performance.

What were the weaknesses of management that led Studebaker to its position in the middle 1950s?

I think labor relations were on a friendly, paternal order of things to a larger degree than was absolutely practical from a satisfactory operating standpoint. And I think that was one of the basic weaknesses—*the* basic weakness of management, particularly in relationship to labor negotiations. They were handled not by systematic directives. They were handled lots of times in a paternal relationship. "Well, sure, you can have this." Our personnel people, our director of industrial relations and the vice president of manufacturing and people that were directly affected by having responsibility for the management of the labor costs were oftentimes circumvented in the negotiation process.

Are there any other areas that you think that management might have been deficient in that would have led to Studebaker's situation in the middle fifties?

Lack of capital. I think there is another one. We've beat that to death, but it is important in this respect: that after the seller's market ended in 1953, the automobile industry—where capital was abundantly available—stimulated sales by frequent changes. Now, I don't mean controlled obsolescence. Styling took over. Product performance was accepted, and styling became an obsession with people. They had to have a new automobile every two or three years to keep up with the Joneses. This is part of the affluence of the American people. It's really a sociological question, and I think that the answers are sociologically available to a great extent. But they produce conditions that put value on a high degree of capital available. The independents and Studebaker did not have the availability of capital that was necessary, and maybe it wouldn't have been prudent to use it if we had.

By 1960, it began to decline once again. Sales began to decline.

Yes. Our smallness and our capability to manufacture let us get into the market before the Big Three came out with next model year with models that were directly competitive with the Lark. There was the Valiant, the Falcon, and the Corvair. The market was there, percent of industry was there. And we got a hunk of it. We got a hunk of it before they were able to come in and gobble it up. Now, that's what happened to the Lark. The Lark didn't fail. It didn't compete with the saturation of the market by the Big Three in the industry.

Were they able to underprice you?

Pricing was not it. It is distribution. It is the covering of the market by, well, there must have been about 10,000 dealers involved in it. I think Chevrolet had 6,000. I'm sure Ford had 3,000 or 4,000 dealers. And Chrysler probably had 2,500 or such matter. So that you got a broader coverage of the market that was available. Statistics show that. The success of the small manufacturer has been, throughout the history of the business, his ability to get into specialty items. And once he gets out of that field, he's lost. The best example of that's the Jeep by American Motors.

Odell Newburn moved with his family to South Bend when he was about seven years old. He first worked at Studebaker in 1939.[8]

[8] Interviewed by John Wolford, 10 July 1984, South Bend.

Mr. Newburn, could you just tell me when and where you were born, what your parents did, that sort of thing?

Newburn: I was born in Henderson, Tennessee, April 18, 1918. My father, [due to] the big ads that were coming in the papers in the South, moved to South Bend. And we followed after he was employed at Studebaker, about 1925. Studebaker was having big ads in the newspapers for workers at the Studebaker plant, and that's what drew him here. He sent for us later on after he was working and found a place for us to stay. And we came here, we joined the Pilgrim Baptist Church, and I attended grade school at Linden. And from there I went to Central, where I finished. Participated in football and track.

After graduation in '38, the year after graduation, I went to work at Studebaker, one of the dirtiest jobs at the Aviation Plant. I was a spray painter in Department 34. I spray painted until, oh, I was there twelve years spray painting, and then I moved over into the foundry. I was working in what was called the mill room. That's where we grind the pins off of the manifold pipes and clutch housing. And at that point, after a year in the mill room, I went on supervision.

And there was a period of time that I left to go to the navy. I went to the navy, and I was there for two years. And I went to Great Lakes, from Great Lakes to Millington, Tennessee, petty officer school. From petty officer school I went to San Diego, from San Diego to Pearl Harbor. And from Pearl back to where I was released from duty. I was there at the time that Roosevelt died.

And then I left. When they closed, I went to the Sheriff's Department. I was there for six years. And after leaving the Sheriff's Department—I didn't enjoy the work so much, because my first assignment one night was a suicide. He was a young Studebaker man who sent his family, wife and two kids—they lived in North Liberty—he sent them downtown. He was so depressed about the loss of work, he went out in the backyard and put a shotgun in his mouth, and he used a yardstick to end it. That was on the Sheriff's Department. I didn't like the work so well.

So finally I went to work for Kaiser Jeep. Kaiser Jeep was soon sold to American Motors. And after a year, which you had to get your seniority before you could run for any of the union offices—after the year I went for president in '68. I've been president, off and on, since '68 or so, of UAW Local 5. See, when Studebaker closed, Local 5, which is one of the oldest locals in the UAW, rather than lose our status, we went into an amalgamated local. The president had ten units in this amalgamated local; therefore, we eliminated the possibility of this local closing and international taking over all of our property and assets. And now, as long as we are an amalgamated with any unit in there, we will still be operating.

When you were growing up, did you have any aspirations for a particular type of job?

We graduated in '38. The only thing on my mind was football and track at that time. When we graduated, Ziggy [a friend] and I both applied for work at Studebaker. Ziggy was employed and I didn't get a job. And I went, and I'm honest, I said, "I didn't get a job because I was black." And then I sat down, and I did a little soul searching. Hell, they didn't have any football teams there, they had no track teams. I said, "What did I have to offer?" And that's where—that's where I realized that I think my time was wasted in school. If I'd have been concentrating on something in shop and set a goal. . . . But, take the average black along in that period of time, there seemed to be no avenue of advancement. They didn't have that will to go to college or to do those things, because they thought they was blocking them. And I'd fallen into that same attitude, frame of mind, which I regret now.

And we posed a threat to somebody else who was getting jobs then. You know, when I went on supervision at Studebaker, there was a foreman over me that had to come to me to get answers to their problems. And certainly he had that job because he was, well, there was no question about it, he was white.

Were union leaders strong?

Odell Newburn (second from left) presents back issues of Local 5's *Studebaker Weekly News* to Wayne State University
Archives of Labor and Urban Affairs, Wayne State University, Detroit

Our union leadership—Louie Horvath, Bill Ogden, Rayburn, Hill—they'd set with management and they'd bargain, and bargaining hard people they were. People that were qualified to do that, that bargaining. And they took the position, they're not going to kill, but they were going to get—we got insurance and other benefits that we got at Studebaker, Walter Reuther and them were upset because they were unable, at that time, to get those benefits with General Motors and those bigger plants, Ford and those, they were upset about it. I know that's the time international was quite upset about Studebaker.

Was anything else different about Studebaker at that time?

The management had their setup for management training at Notre Dame, and I went there. And they also had, within the shop, a classroom where we got on-the-job training, too, from management. I never thought I'd be reading the *Wall Street Journal* and journals. And then I got to seeing why stock market reports and those things were vital to a company, to see how their stance was affecting them. Never gave it any thought, or why I would be able, would be in anyplace to use that kind of—or what are they going to give this to me for? I've had an interesting time in the labor movement and at Studebaker, and the training that I received from the union and management has been helpful to me in other programs. I found myself involved in an awful lot of those things. I hold state commission on Bureau of Land, Fish, and Forest; I'm on the State Vocational Board; and all because I know where the salvation of minorities in this country lies—in the education.

You take a lot of the training that I received at Studebaker has been very central to me after Studebaker closing and getting involved. I know when she closed and I went back into it, I was concerned about it from my education standpoint—education of our children in the school. That's why I got involved in the Linden School.

Oh, you did?

That was, let's see, I went in in '68, that was about '69. We were having a problem with the school because it was old. I had gone through Linden School. And now my kids are in Linden School. And I had tried to get the state board to act, and the local board to act, on doing something to the school. Pull the kids out for two days. The state finally said they were coming in to see it and check the school. They went to the school board. While they were in session at the school board, one of the teachers noticed the ceiling in the room begin to sag. And she just got her class out in time—the whole ceiling fell. They went back to Indianapolis, the school was torn down, and we got a new school. So those were the kinds of things I've become involved in.

There were quite a few walkouts at Studebaker that people complained about, and people, of course, blamed the union for that?

We had these working conditions and especially during the time when it would be ninety degrees, and just imagine being in that foundry. Oh, you always were running up into the nineties and near hundreds. I've seen one hundred degrees inside of there. I've seen a lot of people that sweat so that when those clothes dried they just, like, crumbled, because of the salt and stuff that came out of their body would just, the clothing was that way. Those were some of the things that caused the majority of labor problems, and especially in that foundry.

It was more or less seasonal work at Studebaker, anyhow. Because I can't see why you have to change models and body designs. That was one thing that Studebaker refused to do and that was hurting. You had to deal with according to what the consumer wanted, and Studebaker refused to do it. They said it was too costly. Which was a costly project, changing the body design every year. We would work seasonally because there would be a mad rush.

I'll tell you, that foundry—that foundry group, because of the heat, the gasses, it kept people irritated all the time. I was always irritated because you have fumes, gasses, heat; all those contribute to the attitude of the people. And the majority of the time the guys even coming in, they realized what they were going to face. We were running three shifts. Three shifts.

And my dad died from the sand and stuff that he

accumulated. At that time they didn't have brain operations and things that they have. The doctor told me that it had accumulated, dirt and dust had accumulated in there.

***Several of Robert (Bob) Hagenbush's family members worked at Studebaker, where he also served in several offices of the United Automobile Workers.*[9]**

When were you born and where?

Hagenbush: Nine, nine, twenty-three, and in Walkerton, Indiana. I was six months old, and we moved to Argos, Indiana. And I lived there until we come up here to South Bend in '60, 1960.

Up to that point you were commuting to South Bend?

Thirty miles a day one way, sixty miles round-trip. We had most generally a carload—five of us—riding back and forth, see.

And some of them was on a different shift and they rode with different people. But most generally it was people from Argos, Rochester, Richland Center, Culver, and Plymouth that we rode up here together. Sometimes I had to go by myself because I was on the bargaining committee here for Local 5.

Studebaker's hired a lot of people from that area. In fact, at one time when we had about 22,000 employees, there was a lot of people from Plymouth, Argos. In fact, about three-fourths of the whole town worked up here. That and Bendix-Studebaker and Bendix.

Back there then about the only big industry was Studebaker's and Bendix. Back in Argos, all they had was the lumber mill and that's it. That was a farm community.

When you were growing up, was there any special job that you were aspiring towards getting?

Well, when I first went out and worked—really

Robert Hagenbush puts tie-rods in chassis, Department 156, 1946
Studebaker National Museum, South Bend

went out and worked—I was in apprenticeship on trades, and—until I went to the army. And then when I got out of the army, I never followed the apprenticeship up. I goofed around for a few months and then decided to come to work for Studebaker's. And that's when they was really hiring. Back in '46, they was hiring a lot of people, after the war.

Then I went to work at Studebaker's. And I liked it. When I first got hired I was in assembly on the frame line. Well, I was in assembly for, oh, I'd say approximately a couple months, and then a utility job came open, which was most generally—in utility, you do everything. You cover for absenteeism or wherever they needed you—the extra help—why, they'd throw you in there for a while. And I went on the utility job, and I was on that utility job until I was elected chief steward on the final assembly line.

Then I ran for chief steward of the final line and naturally the chief steward of the line was, because of the three floors and three buildings, that was a job that

[9] Interviewed by John Wolford, 24 July 1984, South Bend.

serviced the stewards and problems of trying to keep the problems down on the final line.

I liked the labor movement. I've always believed in the labor movement. And I wanted to get into the labor movement, that's why I ran for steward, chief steward, and the bargaining committee. And I'm still doing it, helping people.

I mean, we had good labor relations with Studebaker's, there was no question about it. And I can remember a lot of things that happened. But anyway, we had good labor relations.

Now, you were just one of several members of your family at Studebaker. Your father was in carpentry?

In the carpentry shop. And my brother, one brother worked in the small press room, then he came up on the wheel line and worked. And that was the brother next to me. And then I had two other brothers, one worked on the truck line and one worked on the wheel assembly. Tire assembly, rather, not wheel assembly.

They hired people on family lines. There were several families but that, you know, it's been so long I've forgot, some of them, who they were, but there were a lot of families like that. That all in the family worked there.

Some people have said that after the war the family tradition seemed to drop off more and that contributed to the decline.

It did drop off later on, but not right after the war. Right after the war they still had family—you know, people still hired in as a family deal. I think later on it dropped off, really.

Now there was the complaint back then that people didn't work as hard. You know, they would just do so much and then just loaf around the rest of the times.

Well, what they'd do—and really, you couldn't

The Hagenbush family 1947. (Left to right): Robert, Donald Lee, Ivo, Jr., Charles, Mr. and Mrs. Ivo, and Evelyn
Studebaker National Museum, South Bend

blame them—it was mostly, I'd say, management's fault. Because once they set the standard on the job, then a person is going to get their incentive built up, their initiative, built up to do that job. And instead of eight hours, they're going to do it in six hours, they're going to do it in four hours, see, or around four hours. But they did their daily production that was required of them.

I think their [management's] standards were too lax. They had an industrial engineer. I don't think . . . really, my job was to get the best pay and the best working conditions for the people, and that's what you do. And lo and behold, after you do this, there's always people finding angles, the short way to go and still get the work done. And you do, and this is what happened. So where they got the idea of one working four hours on and four hours off, or something like that there, instead of getting paid for eight, that came from the people working their piecework and getting their production out. And Studebaker was happy because they got, they set the standards.

How did that come about, that people could actually manage it so that they'd work half a day and still get . . .

Well, most generally it come about, as I said, through their efficiency. The employees, after their standard had been set, their time-studies were set, and so much time for each piece, they would build their efficiencies around that to get extra time off and work that much harder. Instead of working at a normal rate of 100 percent at a steady pace, they would just work really fast to get it done so they could . . . but in the spray booth it was a little different. You couldn't stay in the spray booth. You had to have that time off in the spray booth, because you couldn't stand to be in there that long time in them obsolete spray booths: fumes and sprays and so forth, and air, because you're in a mask all the time. And myself, I wouldn't work in a spray booth. I represented a lot of people that did.

Were you looking [for another job] before the [plant's] close?

It was amazing. I wasn't looking. Because it was amazing how we got the word they was going to close.

We had to go back and tell the people. I mean, it was just like that. And as soon as the line finished off, and they finished off the bodies off the line, that was it.

Right before Christmas?

Yes, and everybody was bawling and crying and especially old-timers because they couldn't get jobs anywhere else. And it was just a hassle, I mean really. And if you ever got hurt, that's when you was hurt, seeing these old-timers bawl.

They spent all their life . . . lived there . . . livelihood they spent at Studebaker's.

Right. Did anyone anticipate the end coming?

Not really. International—back here when we took the wage cut—said they would if we didn't do our share. So we felt we did, but we hadn't really heard no different. But we knew something was wrong because no corporation would stay in business and have nine presidents at one time being paid.

And when Egbert was there they had several presidents on the payroll. They already had that contract and had to pay them. Then you had a bunch of directors in New York running the show. And they were merging, buying up things at different organizations, and you knew they was in trouble then. Like I said, it came to a real blow to us that it was that way, and I still think they could have been saved if they would have made the advance [investment]. But the board of directors said, "No, we don't care what they give us, shut it down." And they did.

What do you mean, if they'd have given the advance?

Maybe we could have worked and come up with something. As some of them are doing here; like Chrysler's did here a while back.

[Studebakers], they were good cars. I had three of them. I bought a '47 new, a Champion. And I drove over 100,000 miles and got more money for it than I paid for it when I sold it. And I believed firmly in my Studebaker product. Because I figured I'm working there I should support their product. We had a lot of people who didn't. They got into other makes of automobiles and stuff.

That's the point of a lot of wildcats [strikes]. When they got in trouble at Studebaker's—they knew Studebaker's was in trouble—there were a lot of wildcats. Because a guy would come in one day and he says, "I just bought a new Chevy today, to heck with Studebakers." And they wouldn't work with him. They'd sit down on him. So the corporation had no alternative but to fire the guy, because in the contract there was language that no one or nobody could instigate or agitate a wildcat strike. If they did, they were fired. So they come in and talk about it and brag about, people would just quit working with him and Studebaker's had to fire him.

Robert Hagenbush, 1984
John B. Wolford

So December of '63 came and everybody was shocked.

Told that Studebaker's was leaving and everybody was in shock. It was a good Christmas present. Well, just before that, too, was when John Kennedy got assassinated too, you know.

We set our sights highly on Kennedy. You know, they liked what he was doing and that was a blow to *the people.* And then it wasn't long after that, we got the blow of closing the place down. They told them to close it.

The government put some money in here then to train people to do other jobs, especially the ones that were up in years that never did anything else, only just worked at one given job all their life. And they really tried to absorb them. Some of them went to Chicago and worked for Ford. They just went all over, wherever they could get a job—Kokomo.

The skilled workers, there wasn't too much trouble with the skilled workers. It was trouble where people wasn't skilled, just on assembly, you know.

Whiting

In this chapter nine individuals relate stories from the community of Whiting in northwestern Indiana. Some people speak of their experiences over the many decades they inhabited the town, and a few discuss their reasons for leaving late in their lives and moving to Arizona. This chapter allows the reader to enter the world of the region's immigrant communities that were formed early in the twentieth century and learn about the strong feelings of attachments that women like Sophie Gresko and Clementine Frankowski felt to those communities. Frankowski tells a remarkable story of a young woman leaving the community to become a physician only to return to serve its members out of a strong sense of obligation. This chapter also relates another story of corporate decline. In this case it is the tale of the Standard Oil refinery in Whiting and the effect its layoffs had on people who had placed a great deal of faith in its potential to reward and sustain economic and community life.

Sophie Gresko was born in Slovakia in 1902 and came to Whiting with her family in 1911. [1]

Gresko: I was born in Cervenica, Slovakia. At that time, it was Austria-Hungary. And my dad lived in USA in the section of Robertsdale on 119th Street, right behind the St. John Church. My father was named George Dvorscak. He worked in Whiting already. He was working in Standard Oil as, as still cleaner. That was a hard job. And my mother worked very hard on a farm, and she thought, "I better go and see my husband in America. What is he doing? He's not helping me anything." Well, he stopped sending money back, whether it was due to his work, I couldn't tell you.

Did he write your mother and tell her to come to Whiting, or did she surprise him?

Finally, I think, he got a telegram from New York, "Your wife will be arriving, and children, on Baltimore, Ohio Railroad in Hammond." So he came to see us; he came to meet us, and he brought us to his brother's home on 119th Street to see [the] Dvorscak home. And then he rented a home on Myrtle Avenue and Lakand, and our home is still standing there, that's where [we] settled.

They [Austria-Hungary] wouldn't give us a passport, you know, to go, so we had a guide to take us to the country line [border], and we were traveling all night. And then we got lost in the forest, and the guide said, "You stay here. I'm going to see where we are." And he hasn't been coming back for quite some time. We all started to cry. Where we going to go in the forest? We don't know which way to go.

And then when we came to Poland we were free. And then we went to, well, to Germany, and we got our ship over there, in Germany.

And, oh, we had a rough trip coming down here. On the [ship], they don't treat you as a human being, just like a bunch of cattle. They throw you down there, you know, and you had your sleeping quarters, you know, just like on layers, and tin cups up over your head. And then we had a storm on the ship, on the ocean. That was really bad storm. And then, you know, as we were coming down here, and I'll never forget my mother, when we were on the deck, and she saw Statue of Liberty. And she says, "Oh, thank God, we're close to America, because there's a lady standing in the ocean."

Sophie Gresko's father, George Dvorscak (left), and Steve Kendra, Whiting, ca. 1920
Sophie Gresko

I tell my grandchildren this story. And I didn't know where the lady was, you know, she had to show me. And then when you, when you come in that Ellis Island, you know, you had to be examined. . . . Well, if you were healthy, you passed. If you were sick, they put a number, they put a little white card or whatever, with a card on you. You were shipped back again where you came from.

I wasn't afraid. No, neither [was my brother] John. We were, oh, we were just full of life. No, we were not afraid, we were not afraid at all. And then we got a piece of pie, we didn't know what it was, how to eat the piece of pie. Orange was a great thing for us.

[1] Interviewed by John Bodnar, 12 March and 11 October 1991, Whiting.

Still cleaners, Standard Oil Company, Whiting, 1920
Whiting Record, May 1920

And your father was working in Standard Oil?

Standard Oil. They break the coke here, you know, the coke that you threw, they had that in the oven—I've never been in the oven—and he used to wrap his face in flannel, and you couldn't be there more than five minutes in those ovens. So hot he didn't have any eyebrows. All parched, it was all parched. And I don't know what kind of shoes he been wearing, what kind of shoes they were, but they, to go inside of those ovens to break the coke.

Oh, I think they didn't work any longer than about three, four hours. That was a shift. It was terribly hot. It was terribly hot. And after that, our Slovak people wouldn't go there anymore, then the Turkish people used to take care of it.

Why wouldn't the Slovak people do it anymore?

Well, it was a hard job. It was a hard job. They thought they could do better. You see, they thought, "We're just like slaves," you know.

When you come to Whiting, you're a young girl. What do you do? Did you go to school? Did you help your mother?

I went to school, to St. John's school. They put me in the kindergarten. . . . They were teaching ABCs, and I was repeating those letters, even walking down the street home, "A-B-C-D-E-F-G," because I wanted to get out of that place. I mean, I wanted to know the language, and I wanted to understand. And I tell you, the nuns were very nice to me, at the St. John's. And before I know it, I was in the third grade.

And then when I was around the yard, playing with the other children, and some of the children, of course, who couldn't speak pretty well, and some of the children used to call me greenhorn, yellowhorn, you know, five cents a popcorn, and this did hurt me. I was so mad. And then, when I knew how to answer them, I came back at them, and of course then was the finish of it.

I graduate eighth grade, St. John's. Then I stayed with my auntie, Helen Kocan. She had a saloon business. And some way, other way, I got next to her.

So I stuck around her. And then when she, you

know, she had a little money because she was her own business, and when she bought me a nightie to sleep in bed, I thought I was in heaven because I had a nightie to sleep in. That was something. And, you know, then I just stuck with her. Working around, well, we done, just cooking, cleaning, helping, and that's what you did.

Did you serve meals at the saloon?

Yes, on paydays, on paydays. We had hot dog, sauerkraut, and what else? There was fish.

Did you want to do that? Did you want to make it easier for your mother?

Yes, I did. Well, I saw my mother all the time, but I liked to be with auntie, because she used to take me, we'd go together, and, or in the afternoon we'd go out, and she took me to ice-cream parlor, there was something I didn't get it by my mother. You see?

How long did you stay with your aunt?

When I married, two years after I married, or three, about three years, my husband was injured in Inland Steel, and he was not capable of working anymore. And then I had to go out working. I didn't have an education to work, but I tell you, auntie didn't want me to leave. When I think about it, she didn't want to lose me, see?

And there was a Judge Federhoff, from Whiting. He had offices over the bank on 119th Street, if he wasn't in our house, down at the Front Street. When I graduated from St. John's school, I was fourteen going on fifteen, you know, and he wanted me to go to school to take typing and to work for him because I could speak Slovak, I could write Slovak, and he had business at that time.

And aunt says, "Oh, no. I can't do that, I can't let you go to work!" That's working but I was working more home than I would've been working at, at that time. And then I was seventeen, got married, I was married about three years, my husband was injured, my life was tragic.

Kocan's saloon, Whiting, ca. 1917
Sophie Gresko

Sophie Gresko, Whiting, 1991
John Bodnar

My husband had his skull fractured. He was a mill rider, and some kind of roll fell off the track. That's what I was told. So he was only about four months on the job, and they were lifting these rolls, and some fellows were hit. This bar, long steel bar, flipped out of his hands and hit him over the head.

And at that time there was no Social Security, no benefits of any kind, no kind, no benefits no place. Inland Steel took care of the hospital and took care of him in the hospital.

So I had to go out and work, scrub the Whiting Community House. I'm not ashamed of it, you know. And I was working there twenty-five years.

After twenty-five years, well, I had some little surgery, and I didn't want to go to work there. And I told Mr. [John] Sharp, the manager of the Whiting Community House, I says, "I would like to get a job at the desk. I could take the reservation, and I could take, give change, I could give a receipt, and I could do these things, why couldn't I?"

Your husband, then, couldn't work anymore?

Just sitting around, that's all. Sweeping the basement, shining my, my washing machine, shining my pots and pans, like that, he could do that. And he used to get convulsions quite often.

How long did he live?

Nine years after the accident. My children, a boy and a girl, always say, "I don't know my father." I says, "Well, neither do I," I says, "I don't know your father either."

I took care of them. Of course, it was nice with company in the house, auntie was downstairs, and she was busy. She held an office in the fraternal organization for thirty-three years as the national president [of the First Catholic Ladies Slovak Union]. So she needed me here, see? But I didn't get no pay on that.

You lived in the house with your aunt, and your husband of course?

That's right.

Did she keep the saloon business?

No, she wanted to get out of that place very bad, very. Oh, yes, she didn't want to have anything with that. Prohibition, there was no business, there was just soda pop and tobacco and candy and your beer that hasn't got anything, you know, there was nothing in it, and she said, "I'm getting out of here." So she bought this home, see, bought this home. And of course, she was elected as a president, so she wanted to be in a better place, too. She wanted to have a little prestige for herself, you know.

And this was a nice neighborhood in Whiting?

Of course, we're here fifty years, over fifty years we're staying in this home, there's a change in people. The homes got older, the people are different coming in, you know. They don't keep it up as nice. It irks me.

Next door, that place was just beautiful. It was just beautiful. And we used to keep our lawns and our, everything as much as . . . I still do, do as much as I, as old as I am, I still do keep it up. Next door here, she's in a wheelchair, there's no husband, the daughter is in Chicago, she's a schoolteacher, comes here on the weekend, and she has a woman taking care of her. Next door, on the other side of the home, my home, another people came in there. They just, they don't care about it, don't care. And they, they don't rake, they don't cut the grass, they don't do anything, just, just live in the house.

How do you remember the depression? Are these rough times for you or were you able to, to find some jobs and keep things going? I mean, you've got young children. . . .

I'd even wash clothes for people. And I was working at the Community House, you know. They paid about thirty-seven cents an hour. And, well, that kept me over, you know, that really helped a whole lot, because I had that job, and they need somebody there, see, so that kept me going. That paid pretty well at depression time.

John Sharp was our manager. And he was too particular, you know, you couldn't stand a minute, he wanted you to keep on working, continuously working. He was a driver. John Sharp wanted to show it to the stockholders and to the big fellows, you know, how clean everything was. And he had three people during the day working like mules. And that was not only that time because he was always that way.

What did people use the community center for?

Well, there was swimming, there was basketball, practices, exercises, lot of games were there in the men's gym, in the women's gym the same thing. They had a girls' director, they had a boys' director. There's a little kitchen there; a lot of meetings. They used to have flower shows, where people raised flowers. There was like, during the gladiolus time, roses time, they would have exhibitions. They would give prizes for the best rose or best flowers, there. It was always used—card parties. And I want to tell you, every morning I looked at the book, what was on the agenda, and it said, "Twenty card tables to be put up" in that room.

How long did you work at the community center?

Twenty-five years. I told you that I had a little surgery, so I didn't want to go back. And so finally they need a woman at the Liberty Loan, as I said it before, and I got a cleaning job again. That was very early in the morning, cleaning job, see. Early in the morning, six o'clock in the morning, and then we had a Slovak Dom here, right across the street. Slovak Dom, or Slovak Home, and they had a hall upstairs, they had a kitchen upstairs, and the hall was rented almost every Saturday. There was a wedding, and I took care of giving dishes out, checking the dishes out, checking the dishes in. And then the next day cleaned the kitchen, scrubbed the stove, scrubbed the table, that was my job. So many Sundays, instead of sitting home, I was cleaning the Slovak Dom kitchen.

You were talking before about you lived on La Porte Avenue here in Whiting, you said that you think that people don't keep up the houses and the properties like you remember thirty and forty years ago. What else has changed about Whiting?

You take the Slovak Dom. No activities there. And there was always, music every Saturday. And, and what else could I say? The people are different. Different people moved in. They're more to themselves. I go to St. John Church, I don't know my people anymore. It's all mixed up. See, it's a Slovak church, all Slovak families, all Slovak sermon. Now you have everything. Of course, that is all over the country. Because, you know, when Slovak people came to, to America, that's the first thing what they look is to build a church. And the church had a school. So they always took care of the people. They never tried to get on somebody else's property. They always like to be independent themselves. And they stuck together, see. They stuck together.

The young people, you see, when—I'll tell you like this: when I was a young, married woman, I couldn't afford to go for vacations, never thought of going vacations. We cooked at home, we baked at home, we wash our clothes on the washboard. And iron our clothes. You know, today you don't do that. Even my daughter didn't want to live like I did. She wanted to have a lighter life. She told me that herself. She says, "I want to have a lighter life than you had." And so that's, she wanted to go to school, and she made something out of herself, she did.

Our people, the first settlers, they didn't go out. They didn't go for vacations, and if somebody went on vacation, "He must have a lot of money." Today, whether you have money or you don't have money you go for vacation.

You never drove a car?

Never. I walked all the time. I went to the park, they told me, "I think that's why you're walking so well, because you never, never rode a car." I don't say that I don't, people pick me up and I go, but I never own a car. I think that's why I'm holding up pretty well.

Slovak Dom, Whiting, date unknown
St. John Catholic Church Collection, Whiting

Slovak Dom, Whiting, 1991
John Bodnar

You were telling me that Slovaks formed a bank in Whiting in the 1930s when a lot of people were worried about losing their homes. Do you remember that?

Mr. Michael Kozacik, he was our businessman, he was our first man in Whiting. He had a hardware store in Whiting, and he was quite a popular man. He had money, so he looked after the people that had it in the banks. That was before the depression. And so he says, "Why can't we Slovaks have our own bank? We go to other people's bank and they're making money and they're popular. Why not the Slovak people organize themselves and put a good name for themselves?" So he, Kozacik, organized, if I'm not mistaken, the Liberty Loan Association.

Every one of them was Slovak, see? Mr. John Ciesar was the president. He was in the automobile business. First he handled a horseshoes, like a stable and he was horseshoeing the horses. And then he went to automobile business.

This was a loan association, you see? And these were the directors: Urban, he was in the saloon business. Stodola was in the grocery business. Michael Tuhas, he was in the bowling business, in the Slovak Dom basement he had bowling. Kalapach, he was a bricklayer. George Fedorko, he was in building business.

And the Liberty Savings was right in the Slovak Dom?

That's the time he had started banking. Again there were all Slovak people.

What was the name of the bank Kozacik started?

American Trust. And then he went out and asked all the Slovak organizations to buy stock. We had some from our First Catholic Slovak Ladies Union Branch 81. We had for $1,000, and our junior order had for

$500. Our men's organization had their [stock] too. At that time, some ordinary family man couldn't afford to buy $100 worth of shares.

Your aunt's saloon was an important place for Slovak immigrants when they would first come here. Now, you said they would come to the saloon and then what would you do with them?

Well, the family of the immigrants, when they were coming home, they would call us on the phone and say, well, "Mary is coming," or "Susan is coming; you meet them at the station and bring them to your saloon, and then we'll come and pick them up." So when they came over, we would prepare them, many times bacon, eggs. Yesterday a woman called me: "Sophie, I remember when you brought us the bacon and eggs at the table when we came from Slovakia, and you called my husband to come and pick us up. But first you fed us here."

That's the only place you could call from because there was no phone in the people's homes. Only, as I say, the priest would have a phone, the doctor would have a phone, the butcher would have a phone, the saloon would have a phone. Not even the midwife didn't have a phone either, you had to run after her. And the midwife was delivering the babies at that time, not, not doctors, the midwife. And the midwives would wash the baby clothes, and they would also cook for the new mother.

Sometimes the wife would every year have a baby. It was not easy. It was not very easy, you know, to raise children, where you had one of them in sink water. You had to heat your water on the stove. You first had to make a fire in the stove, and bring the wood and coal and heat the water, and put it in a washtub. Then you had to iron, and irons were heated up on the top of the stove. I had one, so I know what I was ironing. When I got my first electric iron, why I, that was great! Oh, that was great! I was maybe about fourteen years old.

What's your saddest memory?

I tell you, the saddest is my grandmother.

Why?

And she died in Europe. But I was in Europe, I was born in Europe, and she, I think she loved me so much, she pampered me so much, and when we were going to America she cried so hard. And you don't forget that, see.

And now, and all the time, "Come, Sophie, I'm giving you butter and bread," you know. See, that's a time, you know, when you're hungry and somebody gives you a piece of bread, you never forget that. Your love for that person never, it never fails.

You never went back to see her?

Never. And I always was telling myself, "I don't want to die before I won't see my grandma." And then here I get a letter, "Your grandma died." And there was somebody here from Europe, and that was during the depression, and he was going back to Europe, that part, so he was in Canada and then he came here to see some of the countrymen. And I gave him the big two dollars, you know, that was during depression. And I says, "When you go back, you give that two dollars to my grandma."

And here I get a letter when she died, and they telling me that "Mr. John Adzima just arrived home, when we were carrying your grandma up to cemetery, and he was telling us that you send her two dollars. So we didn't give that two dollars to nobody, we gave it for a mass, to church for her." Just think!

He was here, you know, and he came to Canada. He wanted probably to make a living here someplace. So he came to Canada, and from Canada he came to America. So he came to Whiting because there was a lot of countrymen was here, see? And I think he didn't like it, you know, so he thought, "I'm going back home. I think I liked my home better." So when he was going back home, I said, "How about remember me to my grandmother?" I gave him two bucks. I said, "Give it to my grandma." I still have that letter.

Born in 1911, Betty Gehrke is a native of Whiting and worked as a librarian for seventeen years. Her father, husband, and several other family members worked for Standard Oil in Whiting.[2]

[2] Interviewed by John Bodnar, 28 September 1990, Whiting.

Clarence and Betty Gehrke, curators, Whiting-Robertsdale Historical Society, 1991
John Bodnar

Gehrke: I've always thought of the two world wars as being very important events in my lifetime. I must have been six years old going on seven when World War I began. And from what I heard people say about it in conversation made me think that the noise, the shooting was coming from Gary. But I remember especially Armistice Day, jumping in the car and rushing down to Michigan Avenue in Chicago to see the ticker tape parade. This was November 11, 1918.

And then there was World War II, and I had a seven-year-old daughter in the hospital having appendix out, and she had the only radio in the ward when VE Day occurred. So that was an exciting day. She got to entertain all the nurses and all the doctors who came in to hear the news over her radio. When Japan surrendered, again we jumped in the car, but we couldn't get any farther into Chicago than Seventy-first Street. So we parked the car there and got into the IC train along with other people who were even climbing in through the windows and went to downtown Chicago to see the parade. It was more like New Year's Eve. You just couldn't move on State Street. It was very exciting, and perfect strangers were hugging and kissing each other.

So those are your most important memories as well?

Of course I remember the fire at the Standard Oil Company in 1955. When I worked at the University of Chicago, fellow employees couldn't understand why I would live anywhere near the Standard Oil Company for fear of an explosion. But there had never been anything serious until the fire of '55. That was probably the worst.

I lived in Robertsdale, on the west side of town, and the explosion blew our french doors open on our front porch. And we knew something had happened. We ran upstairs and looked out the windows and could see the smoke downtown on the south end of the Indianapolis Boulevard. So we jumped in the car and went down there, and we walked all over the place where the big piece of metal had landed on a house and killed a child in the bedroom. We were able to do that because they roped off the place after they knew how dangerous it was, and the oil spilled out of the storage tank and flowed down Indianapolis Boulevard. It was just a steady stream of fire and smoke.

All down the street, and it hit the railroad tank cars in the Standard Oil Company yards and all kind of metal just bent out of shape. And we watched from the top of the Administration and Engineering Building where my husband was employed. That was the tenth floor, administration on the eighth and ninth. So we had a good view, but it burned for three days, and in the meantime we heard from Holland, Michigan, that they could see it over there, and we ourselves went up to the planetarium on Chicago's lakefront on the third day and watched it from there, still burning.

[It burned] at least three days, and it was considerably longer than that before anybody was allowed to go back to their homes or to look for belongings or anything. And then it was my brother, a lawyer for Standard Oil in Chicago, who was in charge of buying the homes from the people and making all those settlements. And they leveled off the property, and now it's full of storage tanks.

Temporary quarters were set up in the community center and first aid was administered to anybody who needed it and food, clothing, things of that sort were supplied. I think, on the whole, people were well taken care of, but it improved the town spirit in a way which brings to mind the fire of 1980 on 119th Street. I can't tell which block it was. I think it was the 1200 block. Most of the stores burned, Star Sales burned, then the Newberry building and a number of others, but we had help from so many people and from surrounding towns, from fire departments from surrounding towns. And first aid and instant assistance from the townspeople, and that's what brought the townspeople together again in a spirit of community.

The town is very highly organized socially; there are all kinds of clubs and societies and lodges. And many churches and everybody, they all just united in a big attempt to take care of that fire.

In the forties you had three young children; what was your typical workday? Describe it.

I was a homemaker, and I had three children at home and I did a lot of walking and buggy pushing. And you hardly see a buggy anymore on the streets. I joined all the clubs, did everything I was supposed to. I enjoyed it, but it sounds dull now.

Why do you think it sounds dull?

Well, so many women today have careers, and I know that's a lot more exciting because I had a career too, *after* the kids were grown. I think the youngest was probably ready to go into high school when I became a librarian.

The Hammond library system needed a librarian in the local branch, which was around the corner from my house, so I took the job. I was there for seventeen years.

I always liked a challenge. And certainly raising children is a challenge. And of course the library was too. The thing that made the library a challenge was that the Russians put *Sputnik* in the air about the time I started there and that began the knowledge explosion. I think probably the year was 1952 when I took the job, and there were fifty bookshelves in the branch, which quickly filled up with "How to do this" and "How to do that" and all kinds of science books. Whereas before, nobody read anything but fiction. It just changed the reading entirely.

How is your life different from the life of your parents?

When my parents came to Whiting, the streets were muddy, the sidewalks were wooden, and they spoke considerably about the mud. And if you went out at night, you had to carry a lantern to see that you didn't fall off the sidewalk into the mud.

But that was their life and they, everything they did in the way of entertainment, or most of what they did to entertain themselves was self-propelled instead of sitting to be entertained. The nickel shows came to town, there were two theaters early on in Whiting, and then there were two more and then there were two still bigger ones.

The streetcar tracks and bus lines had come in my lifetime and electric lights and streetlights and paved streets and so forth. And everything was so much easier, it is better for the next generation today.

We lived through the depression. My folks were pretty far along in life during the depression. My father had retired during the depression on a very small pension and moved to Florida, but we were married in '32, and it was the first wedding the church had had since the church was built in about 1926 because nobody could afford a church wedding. And things were just beginning to pick up, and of course, the depression has scarred a good many lives and changed a good many attitudes. But I think probably for the better.

How?

In our generation, we knew how hard it was to come by things and make money last and so forth. We never had too hard a time living in Whiting because Whiting was in pretty good shape. My husband wasn't laid off for more than a short time, and I was working at the University of Chicago then and their attitude was that if a married woman was working, she needed the job.

I worked for Charles Hubbard Judd, who was chairman of the Education Department. I worked at his editorial offices. He had academic offices and editorial offices. He was editor of several publications and did a lot of the writing himself. But while I had that job, things were fine and so we had nothing to complain of during the depression. Whiting was in good shape.

I didn't worry about it [the depression] too much coming back, but it was something that stayed with me because I realized how quickly it could all be taken away. During the depression, families moved in with each other. They were just living in attics and basements and crowding together, and so many places stood vacant, you know. And it just made me careful for the rest of my life.

No, things are too easily replaceable these days. We had to take care of things because they weren't in our time until after the war, when things got so plentiful.

Would you tell me about where you were born and your parents and what they did for a living?

My father came to Whiting as a professional baseball player. They wanted him to play for the Whiting Greys. He came from Chicago. He was a member of a family of eight boys and one girl. And they were raised on the southwest side. They were close to the O'Learys, and in October 1871, during the Chicago Fire, they dug a hole in the backyard and buried their piano and furniture and moved father west away from the fire.

Why did they bury their furniture?

To keep it from burning. Fortunately, the fire went the other way, north. And that goes for the Gehrke family, they were there at the time of the fire, practically in the same location. They came to Whiting to buy a farm, because Mr. Gehrke had had a livery service, and they took all of his horses but one to fight the fire. My father worked in the loading yards of the Standard Oil Company until he was injured. He was crushed between two tank cars and then was given an office job for the rest of the years he worked for them. He retired at sixty-five and moved to Florida.

My mother was raised on a farm in Edwardsville, Illinois, and was the youngest of thirteen children and

One Hundred Nineteenth Street in Whiting after the Second World War
Whiting-Robertsdale Historical Society, Whiting

met my father at a baseball game in St. Louis. And they were married and came to Chicago the year before the World's Fair of 1893 so that the fair itself was their honeymoon.

My father's family had been members of the Church of England, but he could trace his ancestry back to the Puritans and the Pilgrims. So he was kind of straitlaced, but he was absolutely unable to hear anything, so he didn't go to church. By the time I came along, he was stone deaf. But my mother was very active, and they belonged to the Plymouth Congregational Church, which to this day is absolutely autonomous. They have no connection with any other church or hierarchy.

Did your parents have views about a young girl working?

Well, I was never allowed to work. I wasn't even allowed to babysit. That was just becoming customary. I was the youngest in the family and had no younger sisters or brothers to take care of, and once in a while, I got to push some neighbor child up and down the street, but to make money, I never did it. And if you graduated high school, you would have gone to college if you could and then got married and raised a family.

And then I went to the University of Chicago, and I went to business college on the south side of Chicago, and then I got my job at the university. And that's pretty much what they expected me to do. My sister graduated from Whiting at sixteen and was too young to go to library school, but she had worked in the Whiting Public Library as a page, without being paid. I think you had to be twenty to get into the University of Wisconsin library school, which was a one-year course and you didn't have to have any preliminary degree. They finally took her at eighteen. So she went away for her one year of library school, and then she came back and became a librarian at Whiting.

How did your father make a living?

He was a clerk at the Standard Oil Company. I don't know how long he played baseball, but when he was injured in that train accident, he was given a clerical position and he was a clerical employee the rest of his life, in the storehouse.

When you were a young person, did you have roles or aspirations about what you wanted to do with your life?

At one time I wanted to be a musician, a pianist. But there was no, that was not a career at the time. You couldn't support yourself that way. Unless you were extremely good.

Leo Kus was born in Whiting in 1919 and worked at the Standard Oil refinery.[3]

Kus: I started out in the Standard Oil in boy's work, as a messenger. And I used to be a messenger, pick up all the books and night reading and bring it to the main office for computations for all the units, how much they put out for the night and everything for the day, every day, every morning I would pick it up so they would run it. And the other thing was mail. Then I got to be a clerk in the office and run the IBM machines. And then we had a major fire on the Buffalo side, the north end. I was fighting that fire there, all my beautiful clothes got all messed up. And after that I got drafted in the service, and I was gone.

And I was gone for four years and when I came back in 1946 they asked me if I wanted to go back as a clerk, you know, or somewhere else. I have a choice. Well, when I came back to Standard Oil, the fellows in the office says, "Hey, don't come here, Leo. No way of making money here. If you want money, you better go to the refinery, that's where the money is." So, it's known as the refinery, you went to the refinery.

So I went and said, "I'll take refinery." Because I needed money. I was the oldest in the family, and we went through a hardship when I started working. No sooner than I start to work, in 1937, I got laid off in 1938. And I got laid off in '38, came back in '39, and I worked there for three years and here, boom, I went to the service. I was the oldest boy, so I was able to help out the family. So I didn't put anything for myself,

[3] Interviewed by John Bodnar, 10 November 1991, Griffith.

didn't save anything for myself. All that money I made was given to the family.

But then we went to school [after the war]. They started up a school because we had a lot of problems there. People came from the service, and they didn't, weren't quite schooled in the rights and wrongs because they were getting their information from old-timers, and the plant was modernizing and it wasn't quite up to what the company wanted. You see, we were not getting good information, so they decided to set up a school in the Frame Building on the north side. We went to school during the day for I think that was six weeks, every day, eight hours a day. Three times a week, I think it was. I don't quite remember, but I believe that it was. After we finished at school, the state wouldn't recognize it to give us credit for it because there were no educators in charge of it. So they asked us to go to night school, and we had to go away from the refinery and we went to night school in Whiting High. And they had set up a school there with the educators. We went through that school on three nights a week, and we got credit for it. They taught us all these things, how to measure, how to caulk units, a pipe, and everything. Right there in that school. From that time on, we were more sure of ourselves, and we did it right.

People have told me that after the fire in 1955, which is the big fire they had at the refinery, that the company started to modernize even more and that that led eventually and slowly to a decline in the workforce.

Oh, that's absolutely true. See, they were talking about modernizing way before the fire, and the fire was in '55. We had various fires that had become a problem and in a way, we were kind of edgy about fires. And they were saying, "We got to modernize because things are not working up to par." And in '55, they built a new unit. They were starting it up, and it happened the unit was new, absolutely new. And nobody quite knew how to run it. Well, they knew how to run it, but they had no experience in it because it's a new unit, completely. And they had problems with it and eventually that's the thing that set the fire off, because it exploded.

What happened is that this piece of metal landed on a house, and a roof caved in. See, the roof was

Wedding of Leo Kus's parents, Whiting, 1915
Leo Kus

knocked down. It went right through the roof, right through the ceiling and killed one of the children. It killed a person, a young child, and another one, it severed his leg, the way I understand it. And, yes, so after that, there were all houses on the 129th Street there. If you go by there now, Standard Oil bought up all the homes and demolished them. That whole area was after a while demolished because they didn't want any more homes in that area in case something else happened like this. It's very dangerous for people that were living right next to the refinery there.

Then after the fire, the fire did exactly what the company wanted to do, only they have accelerated immensely. Whatever units that were left, that were old, they dismantled them, cut them out. And they started on a remodeling program. The whole refinery was filled with units and when the fire demolished a lot of them, and they finished it. You have big spaces in between now. You had people in there that cost the company a lot of money, so that after they demolished that, they had excess people.

Let me put it to you this way: we come back from the service, World War II, we had started replacing, there were women there at that time, we started replacing them. And a lot of the old-timers were going on pension. But when the Korean War broke out, they were afraid that they were going to get short with personnel again, so they hired up a lot of people just to make sure that they're not going to be shortchanged. And when the Korean War finished, then we had an excess of people.

Now I was a pipe fitter, and I was like a leader whereby people depended on me to fabricate, line up things. I sketched them, and I lined them up, measured them. And I'd have maybe three, four, five, or six people working with me, a welder and then various other fellows and pipe fitter helpers with me. Well, sometimes I just had enough work for two of us or three of us. And I would be getting three or four more men, and I says, "Hey, what am I going to do with them? I haven't got anything. Give them to somebody else."

They had to lay off. They started laying off in '60 and they ended up in '65. That was the first time Standard Oil, in my knowledge, that they laid off people with ten years of service or more. If you had ten years in Standard Oil, they would keep you regardless what the conditions were. If, like in my dad's time, why it was depression days, they laid them off as a last resort, but they cut down the weekly or hourly rate, thirty-six

Pipe-fitting gang, Standard Oil Refinery, 1920
Stanolind Record, *November 1920*

Pipe-fitting gang, Standard Oil Refinery, 1979
Leo Kus

hours they went on. They cut down the hours per day and they also made no overtime. If you took overtime, you had to take a day off on that, so consequently that kept people working. And they asked people to shorten up the work week. That is, you worked three days a week and this way, gave more people jobs. The work week, in other words, they would work maybe three days out of a week rather than six days and have all the people working than none.

Was there a change over time from the thirties to the sixties in Standard Oil's management where there was more of a willingness to try to preserve jobs then and less of a willingness by the sixties?

It wasn't as drastic as some other companies, but I think looking back, in retrospect, they had the right idea because at that time they had a surplus of personnel. But at that time everything else was booming in this area. You can go from, if you're laid off today, tomorrow you go to the steel mills. You'd get hired because they were always short on help there. See, Standard Oil was one of the jewels of the working force, they had the best, highest pay. They had the best benefits, they had sick benefits, whereas no other companies had it. They had, gave you a death benefit that few companies gave to their employees.

And you had sick benefit, in other words, before you had to be off two weeks before you got paid, but then you got paid. If you were off six months, you got paid for six months, that was real good. No other company was doing that, see. Well, most of the people that were working in the steel mills every time they got a chance and got a call from Standard Oil, they would run to Standard Oil. They would quit, see? But then the steel mills caught up with some of the benefits and then in 1965 when they were laying off, people went there [steel mills] to work. They didn't lose nothing by it—they lost, but not drastically.

It was a tougher attitude, and it had to be in order to compete, I think. Now at that time I thought it was pretty bad. In fact, when they laid off that last bunch that already had fourteen and a half years of service, that was the last bunch they laid off. I understand through the grapevine that the company thought that the last layoff should have never happened because they thought they would be hurting by it. And it proved them to be correct. They had to rehire some of them. Yes, because they ran short, they rehired some of those people. Not right away, but people lost their service.

That was a great surprise, although before this all happened, our supervisors were telling us that, of course, like I told you before that we were tripping over one another, and they were telling us, "We've got to be more productive." This was stressing more production, more production, because other companies were getting, selling gasoline cheaper than they did and only because they cut their personnel down and things of that nature.

Were you a member of the union?

We had an independent union. It was a local independent, within the refineries itself. Standard Oil. And that Standard Oil had this independent union since my father's time, the CIO never could break into Standard Oil. They tried it, they never could.

Now when would this be?

Nineteen sixty-six, 1967, somewhere around there. To be frank, we were kind of disgusted with the fact that we had such a big layoff and then we felt we have to stop this.

What happened then? Did you force a union election?

Yes, we had an organizing campaign, and we campaigned throughout the refinery. And asked if we would help them out, and I was one of the organizers there.

The question was to sign up with the international so that we would have more strength in dealing with the management because the management is dealing with strength, and we cannot do anything because we're independent. We didn't have no way to force an issue by a strike. Because if we did it, absolutely didn't make any difference. We struck here in Whiting with some other refineries, Standard Oil refineries. It didn't hurt them because they were able to produce in other units.

We failed, we didn't get a majority. Twice we had an election, twice we failed. The last time we failed was pretty close, but nevertheless we did lose out.

Some people feel that the degree of loyalty isn't as strong and you don't have the same type of worker that you had there in an earlier generation or at an earlier time. Would you agree or disagree with that?

I would agree with this. I have to agree because this is the thing that really struck the old-timers the most when we were going on pension.

And you couldn't say anything against Standard Oil [to old-timers]. As I told you, Standard Oil was ahead of the time in various benefits the other companies didn't give. But anyhow, we had to some degree the same type of loyalty. But with the younger generation, especially after the Vietnam War, when they hired people there, they didn't have that kind of attitude anymore. It was a job and that was it. And the attitude in the United States has drastically changed and their outlook to what they call "work ethic." The people in there thought that all they had to do was come and show themselves to the plant and they should be paid. In other words, it was an honor for the company to have them.

That's the attitude we got as old-timers because we had a hard time pushing these younger fellows to a normal type of work. Many a times we were appalled and says, "Why did you come here?" They would come here and fall asleep standing up. I had one fellow, he almost fell over, hurt himself, and I was trying to show him how to do the job. And I had a top job as far as, what you call, piping is concerned, one of the top jobs because the other one is in the research. That's one of the better jobs too. But I was showing him, I was willing to show all the people that came to work everything that I knew because I knew I was going on pension, and I know how hard it was for me to learn, so I wanted to pass on some of my knowledge so part of me would be with them, see?

I was trying to teach him. It was amazing. They absolutely, their mind was on sports, good times, and what they're going to do next. All they were waiting for was payday and Friday, weekends.

So you feel then that that latter generation after the Vietnam War, after the sixties, simply didn't have a sense of responsibility?

Right. Basically the responsibility wasn't there. I mean, I fought it with my family. I didn't fight it on the outward. With eight children I had to make sure my family knew where I stood, how I stood about this whole situation.

Well, see, my oldest went to Purdue. It wasn't such a bad problem with the Purdue school there as it was with Indiana, which is a more philosophical type of schooling versus engineering at Purdue. But he was giving me a problem. He was my oldest. I always, I've also made up my mind too, with eight children I made up my mind that my oldest is going to get whipped, disciplined. Not physically. He's going to get whipped in line first because if I don't get him in line, I can forget about the rest of them.

So I stepped on him all the time. He went to a Catholic school, Catholic high school. He came with some philosophies that they were teaching them there and I told him, "I don't care what they teach you over there. Your dad has gone through life, he has listened and he has seen life. He was around the world," which I was, in the service. "I went around the world, I'd seen other people and I didn't care what that book-learning professor has to say. I've had practical experience. And I tell you that in the long run, I may be wrong as far as the professor is right, as far as his theories are concerned. I'm not going to argue that point, because I don't know. But practical experience has taught me that this is the right way, and you learn whatever you want, but I want you to know that basically this is my belief. This is the way we're going to conduct this family and as long as you're under this roof, this is the way you're going to behave," I says, "no ands, ifs, or buts. I don't care what anybody else tells you. You can learn, and I don't say shouldn't, but in this household that's the way it's going to be."

When did you leave Whiting, and why?

I'll tell you how it was. I got married. I was still in service, I came back from overseas and in one month's time, because I knew my wife, we was engaged before I left. And my wife Mary and I married in the '45. And then I went to camp here, Camp Atterbury, and waited processing. I thought maybe I was going to go to Pacific for completion of a tour of duty, but the war ended and I went to Camp Atterbury and waited for my discharge, for the processing.

But anyhow, I came back and we looked for rent in Whiting and found a rent in Whiting on Schrage Avenue right across from Globe Roofing Company. And our first daughter was born a year and a half later. Two years later, a boy was born. And that was a three-room apartment, so I had to go looking for another apartment. I decided, well, I've saved a little money, I better see if I can build a home. I didn't want to rent. I wanted to build a home. I went all around Whiting and I couldn't find a lot. All the lots that were there were held by people that wanted to have their own children build on. So I couldn't buy. In fact, I had one I was going to buy it, he asked for an enormous price but I was desperate, I wanted to buy it. So I decided I was going to buy and I came in there to complete the agreement and he backed out. He says, "No, I don't want to. I'm going to save it for my children."

So then I had to look out, but I had to move because it was too tight for that three-room apartment. So I had to get a rent, and I couldn't find any in Whiting so I had to go in Hammond. I found a rent there. And it was there that we had two more children, and I started building. I looked all around this area to get some property, and I came across this property in Griffith. This was a new subdivision in 1951, and I liked it.

You built most of this yourself?

I had a person at Standard Oil, was an electrician, and I helped him. So he came here and helped me, put in the electric. I had another fellow at Standard Oil who was a mason, and he put up the brick. And then I finished up the carpentry in here myself.

Yes, we helped each other. That's one of the better things that have come out of an industrial area is that in industry, you have all of these various crafts that constitute building of a home. And if you are cooperative with each other, you can build a home fairly reasonable

Leo Kus, Whiting, 1991
John Bodnar

even today. You don't have to spend no $100,000 or $200,000 for building a house. You can build a really good house because you'll save a lot of money. But I'll tell you, you work like a horse. Saturdays, Sundays, evenings. You hustle. Not only do you have to worry about everything, you're a laborer, you're a craftsman, you're a contractor. It's all rolled in one, and then you've also got to go to work, you know, and put in a full eight-hour job.

Whiting natives Dolores and William Curosh owned and operated a clothing store in Whiting for twenty-four years and retired to Arizona. Mike and Bertha DeLuca also grew up in Whiting.[4]

William Curosh: Well, my parents were both born in Czechoslovakia, in Slovakia rather. And my dad came over first and then my mom came over. My mom was over about, oh, I would say a year and then for some reason or another she decided to go back to Slovakia. And she went back, and she was back about a year. She was only about seventeen years old at the time, and she came back the second time and she married my father. And that's how we ended up in Whiting.

I think my father came 'cause he was a draft dodger. Yes, he didn't want to serve in the army, and I think that's one of the reasons he came. But a lot of people used to do that.

He first came to Joliet because he knew some people in Joliet. And he lived in Joliet, and he worked on the railroad in Joliet for quite a while. One day he had a fight with some other fellows that worked on the railroad with him. The story goes, my father hit this fellow and the police were after him. So he took off for East Chicago, where my grandmother lived, and he lived there, and he went to Whiting.

I think my mother ended up in East Chicago 'cause that's where my grandmother and grandfather lived. And then she married my dad, and they moved to Whiting because it was closer to work.

My dad used to clean stills in Standard Oil. In the olden days when they ran the still for so long, it formed coke around the still and when they discontinued that

[4] Interviewed by John Bodnar, 2 March 1992, Sun City, Arizona.

still, they went to another still, but while this still was hot, there was coke around the still. So my father used to go in there with a great big iron, long iron bar, like a pole vaulter's bar. He would chip the coke off of the sides of the still. But they had to go in there when it was hot, before it dried and stuck a lot harder. So they would go there while it was still wet, I mean, it's hot. And they would chip all that coke off.

It was real hard work. Very hard work. One of the things they used to let them do in those days, if you finished the job in six hours, you could go home. 'Cause you were really soaking wet and that's what my dad used to come home at all hours in the morning, I'm not talking about the afternoon. He'd generally come home, one, two o'clock in the morning.

So they wore gloves and long underwear, and they would go in there and work real hard. My dad couldn't speak English so that was the kinds of jobs that were available. They [immigrants] either worked as still cleaners, but they worked as manual labor, you know. Really hard work. They worked on railroads. There's a lot of them worked on the railroad and a lot of them worked in the grease works. They used to do some kind of work in the grease works.

My mother worked at home. We had nine children. My dad died when I was about five or six years old. He died of pneumonia. He came from the job, and he came home, and he got a cold and was sick. And he laid in bed, oh, I would say about a week, if I can remember correctly, and he just never got better. And died.

What does your mother do with all those children after that?

Well, there was nine of us in the family and my sister, Anne, she was working. And my brothers, my brothers all had some kind of job, you know. And then we just supported ourselves. You know, and as one got older and got married, the other ones took over the job. And all my brothers when they worked, they got a paycheck. They never cashed the paycheck. They never spent it. That's a tradition or something, but they used to put it on the little mantle when they got a paycheck. And that night if they wanted to go out, they'd ask my mother for one or two dollars to go out. And that's how we survived.

All my brothers worked in Standard Oil. Mike, John, Joe, and George all working at Standard Oil. I was the only one that never worked in Standard Oil from our family.

They used to have an employment agency, and they would put their names in the employment agency. And you'd have to wait until they called you or somehow or other they would call you up. There was a fellow that I remember really, really well, his name was Brown. And everybody used to be afraid of him, and he used to do most of the hiring. And everybody had to get on his good side to get a job, really.

Did Standard Oil have pensions?

They didn't have the pensions until I would say, in the thirties they started to get more generous. And I wrote a thesis on pensions, and the theme of my thesis was "profit sharing through stock ownership." At that time Standard Oil was one of the first companies that gave stock, matched stock sharing plan. In other words, I don't know what the plan is now, but at that time, if you put one dollar in, they matched the one dollar per dollar. And they put it in the fund profit sharing plan, and that was part of your pension. And that was, I wrote it in 1940. I had to write a thesis to graduate from St. Joseph's College [in Rensselaer, Indiana].

What was your neighborhood, Mr. Curosh?

I lived at the south side of Whiting and they say that the further south you live, the tougher you were. And we lived at the most extreme end. We all lived on the south side, and we ran around barefooted all summer. And all got, I think, most of us got a crew cut haircut, and we were out in the mud lake. And railroad tracks, we hung around the railroad tracks all the time. The railroad tracks were right across the street from our homes.

Well, we used to go swimming in the nude. Pick strawberries and play baseball out there. Chase around. We never wandered into town. I don't think I ever went into town very, very often until I was in about eighth grade. Then I'd go to St. John's school and go right down the boulevard right back home. Never went into town. We hung around there, we all knew each other. There was a large family down the street, and we had nine, someone else had two or three.

And in the evening we all, there was a big streetlight and we'd all end up by that streetlight like a big circus. And we'd play a game called "Railroad, Railroad, Run Chief Run." We'd run all around the neighborhood, screaming like heck.

I stayed right at St. Joe 'cause I was a fairly good football player and a fairly good baseball player. So I got a scholarship at St. Joe and went there for four years. So I didn't come home until I was out of college.

And I got a job at the steel mill [in 1946]. Inland Steel, really. And I worked there, oh, I don't know, not very long, maybe about six months. I was cleaning the stills. Then I got a job at the American Trust and Savings Bank, and I worked there until I went to the army.

When I came back from the service, frankly, I didn't want to work at the bank. But I was only home I would say two or three days when Mr. Grenchik came to the house. And he said, "Would you come back to work at the bank?" I didn't have any idea what I wanted to do, but I knew I didn't want to work at the bank because he [Grenchik] had a large family, and I could see there was no future at the bank. I mean, I didn't think there was much of a future at the bank. Mr. Grenchik had about four or five boys. And they were all working at the bank.

[It was a] family business, and Mr. Kovachik was the brother-in-law of Mr. Grenchik and they were all interrelated. So I went back and I worked until, if I remember correctly, it was Valentine's Day in February. And I told him, "I'm leaving."

In the meantime, a priest friend of mine named Father Lefko, he's still living at St. Joe College, came to the bank one afternoon before this was all decided. And he wanted to take me out for lunch or supper I should say, 'cause it was about four o'clock. Well, I'll cut the story short. Took me out for supper, we talked. And he said, "Bill, I got a job for you." He said, "You'll like this job."

I said, "What are you talking about?"

He said, "It's a ladies' shop."

I said, "What are you talking about? I don't know anything about that kind of . . ."

"Oh," he said, "you'll learn, you'll do well there. I know you will. I'll help you, and we'll get some money somewhere."

Dolores and William Curosh in front of their store, Whiting, late 1940s
Curosh family

Well, anyway, we talked, and he drove me down the street and showed me to the store. And I said, "This is crazy," I said, "I don't know anything about this business."

But Father Lefko insisted, you know, he said, "Bill, just think about it. Think about it for a few days. You'll do real well."

Dolores Curosh: It was located on 119th Street, right across from Baren's Funeral Home, if you know where that is. So we had it for twenty-four years. And then I think I convinced my husband to sell it. He wanted to stay for a twenty-fifth anniversary. But I could see the writing on the wall that Whiting wasn't going to go up, it was just going to go down. And there were all these big stores and supermarkets moving into town.

What is about that time? When are we talking about?

Dolores Curosh: 1970, when we left Whiting.
Mike DeLuca: I've been told that between Bill and

Dolores and William Curosh, Sun City, Arizona, 1991
John Bodnar

Dolores they ran such a tight ship that if you were to call him at the store and say it was your wife's birthday, they knew her bra size, her panty size, her hose size, everything. And he would make up a package for you to pick up, which was desirable to your wife.
Bertha DeLuca: Not only that. When you went into their store, Bill Curosh would greet every person personally by their first name. I mean, everybody just thought he was fantastic. "How's so-and-so? Your brother or your sister or your mother." He took an interest in you personally, and they had a very, very good business. They really did. They were very, very good to deal with.

You didn't want to sell the business?

William Curosh: No, I didn't want to sell it. I really didn't want to sell, I didn't want to go. We had come to visit Arizona, my nephew was an orthodontist here in Phoenix.
Dolores Curosh: And we were instrumental in getting him over here. He had been out of dental school, and he was working in McHenry, Illinois. And his partnership broke up, and he was looking for a new place to settle. And they were looking in Highland and Munster. And then we had a friend that we met, don't ask me how, that lived there in Scottsdale. And he really romanced us. He told us all about Arizona, and it was like heaven. So my husband suggested that Dr. Curosh have a look out there. And he did, and he settled out here.

Do you all remember the fire?

Bertha DeLuca: Let me tell you about the fire. That particular morning Mike had gone with another friend of ours and our son, who was only about three years old, four years old. They had gone out to southern Indiana hunting for whatever.

So it just happened. It was August—very, very hot. I woke up—must have been about five o'clock in the morning, opened the front door so that I had some air coming in. And I had, the baby was asleep, she was only about a year and a half old in the other bedroom. And I walked around the house and opened the windows, like I said. And I just got back to bed and it happened to be around ten minutes to six, I do believe. Whatever, the tremendous sound threw me out of bed, scared me half to death. I jumped off the floor, and I ran to the back bedroom to see if the baby was all right. I knew it was an explosion at Standard Oil immediately. As I came out of the bedroom, there was my kitchen, the window was broken. There was just glass all over.

Immediately I ran outside, the baby was still asleep. How she slept through this, I'll never know. I went outside, and there wasn't a soul out on the street. I did not really know what happened outside the windows, the picture window was all blown out and whatever. And running down the street was Joannie, who is the woman who lives next door. She had just come back from her mother's, who owned a grocery store about five houses down. And all I could recall was her whole face was black, all I could see was her white teeth. And I says, "My God, Joannie, what happened?"

And she said, "I think my kids are dead."

And I wanted to run into the house with her. There wasn't another soul out in the street at that point. And she said, "No, no, no. I don't want you to come in. I don't want you to see this." I'm telling you this just scared me to death.

So I ran back into the house, I ran upstairs. And her husband was a policeman, Tommy Dencovich was a policeman. He's working midnights. She also had two children like I did. And her house was, it was just all dust. All the plaster, you could just—dust from plaster. She was just covered from head to foot with all kind of debris. And I said, "Franny, where's the kids?" And she was in a state of shock, this woman, she was a basket case. We were both the same age, we were in our twenties.

In the meantime, her mother and father came from the corner, they lived on the corner. And she said, "I saw that the children were OK."

And I said, "Well, I'm going to see what's going to happen next door." In the meantime, there was fire engines and everything, the 650-pound cylinder laid across the bed over there . . . and it was so hot they could not pick it up. They could not take it off the children. It cut off Ronny's leg, severed his leg. He was six years old. The other one was killed.

One child was, he was the only casualty. And that was next door to us. And in the meantime, Mike heard about this when they were on their way home. Anyway, we were all evacuated, and we had to leave the area because of the gas lines.

When you decided to leave Whiting, why move to Arizona? You had people here, you had contacts. . . .

Dolores Curosh: I was happy here [in Arizona] from day one. My brother and sisters were, like I said, older than me. One sister two years older than me lived in California for many years. My parents were both deceased. So I didn't really have that many family ties. So it was easy for me to leave. But it was difficult for Bill to leave because his family was still there.

You still had young children when you moved?

Bertha and Mike DeLuca, Sun City, Arizona, 1991
John Bodnar

Dolores Curosh: My husband retired at like fifty-two. And he came here with no occupation and we had five children. Two were in college and one was a senior in high school and one was an eighth grader and one in the fourth grade.

What did you do then? Did you get a job down here?

William Curosh: I used to go in the alley and cry.
Dolores Curosh: No, he didn't get a job. We had enough money to see us through for a while, and then he just got a job just so he'd have something to do, 'cause he was bored.
William Curosh: I went to real estate school for lack of something else to do. 'Cause I was really homesick and bored and everything else. So I went to real estate school, and then I still didn't sell real estate. Then I went to broker school to get a broker's license. No, I never sold any real estate. In the meantime, I had a broker's license and never sold any real estate. Then I started to sell real estate and that's what I did.

How would you compare life here to Whiting?

Dolores Curosh: Much, much better. It's cleaner. I'm sorry I didn't come earlier.
William Curosh: You walk the streets at night.
Dolores Curosh: Yes. I'm sorry we didn't come earlier because we didn't have all those galoshes and all that stuff to go through bad weather and all. I just love it here. I could stand the heat, I mean, I never did like the cold. Even as a child I didn't like the cold. I didn't go back for seven years or something like that.
William Curosh: But I went back. When I first got here, I was deadly homesick, really. I really was so homesick I didn't know what to do. Driving me crazy. I would go to church and I would see different ladies and they would remind me of the ladies in Whiting. And I would go down the street and I'd see somebody I thought I knew. And I would go to the bank and they'd say, "Have you got any identification?"
Dolores Curosh: That burned him up.
William Curosh: I said, "Are you crazy?" I used to go to the bank, I never had identification in my life. And always, every time I went, they'd ask me that same question. So one day I went in the bank and I was homesick and the girl asked me for identification. I told her, "Listen, my name is Bill Curosh." Her name was like Dorothy. I said, "Your name is Dorothy. Next time I come in here, I'm going to call you Dorothy, and by God, you better call me Mr. Curosh. And remember me, look over my account now so next time I come, you don't have to look over the account." By that time, one of the managers come running out. I didn't realize that. But that's how I felt, you know, in Whiting, you knew everybody. You didn't have to identify yourself. If you wanted a loan they didn't even ask you how much money you had. So that's, I was really homesick but I guess I finally got over it.

Let me ask you this question: How has your country changed? Regardless of where you were living, in Arizona or Whiting, in your opinion I mean. How has your country changed in your lifetime?

William Curosh: Oh, I think it's changed. I mean, there is a lot more liberal politics going on. Everybody wants their own way now, and I don't think people respect the law like we used to. There's more robberies and more killings. Like in Phoenix when we first moved here, we heard of a murder or something once or every two or three weeks. Now every weekend there's someone who gets killed, someone shooting each other, there's highway shootings and all that stuff. And I don't think that used to be, even ten years ago.
Bertha DeLuca: Because it's a different society. The children, our children, they're entirely different mannerism. They behave differently. I don't know why they do that, because do you think that maybe we had been a little more liberal with our children? Our parents would not permit us, we could not go out at any time we wanted. We could not have cars, we did not have the things that children have today. They've got it all. And we did this. My children have had it all. They had cars when they were sixteen, seventeen years old. I was dating and I was eighteen, nineteen years old, the fellows didn't even have cars. So it is, it's a different society. They're promiscuous, they think nothing, sex is too open as far as I'm concerned. Which you would never have had in my day.
Dolores Curosh: In part because women work now, you know. The parents are not home, there's another thing.

Bertha DeLuca: That's why in my married life, Mike never permitted me to go to work, and I kid you not. I only worked part time for twenty-seven years. Everybody else, my sister went to computer school, and they all got good jobs. They've got pensions today. I get absolutely nothing because he said, "No wife of mine is going to work. You're going to be home when the children are home." So I went to work part time. I used to work from 9:30 to 1:30. I would take my children to Sacred Heart School, and he did not even know I worked for a long time because I was home at 1:30. Then I'd pick the children up and his dinner would be on the table. It was just like my family used to be, my parents. But Mike never, he never would let me go to work such as anyone else. He wouldn't.

Dr. Clementine Frankowski is a native of Whiting, where she operated her own medical practice.[5]

Frankowski: I was born [in 1906]. Now it's outside Whiting, because I don't know when this happened. It was considered Whiting, even the post office was Whiting. It was a little farm and my folks had the farm. And they didn't own the farm, but they farmed it. And I was born and that house is still standing. It's in the midst of a motor lodge.

Well, my father's name was, he's got a real Polish name, Konstantin Frankowski. And my mother is Pearl. They didn't know each other in Poland. When they came to the United States my mother's maiden name was Stanizeski.

First of all, my mother first came to Chicago and settled there and so did my father. They both settled there and they met. And they were married in Chicago. In fact, they were married over one hundred years ago.

I think at first he worked in the butcher shop. And my mother, I don't know. I don't think she worked at all. And I don't know how soon after they came here that they were married. But they came before because they were married in 1891.

When my father left Germany he was enlisted to go to the German army, they had conscription there. And he used his brother's passport because he didn't want to go into the army, and he left Germany.

[5] Interviewed by John Bodnar, 14 August 1991, Whiting.

They were married in Chicago, and I don't know whether he worked in the business but the neighborhood that they lived in was very bad and there was so much robbery and so on. So they came out to Whiting to live, and we've been here ever since and our whole family was born in Whiting.

They came out here and built a little hall, and he went into business. He had a dance hall where most of the entertainment [took] place among the ethnic people in Whiting. They had all the weddings and all the dances. . . .

And then he had a store. A liquor store and tavern. And then when Prohibition came on he got disgusted, and it was turned into a candy store. There was a school built right across the street, and the kids come in after recess and bought all their penny candies.

There were six in our family, and when I grew up I didn't know any of them but two brothers that were still alive. And one died when I was just about five or four years old.

What was happening?

Well, they died of diseases that were very prevalent in those days. My mother lost the first child, which was a girl. She died of this dysentery and diarrhea that so many babies died of in those days. And she died at the age of two. My brother died, his name was Leo, at the age of six months from pneumonia, which they had no medications for at that time. My third brother died at the age of eighteen. He was a senior in high school, and he played basketball. It was the one time that Whiting was in the state finals, that was in about 1912. But he died in 1911. He didn't live to see his school enter the finals.

We all went to Whiting High School. He was the only one that was alive. My fourth brother died at the age of ten of scarlet fever.

Well, it sounds like your mother had a very difficult time then. Do you remember or recall your mother's reactions to all of this?

Oh, it took a long time. She was very depressed when my brother Eddy died. That was the fourth one. And he died in high school. I remember that I was just a small child, and he had a nurse at home taking care of him. And he was sick just about a week, and he expired on Thanksgiving Day. He died of pneumonia.

She was very depressed. She couldn't eat. She couldn't sleep. And she, she felt very terrible until one day, I don't know whether it was actually a dream or whether it was his spirit that came over to her. But during her sleep she dreamt of him, and she said he came to her and he was dressed in a white, in a white uniform as if he'd been in the hospital. And he came, and he told her that he was very upset that she was crying and carrying on. That he was very happy, and he would never want to come back.

She felt much better after that dream. Whether it's dream or it's actual spirit coming back, we don't know. It was in her dream. So after that, she stopped her weeping, and she began to get better. But up to that time she was very, very depressed.

How long did you go to school?

Dr. Clementine Frankowski, Whiting, 1991
John Bodnar

I graduated Whiting High School in 1925. Then I don't know where the idea struck me, because my brother was going to be a doctor. So whether that idea fell into my head, after I graduated I made up my mind that I was going to go into medicine. That was the only time that I made up my mind. I didn't think of medicine at all during my high school days, but I was the valedictorian of my class.

There were just only four of us in the class [in medical school]. In fact, many of the schools didn't accept women. I applied to Loyola [in Chicago] and that's the only place I applied to and got in because of my scholastic standing.

And I graduated from Loyola in 1932 but at that time our fifth year of school was an internship. And the hospital I went to, Mary Thompson Hospital, which is first known as Women's and Children's Hospital, in Chicago.

And when I came to it, it was just a hospital for women. Right now, it's coeducational. So they have both men and women on the staff.

And I says, "I'm going to go to OB and GYN. 'Cause I like that." And then I didn't make my decision because in a small town like Whiting, I had as many men to take care of as I had women, and I still do. But I didn't have as many, most of my patients were women and children.

When I graduated I decided I would stay home in Whiting and stay at home. Because we were needed, we didn't have any women here. I was the only woman. In fact, I had a hard time getting on the staff of the medical hospital. In fact, I was denied an internship at St. Margaret's Hospital [in Hammond] because I was a woman.

Whiting was home. It's my home, and my mother was here. And I didn't want to leave her. She had enough hardness in her life as it was without me springing off. And my brother, he was a cripple. He had a curvature of the spine; he was hunchbacked. And that's why my father talked to him and he says, "Now, Matt," his name was Matthew, "you've got to decide what you want to do, because you cannot do any laboring." In fact, he went and worked at the Standard Oil Company, my father knew some people there and they gave him a job at the Standard Oil. And he worked at the can factory. And he worked one month, and he decided that that wasn't for him. So he decided to go to school. And he says, "You better pick a profession that is not

A wedding at Frankowski Hall, Whiting
Clementine Frankowski

going to be too difficult for you to work." So he chose pharmacy.

Do you remember much about women having children like your mother in those days? They probably didn't go to physicians, did they?

No. I was born, my delivery, she had a midwife for me when I was born. I don't know all of them, but there were about three of them in Whiting that were delivering. Mrs. Canjura is the one that I know that delivered me.

Were other physicians resentful towards you, the males, or was it not a problem?

I don't know, but I didn't have any trouble at the hospital because I paid attention to nobody, but paid attention to myself. I did my work and that was all. I didn't go out with any of them [the male physicians], didn't have lunch with any of them. Didn't have any fellowships with any of them, because I didn't want to stir up any trouble. Because they were told that they had previous women in there as interns, and they had difficulties. But I must say I opened the door for women at St. Mark and also at St. Catherine's. Because coming in here and practicing I stuck to my business and had no affairs with anybody. So I'm still single.

It was still a man's world. They didn't think that women could do as much as men. And even in the hospital many times I had difficulty in getting patients in. I would call the hospital and they never ever had any beds for me at St. Catherine's. The only thing I did was OB, but if I had a medical case or something, I still had an affiliation with Women's and Children's. Lots of my patients went to Chicago with me to Women's and Children's because I had [privileges at] that hospital. And didn't have to rely on the men so much.

So St. Catherine's Hospital would actually deny your patients space because they had a female physician?

Yes.

Did these women ask you for advice about how to limit families at that time?

No. It is an issue now. But I'm a Catholic, and I never did give any birth control information because it's not allowed in the Catholic religion. And I never did. I was asked, yes. When you refuse them, that's a very personal matter. And then they knew that I wouldn't do anything as, regarding birth control. So I wasn't asked anything.

I would give them this information: there is such a time in a woman's history that they are not fertile. So I would give them that information and that was about the whole. But they couldn't have any intercourse or anything like that or else they would have to use some measure. And at the time, many of them that didn't want any children, whether it was allowed or not, they used [to] wear some kind of button or something to prevent the sperm from getting into the cervix or they would use some sort of a douche or something. Well, the buttons were dangerous because very often [they] would cause an irritation and would be the cause of cancer.

What about diseases that were work related? Or health problems? Did you notice anything with the population that you dealt with?

Yes, I did, because in Standard Oil Company we have a high incidence of cancer. It's a form of cancer that affects the lymph glands. Or lymphomas. But it's hard to prove. But we do know that exposure to gasoline products and so on and oils is cancer inducing. First of all, it comes on as a cold that doesn't seem to heal, a sore that doesn't heal, bowels that are either diarrhea or constipation, it changes for no known reason. And then bleeding, a cancer of the urinary bladder. If you have bouts of passing urine in your bladder.

I think it's environmental. The environment has part to do with it. And I think an exposure to the smoke and the pollution in the area here. And, oh, there is exposure to other drugs and other chemicals. So we don't know. After all, we don't know the cause of cancer yet.

How did you set your fees as a physician in Whiting? And could everyone pay them?

Well, if they didn't pay them, they just stayed unpaid. I never sent out a collector after my fees. Never. So I have a lot of outstanding bills. From the first day I started practice, I've got bills that are not paid.

How has Whiting changed?

I saw that it began to change, I would say not until the sixties or seventies. They were closer in past times. It didn't make any difference. They helped each other. They would come in and do their housework for them if someone was sick. It was not uncommon to have people come in and help each other out. Do their housework and shop for them and so on. But it isn't that way now.

I have no idea what made the change. It's getting too big, it's not a small town anymore. We're too close to Chicago. We don't know how many hoodlums we have coming in from Chicago too.

I think it's, I told you that my parents moved from Chicago because of the, all the stealing and so on. And we did have to be very, and most of the houses had doors and locks on them that were able to be opened. Now I have a lock that they can't open with any kind of a key. And I keep my door locked all the time.

How has the country changed?

Well, I think, I hate to say this . . . there's so much dishonesty in government. I'm sorry to say that, but I feel that way. And so much graft. The almighty dollar is the only thing that they have any respect for.

Even in the war, I've seen some of the veterans that even the government did not support them. I'm always getting cards from the paralyzed veterans of America and the, all kinds of veterans. And they don't get the support that they should do. They support everybody else but who they should support. And they don't support their own here.

The United States is very kind in giving to everybody and they forget about their own. We have a lot of poor people here in this country that need support, but it's hard as the dickens to get any support.

You could have been a physician and gone to Chicago or somewhere else and left all that. What do you think brought you back here?

I said my mother. I thought she had enough heartaches before, and I came back and I stayed here. I didn't want to change 'cause I was happy here. I am happy doing medicine, and I did a lot of clinical work.

Did you make house visits?

I just stopped making house visits after I couldn't walk too much. I have both rheumatoid and osteo arthritis, and I had two knee replacements because at that time my knees got so bad and I had no surgery until 1978, when I had two knee replacements.

I kept going. I'm still going. I still have patients, but I don't make any house calls. I drove around, but at the present time, because of my eyesight, I can't even drive a car now. I have to have somebody drive me. So you know I can't make house calls now. But if I wanted to go to a meeting or something, they would drive me or to go to the hospital, they'll drive me.

Joseph J. Sotak is a native of Whiting and retiree of the Standard Oil Company.[6]

Sotak: I was born here in Whiting, Indiana, February 9, 1914. And I went to Catholic grade school here at St. John's. I went to Catholic Central High School in Hammond, Indiana. I was hired over at the refinery, which at that time was called Standard Oil of Indiana and has since changed to Amoco Oil Company, on November the 9th, 1939. I retired in May of 1980. I was an official of the union since I had been a member of the union and went up all the steps from grievance man to vice president, secretary of treasury to president. I spent twenty years in the union work, which I kind of enjoyed at sometimes but at other times it was a headache. In fact, it resulted in '71 where I finally got out of the business after our '69 strike. It just so happened that you can't satisfy the employees.

Standard Oil had a lot of openings at one time for kids under twenty-one. They worked in what they call the candle factory. And I just couldn't get in. And so while I was waiting and working at Inland [Steel]. I played professional basketball. And a lot of time I would have to go for a couple of days or a weekend to Indianapolis, Oshkosh, and New Jersey and places like that. So the manager at Inland Steel was a Cornell graduate, he was an athlete, so he gave me the break whenever I wanted to. That was a privilege because I knew I couldn't get that at Amoco, the Standard Oil Company.

You said you couldn't get into Standard Oil in those years. You said they weren't hiring. Did you have to know somebody?

Oh, tremendously. If your father was a supervisor, you got in very easily. I tried to get into the Instrument Department. I finally got into the Instrument Department with thirty-some fellows on the seniority list ahead of me and all thirty of their fathers were supervisors. That was somewhat the premium job at the refinery at the time.

Tell me a little bit about your basketball.

We attracted more crowds on the road because at one time we had four all-Americans. Today you'll hear fifteen, twenty guys on, but at that time it was five men. They had five men. And we had all-Americans. At that time we had Johnny Wooden, we had Ralph Vaughn, Johnny Townsend from Michigan, Jewel Young from Purdue.

We did win the league. I enjoyed it because I was playing with some big shots. See, I never went to college, and everybody else did. I don't know if you remember Bill Harlow. I don't know if you remember, but he was at the University of Chicago. And John Reed from Northwestern, he was an all-American. When we went out of town, we would draw big crowds because the Ciesars came into town with all these all-Americans.[7]

So you were being paid not only for working at Inland Steel but you were making money playing basketball? What did you do with the money?

[6] Interviewed by John Bodnar, 6 November 1991, Whiting.

[7] The team was sponsored by Ciesar's Chrysler-Plymouth in Whiting.

Dedication of St. John Grade School, Whiting, 1930
St. John Catholic Church Collection, Whiting

Well, I got clothes. That was '33, '34, '35, I used to have tailor-made suits, kind of like a big shot. But I lived with my dad, and I was at home.

How did you finally start at Standard Oil?

The way I got in was the owner of the basketball team knew the manager of the refinery. He was a Chrysler customer.

Everybody in Whiting tells me that if you worked at Standard Oil the depression wasn't so bad. How did most people get by then?

There's a hell of a lot of millionaires in this town. The reason why is, just sit back and figure out if an individual employee was in the stock savings plan [at Standard Oil] and continued to contribute to the plan for let's say thirty-eight, thirty-nine, forty years. He has got to have at least about eight or nine thousand shares of stock.

It was a payroll deduction and that was based on 4 percent of your wages. Now there are some who were not in the plan. But in order to be eligible for retirement benefits, which the company would give any employee in '55, that's 1955, you had to be a participant in the savings plan.

Of course, at that time, back in those days when I first got hired, everybody was just putting money away to buy a home. And of course, homes you could buy for about $5,000 back in those days. So the people who are retired today own their own homes, nine out of ten. The town is full of widows. You know, you got one here, you've got another three down here. So they have their own homes, when they die, they're all rich.

What did you do at Standard Oil? How did you move through different jobs?

I went to Inspection Engineers, I didn't quite like that. At that time there was a lot of surveying work done. And it was a good job, I probably should have stayed in it. It had turned out to be a much better-paying job, but I got out of it because a lot of work was out there along the lakefront. The company was getting bigger, and bigger, and bigger and driving stakes and measuring them. And making off corners and building sites and all. I got in the Instrument Department, and they put me right on the unit. That was maintenance of all the instruments in the refinery.

When you went in there, were there still a lot of the old-timers around, that generation that came from Europe?

My dad was one of them, my dad was a stillman at the refinery. If you happen to go by the refinery you see these tall structures, or towers. At that time we called these the still. Now they call it a cat cracker. The still got its name from, at that time they had large vessels, I would say about the size of a house. You know, steel vessels. And they used to pump the crude oil in it, right out of the field. What they call, it came from large storage tanks.

What did your father do in the stills?

He was the operator. He was, depending on the size of the still, he would direct the operations. In other words, he'd have a man, what they called a fireman, and then they had a stillman helper. And he will receive the operation of the unit and if he thought some pressure wasn't working right, he'd say, "Jack, get up there and shut that one down. We're losing our pressure here." Actually, what it did was it heated the oil to a very high temperature of 400 to 500 degrees Fahrenheit.

It heated the oil, and then they'd boil the oil and then—that's why you'll always see refineries with tall towers. Each level of that tower is some sort of by-product and the top one, of course, is the gas. Air gas that is. This is what may be the stock for making gas, the next one would be kerosene, which is a little heavier. That would probably be a motor oil of some kind. A base for a motor oil. And then the bottom was coke.

So by heating it and boiling it, you separated it into these different products?

Yes.

What was your father's name?

John Sotak. He was born in Czechoslovakia. See, after my mom died, which was when I was eight years old, we didn't spend much time talking about old times. He didn't have any of his friends coming over to talk back and forth about where they came from. We made every effort to appease my father's anguish so that he could hold down that stillman job, you know.

He used to hound the devil out of me about, "Forget about playing basketball, and get out and get a job." Jobs were getting scarcer and scarcer at the time. He was always telling me, "You'll get too old. You won't get hired."

You know, so I, after I got tired of playing basketball, I said, "Well, I'll settle down."

So why did you volunteer in '43 for the army?

I had a feeling I was going to get drafted anyway, and I wanted to select a service that I thought I would enjoy, I mean, I would enjoy. So I admired the Coast Guard. I know that the day after Christmas we would report to Chicago, I'll never forget this one. We reported to Chicago to the naval base there that we were going to New York to Manhattan Beach in Brooklyn.

And then I got sick, and to this day I don't know what the hell happened. And I got discharged after a year, a year and a half. I continually had fevers. And instead of taking care of me over there, they sent me back here. They couldn't figure it out. I was in so much [pain]. Well, to this day I have very little respect for them, the Veterans' Administration, the way it's run.

When I came back to my job, I must say they must have had a lot of women. They were in most every department. It sure created a hell of a lot of divorces. As the war kept going on, things got worse and worse. Men and women were working together. It was deplorable. They were fraternizing. Right on the job, you know. I mean, they always leave the men and they have a young girl as helper. These old men would just cater to them, you know, if they had to turn the valve he would go out to turn the valve, "You sit here." And he'd make a meal for them if—that sort of thing.

Were there more layoffs after the great fire?

"WHITING REFINERY was never like that when I worked there!" is what many an overseas serviceman will say when he sees this picture. Seriously, though, the boys who fight are proud of girls like these, whose work in the mechanical labor dep't is essential in the production of much-needed petroleum products. And it is suspected that Foreman Andy Murzyn is also proud of his wartime crew.
In the FRONT ROW, left to right, are Anna Mae Puskas, Sophie A. Gorczyca, Margaret D. Staniszewski, Mary Thornsberry, Mr. Murzyn, Evelyn A. Stephenson, Dorothy Bobos, Dorris Thompson, Doris M. Ring and Mary L. Meeks. BACK ROW: Evelyn Hawn, Mary Quisenberry, Lucille A. Conway, Mary E. Stewart, Ruth Whitten, Marian Strawhum, Grady Hazel Smith, Callie Frailey and Mildred Johnson.

REFINERY, FIELD AND OFFICE

Women workers at Standard Oil Refinery during the Second World War
Stanolind Record, *November 1944*

None in '55. We had a lot of layoffs in '58 and '59 and '60.

Why?

The profitability improvement program. Well, they were just going to cut down forces and justifiably so in my [opinion]. A lot of the people were displaced [by the '55 fire], like the people on the unit that blew, you know. We got two hundred people, what do you do? So we helped those people out with jobs, clean up the fire, get backup. Like a stillman for instance. The younger stillman couldn't hold down a job because of seniority bumped him back into labor. He got a stillman rate, but we used him to dig a trench. And they accepted that because, you know, they had a serious accident.

I was in Wood River, at the refinery in Illinois, in a little dingy hotel. You know, Wood River is a one-horse town. And the guy comes knocking at the door, "Mr. Sotak, you've got a telephone call downstairs."

I go downstairs, it was my wife calling. And the first thing she says, "Joe, you better come home. Whiting's on fire."

I figured, "Oh, Christ, her exaggerating and all."

And she says, "No, they had a big explosion here."

So Joe McKenna was there and I said, "Joe, my wife just called and says Whiting's on fire. She says something caught on fire and blew."

"Oh, Christ, we better get going back home," you know. So we took a train out of Alton, Illinois, and come up to Chicago here. And we took the South Shore home and we were on the South Shore over on the lakefront where the South Shore comes in. And you could see that fire from where we were at. I don't know, you could see the Loop real good from here, well, we could see that inferno from there.

We got home, and we got people from the city lined up where we could get beds for the people who had damaged homes. At the time there was a lot of homes around the refinery. And they set up that program and that's when we got down to this business of how we going to use these men? So we just worked around the clock, and we got a lot of hell because a lot of guys figured, "Hell, no, I'm a stillman. I ain't going to dig no ditch."

"Well, it's either that or you go back to labor, now which do you want to do?" And it's things like that that kind of provoked me.

During the '69 strike I got cited for contempt in court. The judge says, "Sotak, I don't want to see any pickets on 129th Street Gate." Now that's the gate that come out of the refinery, crosses Riley Road, and goes over to the docks and at the docks is where the coke is piled up.

We shut that coke unit because as soon as they get those drums emptied out, those four big vessels in which this coke is put into it, and it hardens and then is cut out and dumped. As soon as we fill those four drums up, they'll have to shut the unit down because they've got no place to put the crude. So we figured, we'll picket the gate and stop those gondola cars from going across the road. And it worked for about a couple of days and the judge said, "Get off." So lo and behold, I'm in court and got cited. So this is about a day later, and the sheriff comes over and says, "Come talk to Sergeant—" whatever.

He says, "Hey, we're having some trouble at that gate." I get over there, this happened to me, that's the second or third day of the strike. Well, you know the first days, two, three, five days of the strike, employees are, as the old saying goes, peeing on the company's porch.

So I get over there, and I says, "For Christ's sake, see that judge's order over there hanging on the fence?" I hung that on the fence, the judge's orders. "Stay away from that gate."

"The hell with him." They accused me of being with the company. Accused me of being with the judge.

I said, "Get off this track."

These are some of your union members?

These are some of the members, yes. And there were about a couple who were half crocked, you know. I said, "You guys are going to have to get off." And lo and behold the skunks, the company's representative when we go to court, they've got photos of me standing right between the two rails with the picket sign. I'm trying to get them off. They're blaming [me]. This was the God's truth. I told them, I says, "I was out there to get them off." And I'm charged for contempt, you know. And he hit me with thirty days or five hundred dollars.

Did you notice a change in the workers in terms of their attitudes toward the company?

There was a big layoff in '58 and '59 before the sixties. There were a hell of a lot of involuntary, and there were voluntary retirements that the company was offering severance pay. And lo and behold in about '63, '64, '65 they started rehiring. Well, we tried to get as many of the people back that got laid off. In fact, the old one president of the union, he was one of them, he went to work for the railroad—Rudy Oberman. He's back as a stillman now. But he was one of them, and there was a lot of them. But then we were picking up more and more and more new faces, you know.

I used to have to pay my hospitalization out of my pocket because I had so little on my check. But then as a supervisor I noticed, I says, "Christ, these guys don't know what a day's work is." And there was many a times you got called a son of a bitch.

And they had a lot of blacks as still cleaners. And they had a lot of, what the hell was it? Turks. Turks. They had a lot of Turks that were still cleaners. Good workers. Just a bull job, and they would go into this big vessel, you know what I'm talking about? And then after the oil boils off, about this far the whole end of the vessel was coked up. At that time they had to do it manually. Send somebody in there, wait until it cools down and then they chop that out and throw it out the manholes on each. And that was the still cleaner job. Nasty job. But if you got that still cleaned in one hour, you went home, you got paid eight hours.

Is there a time when you don't need still cleaners anymore?

Well, they call it "sluciers" now. They retired that system of these vertical stills. I'd say they made that just about before the '55 fire started.

Well, now we've got these vertical towers, they're about eleven or twelve stories high, you know. And the crude is pumped in there and then that coke piles up in there until about eight stories high. And on the top they put a high-pressure water jet, a pipe, and they'd gouge a hold right down the middle. And down below there's a gondola, these cars that they try to pick the stock up. And that would go right into the gondola.

In your lifetime, how has Whiting changed?

Well, the type of people here are entirely different. They're not the type of people, well, going over to the street where I was born.

The people over there, the homes are not kept up. Like you go down this street here and that part of the street over there, hell, that was a nice drugstore on the corner. Now on the left-hand side, a dilapidated home.

They're not the down-to-earth, good, clean-living people and honest people. You know, that's what it is. Now I will say that you take the Poles and the Slovaks and the Irish, I mean, they're proud of keeping their homes nice, you know. You go down to some sections along where most of the Polish people live, the other side of St. Al's, and that's kind of nice. But over here the people that owned the homes died, you know, and the kids get the house, and they don't want to live in this dump. And they sell the house, they couldn't care less who the hell they sell it to. That's the case over here down on Lake Avenue.

The homes over there, you should go down and take a look at those homes. Poor shape.

How has this country changed in your lifetime?

This country will go to hell. I really think so. They're [the younger generation] not responsible people. They're living for today and the hell with tomorrow. I would think that if we were in a real, real big war, a war was coming up that we would have more people running across the border being chicken.

Why?

Because they couldn't care less about defending the country. I would think, we have a hell of a lot of them right now, which is what kind of angered me about President Carter, all of those skunks that ran across the border for amnesty. Don't you feel that?[8]

They're not, they don't believe in saving, they're not the saving kind. They just blow their money, they like to buy big. When I first got [married], I lived with my in-laws, like I said. But back in those days, like I said, people—they started small. Well, I started small too. Hell, it wasn't until I would say in my fifties, I was never too proud to buy a used car. I mean, I was raising kids, and I wanted to feed them, take care of them. And I didn't give a damn whether I drove around in a Cadillac like I do now. And there were a lot of people like that. But today, hell, they believe they've got to start at the top.

You never heard of a divorce around here or even separation. I mean, we've seen some families, well, like, I go back to when the war was on, you know, where I think, "Jesus, this guy's going to lose his wife." But they hung on and hung on, but they lived separately, you know. Finally they got back together again.

[8] On 21 January 1977, President Jimmy Carter pardoned those who evaded the draft between the years 1964 and 1973. *Washington Post*, 22 January 1977.

Appendix

Name	Date	Interviewer	Place
Paoli			
1. Paul Waynick	8 July 1988	Catherine A. Jones	Paoli
	15 July 1988	Catherine A. Jones	Paoli
2. Owen Stout	14 October 1987	Catherine A. Jones	Paoli
3. Louanne Rutherford	21 April 1989	Maria Green	Paoli
4. "Lucy Deckard"	12 January 1988	Catherine A. Jones	Paoli
5. Lotus Dickey	18 April 1989	Maria Green	Paoli
6. Benjamin Minton	9 December 1987	Catherine A. Jones	Paoli
7. Bethel Elizabeth Cornwell	1 March 1988	Catherine A. Jones	Millersburg
	22 March 1988	Catherine A. Jones	Millersburg
Evansville			
8. Alice Hottenstein	18 August 1996	Barbara Truesdell	Evansville
9. Ralph Dorris	11 May 1995	Samuel White	Newburgh
10. Marcella Massey	24 July 1996	Barbara Truesdell	Evansville
Indianapolis			
11. Willard B. "Mike" Ransom	18 July 1983	Greg Stone	Indianapolis
12. Edna Johnson	10 October 1983	Greg Stone	Indianapolis
13. Alberta Murphy	20 July 1995	Richard B. Pierce	Indianapolis
14. William Taylor	14 February 1996	Richard B. Pierce	Indianapolis
15. Anne Malott	24 March 1976	Richard Phelps	Indianapolis
Anderson			
16. Naomi J. Wilson	19 February 1982	Karen L. Gatz	Anderson
17. Joseph R. Wilson	19 February 1982	Greer Warren	Anderson
	19 March 1982	Greer Warren	Anderson
18. Victor G. Reuther	26 September 1980	R. T. King	South Bend
19. Rex E. Roberts	13 August 1979	R. T. King	Anderson
South Bend			
20. Christine Drabecki Louise Dzierla Theresa Grayzck Mary Nowicki Mary Schoonaert Mary Van Daele	25 July 1985	Robin Lee Zeff	South Bend
21. Clifford MacMillan	11 May 1984	John Bodnar	Hudson Lake
22. Otto Klausmeyer	11 May 1984	John Bodnar	South Bend

Name	Date	Interviewer	Place
South Bend, *continued*			
23. Harold E. Churchill	28 February 1980	R. T. King	South Bend
	29 February 1980	R. T. King	South Bend
24. Odell "Duke" Newburn	10 July 1984	John Wolford	South Bend
25. Robert (Bob) Hagenbush	24 July 1984	John Wolford	South Bend
Whiting			
26. Sophie Gresko	12 March 1991	John Bodnar	Whiting
	11 October 1991	John Bodnar	Whiting
27. Betty Gehrke	28 September 1990	John Bodnar	Whiting
28. Leo Kus	10 November 1991	John Bodnar	Whiting
29. Delores Curosh William Curosh Bertha DeLuca Mike DeLuca	2 March 1992	John Bodnar	Sun City, Arizona
30. Clementine Frankowski	14 August 1991	John Bodnar	Whiting
31. Joseph J. Sotak	6 November 1991	John Bodnar	Whiting

Index